Countryside Cooking
& Chatting

Countryside Cooking & Chatting

Traditional Recipes and Wisdom from the
Amish & Mennonites

Contributed by Readers of *Die Botschaft*

and

Compiled by Lucy Leid

Herald Press

Scottdale, Pennsylvania

Waterloo, Ontario

Library of Congress Cataloging-in-Publication Data
Countryside cooking and chatting : traditional recipes and wisdom from the Amish &
Mennonites / contributed by readers of Die Botschaft and compiled by Lucy Leid.
    p. cm.
    ISBN 0-8361-9328-8 (pbk. : alk. paper) — ISBN 0-8361-9327-X (plastic comb binding :
alk. paper) 1. Cookery, Amish. 2. Cookery, Mennonite. I. Leid, Lucy, 1953- II. Botschaft.
    TX715.C8662 2006
    641.5'66—dc22

                                    2005036308

Occasional dialect words spelled according to C. Richard Beam, *Revised Pennsylvania
German Dictionary* (Lancaster, Pa.: Brookshire Publications, 1994). Scripture is from the
King James Version of the Holy Bible.

COUNTRYSIDE COOKING AND CHATTING
Copyright © 2006 by Herald Press, Scottdale, Pa. 15683
Published simultaneously in Canada by Herald Press,
    Waterloo, Ont. N2L 6H7. All rights reserved
Library of Congress Control Number: 2005036308
International Standard Book Number: 0-8361-9327-X
Printed in the United States of America
Cover and book design by Paula Johnson
Cover photos by Paula Johnson

12 11 10 09 08 07 06   10 9 8 7 6 5 4 3 2 1

To order or request information, please call
1-800-759-4447 (individuals); 1-800-245-7894 (trade).
Web site: www.heraldpress.com

Contents

A note from the compiler about some terms in this book:

ClearJel and Thermflo (starch) are for thickening fruit for pies and desserts. They produce a nicer texture than cornstarch and won't turn cloudy. There are two kinds of ClearJel. Instant is ready to use, but Regular must be cooked.

Confectioners' sugar is refined and finely powdered. Look for powdered sugar.

"Dinner" means the noon meal.

"Divided" means an amount to use in portions.

Equal Spoonful can be used cup for cup like sugar in recipes. Thus also, 2¼ cups Equal Spoonful = 1 pound sugar; 1 Equal packet = 2 tsp. sugar; 1½ packets = 1 tbsp. sugar; 12 packets = ½ cup sugar; 24 packets = 1 cup sugar. And so on.

Karo is a corn syrup.

Molasses comes as a table syrup of mild flavor, or full flavor, or blackstrap for baking. Unless otherwise indicated, "molasses" means the mild syrup.

Occident or Western flour is an unbleached, enriched, all-purpose flour gradually bleached by oxygen in the air and thus is off-white in color.

Oleo is oleomargarine or margarine.

Softasilk flour is a Pillsbury brand name for cake flour.

"Supper" means the evening meal.

Sure-Jell (not to be confused with ClearJel) is a fruit pectin for homemade jams and jellies and appears at www.surejell.com.

"Tbsp." means tablespoon, and "tsp." means teaspoon.

Tender Quick is seasoned salt for quickly curing meat, from Morton.

Thermflo: see ClearJel, above.

Cooks can find many of the items in local grocery stores or order them from:

Westfield Egg Farms
165 North Shirk Road
New Holland, PA 17557
Phone: 717-354-4966

Introduction

The weekly newspaper *Die Botschaft*, published out of Millersburg, Pennsylvania, prints news for Amish and Old Order Mennonite communities in North America. News items are written and sent in by "scribes," who often begin their stories with warm salutations, like "Greetings from Indiana!" or "Hello to all from Pennsylvania!" They go on to chronicle events in the life of their communities—births, deaths, where church was held last Sunday, how the crops are doing, how much rain/snow/sunshine there was during the last week, who's visiting, who's traveling, who's home from the hospital, who's getting married.

Printed alongside these items are obituaries, memorial poems, notices, wisdom, prayer requests, address requests, thank yous, classified ads, Ivverich und Ender (a "column for the Hausfrau"), and, of course, recipes.

In the summer of 2004, Lucy Leid of Lancaster County, Pennsylvania, ran a notice in *Die Botschaft* and asked readers to send her "tried-and-true" recipes, along with an interesting story or anecdote related to the recipe or the sender's family or community.

What follows is the fruit of Lucy's efforts, and that of some friends of hers who helped put it all together.

And so we present a cookbook, but also much more. For along with recipes for Sisters Day Doughnuts and Holiday Ham Casserole is a story about traveling home on September 11, 2001. Besides advice on Aunt Fannie's Chocolate Chip Cookies and Sylvia's Favorite Yogurt, you learn that "goats are much harder to keep inside a pen than a cow," and that you should explain to a nine-year-old what "stir by hand" really means. Among the breakfast casseroles, the pies and the cakes, we offer stories about "musty" granola bars, tales recounting "the night of the popcorn," and the day "the guardian angels must have been hovering close by."

There are spiritual nuggets, like this one: "Years ago I heard a preacher remark that people are like tea leaves: their real flavor doesn't come out until they get into hot water."

Some of the stories are composites drawn up by the compiler and her helpers from several anecdotes on a similar theme.

Many of the recipes have to do with more than food. We offer formulas for homemade baby wipes, soap, and bird treats. From the wisdom of generations we offer recipes for a happy marriage, a happy home, and a blessed life.

And doesn't that last recipe, for a blessed life, bring us to the heart of the matter? For what do we gain if we have the best-tasting food but lack the salt of the earth and the light of the world? So perhaps the richest advice comes toward the end of this book, where the author reminds us: "Enjoy the beauties of nature and commune with the Creator as you walk, casting all your perplexing problems and worries upon him. Trust him to work them out according to his will. And thank God for all your blessings."

Michael Degan,
Editor

A Happy Home Recipe

4 cups of love

2 cups of loyalty

3 cups of forgiveness

1 cup of friendship

5 spoons of hope

2 spoons of tenderness

4 quarts of faith

1 barrel of laughter

Take love and loyalty.
Mix it thoroughly with faith.
Blend it with tenderness,
Kindness, and understanding.
Add friendship and hope,
Sprinkle abundantly with laughter, and
Bake it with sunshine.
Serve daily with generous helpings.

Hello *to all. We saw this request for recipes in* Die Botschaft *and decided to send in the above. Love is the main ingredient in a family, and it oftentimes has to be unconditional love, or the result will be a flop, for lack of sweetness. We hope that all of the above ingredients are in stock at our home and will be regularly put to use.*

We had our "barrel of laughter" some time ago (at my expense) when the youngsters came in from doing chores and noticed that I had my dress on inside out! I guess that's what happens when you schussel *(bustle) around too much! We're looking forward to seeing all the recipes and stories in the completed cookbook. Happy cooking!*

chatting

Breakfast Specials and Muffins

My Kitchen

Outside the day is dreary
The sky is dull and gray,
I see no glimpse of sunshine
To shed its cheering ray.

But in my little kitchen
It's cheery, warm and bright,
When in my faithful cookstove
A blazing fire I light.

Cornmeal mush is bubbling
As breakfast I prepare,
The loaves of bread are rising,
Each one is shaped with care.

I sing as I consider
The daily tasks ahead,
They seem to me like blessings
And not a chore to dread.

For in my little kitchen
A haven warm and bright
I feel so blessed with plenty,
With peace and joy and light.

Author unknown

Alma's Breakfast Casserole

2 cups bread cubes	2 cups milk
½ pound bacon, diced and fried	1 tsp. salt
8 eggs	paprika
¼ cup diced celery	¼ cup diced red pepper

Cover bottom of 9 x 13 inch pan with bread cubes. Sprinkle bacon on top. Sprinkle celery and pepper over top of the bacon. Beat eggs and milk; add seasonings and pour over bread. Bake at 350° for 45 minutes. Serves 6 to 8. Ham or chicken can be substituted for bacon.

Country Breakfast

14 slices of bread, cubed	6 eggs
2½ cups ham, cubed	3 cups milk
16 ounces cheddar cheese, shredded	
16 ounces mozzarella cheese, shredded	

Topping:

3 cups cornflakes, uncrushed. (Instead, may use Ritz crackers, crushed.)

½ cup butter, melted

Grease 9 x 13 inch pan and layer ½ of bread, ham, and cheese. Repeat layers. Beat eggs. Add milk. Pour over layers. May refrigerate overnight. Top just before baking. Cover loosely and bake at 375° for 45 minutes.

Favorite Breakfast Casserole

6 beaten eggs	1 tsp. dry mustard
2 cups milk	1 pound sausage or ham
6 slices of bread, cubed	1 cup cheddar cheese, shredded
1 tsp. salt	1 tbsp. minced onion
1/8 tsp. pepper	

If using sausage, fry and drain. Mix everything together and let stand overnight. Bake in an uncovered 8 x 8 inch or 9 x 13 inch pan the next morning at 350° for 45 to 60 minutes.

Greetings *from Indiana! We have a family of five girls and four boys, so there's always plenty of cooking to do. We have several hours of choring to do before breakfast, and so it takes more than cold cereal at that meal. Breakfast casseroles are handy because they can be prepared the evening before and popped into the oven at the proper time.*

I remember one time our two little girls (seven and eight) decided to make a breakfast casserole all by themselves, to surprise me. They didn't follow a recipe, just stirred in what they had watched me putting in—eggs, milk, crumbled milk, and ham slices, etc. It turned out surprisingly well, if you didn't mind a few egg shells and lack of salt and pepper. I added the cheese on top and they were on cloud nine about their accomplishment!

chatting

Farmer's Breakfast

Fry 6 slices of bacon and set aside. Reserve 2 tbsp. grease in pan. Add 1/4 cup onion, chopped fine. Fry until partly soft. Add 4 medium-sized grated boiled potatoes. When browned to your liking, add 4 beaten eggs and bacon. Add salt, pepper, and curry powder to taste.

Layered Omelet Bake

16 slices of bread, buttered

8 slices cheese

½ pound shaved ham

6 eggs

3 cups milk

8 strips bacon, fried and crumbled

½ tsp. dry mustard

½ tsp. salt

1 cup crushed cornflakes

½ cup melted margarine

Using cheese, ham, and bacon, make 8 sandwiches. Put in a greased pan. Mix eggs, milk, mustard, and salt, and pour over sandwiches. Refrigerate overnight. In the morning, mix cornflakes and margarine and sprinkle on top. Bake at 350° for 1 hour. Makes 8 big helpings.

We appreciate *having our own cow and plenty of fresh milk for our breakfast cereal, breakfast casseroles, etc. Our Jersey cow is tame and easy to milk, but she has one undesirable trait. She can find a weak spot (that we didn't know existed) in the meadow fence and slip through into the neighbor's field whenever she has the chance. Naturally, the neighbors aren't very happy about it, and neither are we. We talked about selling her and buying our milk at the neighbor's dairy, but I know I'd miss the extra milk that I make butter, cheese, puddings and ice cream with. I often think, "Why can't she be more contented in our lush, green, buttercup-dotted meadow?" One evening she didn't come up to be milked, and I went on a search for her. I found her wedged between two trees that grew close together, solidly stuck there, unable to go forward or backward. With the help of a chain saw, Dad got her loose. I hope she has learned her lesson—that sticking her nose where it doesn't belong isn't wise—and won't make any more trouble.*

chatting

Gourmet Eggs

6 eggs	3 slices of bread
2 tbsp. cream	1 rounded tbsp. butter
¼ tsp. salt	cheese
dash of pepper	
seasoned salt (optional)	

Put first 5 ingredients in blender. Crumble bread into flat shallow baking dish. Butter the crumbs and dish. Pour egg mixture over buttered crumbs. Bake at 350° for 10 minutes or until firm. Top with cheese slices or grated cheese. Return to oven until cheese is melted.

Peanut Butter Granola

Dry ingredients

8 cups quick oats	1 cup brown sugar
1 cup coconut	½ tsp. cinnamon
1 cup wheat germ	½ tsp. salt

Wet ingredients

1 cup honey	1½ cups peanut butter
½ cup vegetable oil	1 tsp. vanilla

Mix wet ingredients until smooth; then mix in dry ingredients until coated. May add more oats if necessary for right amount. Bake at 250° until slightly browned, stirring often.

I got *this recipe out of a circle letter the first year we were married, which is twenty-three years now, and we have used it almost every summer! At first I used the regular oats, and now in remembering, I think it would be very chewy. However, my sister-in-law informed me that quick oats could also be used—but she said she likes it if it's chewy. I then decided to try quick oats and later decided we like it better with everything mixed together. It's a real favorite with our family, although they also like cornflakes. As for me, I think the cornflakes get soggy, so I still stick to my granola!*

Mary's Granola

12 cups quick oats	*2 tsp. salt*
8 cups regular oats	*1 tsp. cinnamon*
2 cups brown sugar	*8 tsp. vanilla*
4 cups coconut	*2 cups syrup—Karo or maple syrup*

Toast to a nice brown. Add raisins and sunflower seeds.

Pecan Granola

6 cups oats	*½ cup wheat germ*
1½ cups brown sugar	*½ cup butter, melted*
2 cups coconut	*½ cup raisins, optional*
1 cup chopped pecans	

Mix well. Toast to golden brown in slow oven, stirring occasionally. Do not add the raisins until after it is baked.

We like *this recipe so well. It is easy and not so expensive. It goes further in feeding a growing family than cornflakes. And also lasts (sticks to the ribs) better until the next meal than store-bought cereals do. We also like this whole-wheat cereal because it keeps the bowels regular every day. Constipation is not a problem in this house when we have this cereal on the table every morning.*

Grape-Nuts Cereal

3½ cups whole-wheat flour	½ tsp. salt
1 cup brown sugar	1 tsp. vanilla
2 cups buttermilk or sour milk	1 tsp. maple flavor
2 tsp. baking soda	

Mix well and bake in 350° oven for 45 minutes. After the cake is done, let it cool; then crumble real fine and toast in oven until dry.

Nut Caramel Oatmeal

2 beaten eggs	2 cups oatmeal
3½ cups milk	¼ cup margarine
1 cup brown sugar	½ tsp. salt
¼ cup nut meats	

Mix eggs, milk, salt, and sugar. Cook and stir until bubbly. Stir in oatmeal and cook until bubbly again. Add margarine; cover, and remove from heat. Add nuts. Let stand 5 minutes. Stir and serve with milk.

We like *oatmeal for breakfast every morning, usually just cooked, with a handful of raisins thrown in. For special occasions and for variety, we sometimes make this baked oatmeal. Last spring one day when I took a pan of it out of the oven, I set it on the windowsill and pushed up the window for it to cool off before the others came in from doing barn chores. I set the table and then went to the milk house for a pitcher full of milk. While I was out, one of the boys asked for a bit of help with a calf he was feeding, which took some time. By the time we came in to the house to eat breakfast, later than usual, mischief had been done! Our rascally pet crow flew noisily away from the window—he knew he was guilty! He had pecked and scratched at the baked oatmeal, and crumbs were all over! No one felt like eating any of it after his feet and beak had been in it. If we wouldn't all be so attached to him, he wouldn't get away with such things.*

Cinnamon Baked Oatmeal

½ cup butter, melted

1 cup brown sugar

2 eggs, beaten

½ tsp. cinnamon

3 cups quick oats

2 tsp. baking powder

1 tsp. salt

1 cup milk

Cream together the first three ingredients. Add all the rest to creamed mixture. Bake in 10 x 10 inch or 9 x 13 inch pan at 350° for 20 to 30 minutes. Can be mixed the night before.

Apple Raisin Bake

1½ cups water	
1½ cups oatmeal (quick or old-fashioned)	
½ tsp. salt, scant	
½ cup maple or pancake syrup	
¼ cup honey	
½ tsp. cinnamon	
2 medium apples, pared, sliced thin	
½ cup raisins	

Bring water to a boil in a medium saucepan with the pancake syrup. Stir in oatmeal and salt. Cook 1 minute. (If using old-fashioned oats, cook 5 minutes.) Stir in honey and cinnamon. Remove from heat and put half the oatmeal into a 1½-quart casserole; top with half the apples and half the raisins. Add remaining oatmeal; then top with apples and raisins. Cover. Bake in a preheated 350° oven for 20 to 25 minutes. Serve with milk.

Whole-Wheat Flour Pancakes

1½ cups whole-wheat flour	1 tsp. baking soda
½ tsp. baking powder	1½ cups buttermilk or sour milk
¾ tsp. salt	4 tbsp. vegetable oil
2 eggs, beaten	

Thoroughly mix dry ingredients. Combine eggs, milk, and vegetable oil. Add to dry ingredients and mix until smooth. Fry on hot, lightly greased (or sprayed with Pam) griddle.

Apple Raisin Muffins

½ cup whole-wheat flour +	½ cup nuts
1½ cups flour (= total of 2 cups flour)	½ cup coconut
1¼ cup sugar	1 apple, peeled and grated
2 tsp. baking soda	3 eggs
½ tsp. salt	1 cup vegetable oil
2 cups grated carrots	2 tsp. vanilla
½ cup raisins	

In a large bowl mix flours, baking soda, and salt. Stir in carrots, raisins, nuts, coconut, and apple. Mix eggs, oil, and vanilla together; stir into flour mixture until batter is just combined. Spoon into well-greased muffin tins, filling to the top. Bake at 350° for 20 minutes. Makes 16 muffins.

Apple Pancakes

2 cups flour	1¼ cups milk
2 tbsp. sugar	2 tbsp. vegetable oil
3 tsp. baking powder	¼ cup apples, finely diced
1 tsp. salt	½ tsp. cinnamon
1 egg	

Measure and mix the dry ingredients in a bowl; add the beaten egg, milk, and the vegetable oil. Fold in the apples and cinnamon. Drop ¼ cup batter on a hot greased griddle for each pancake and cook until the edges are brown, then turn and cook the other side until browned.

Betsey's Blueberry Muffins

3 cups flour	2 eggs
4 tsp. baking powder	1 cup milk
1 tsp. salt	½ cup vegetable oil
1 cup sugar	2 cups blueberries
¼ cup brown sugar	¼ cup pecans

Sift flour; measure and add baking powder, salt, and sugars. Beat eggs, milk, and oil together. Stir only enough to blend dry ingredients together; batter should appear slightly lumpy. Fold in blueberries and pecans. Drop by spoonfuls into greased muffin tins. Bake at 375° for 25 minutes.

I got these *muffin recipes from my cousins who had joined us for a picnic in the woods one Sunday and brought some along. There was an old picnic table in the clearing, on which we put all our grub while we explored. It was such a lovely breezy day and too early for lunch, so we followed the noisy little brook, wading through ferns and may apples. Soon we heard a splashing sound of falling water and came upon a miniature waterfall! We were so enchanted by it that we almost forgot about eating lunch. When we got back to the picnic table, there were two chipmunks on it, probably stirring around in our things. They scampered off and darted away in the woods. We decided that next time we'd bring some corn or seeds for them.*

Here's our favorite way to make eggs on special occasions. Delicious!

Breakfast Eggs

Grease a 9 x 12 inch pan with 2 tbsp. margarine. Sprinkle with 1 cup shredded cheese. Put 12 eggs on top of cheese. Poke egg yolks but don't stir. Sprinkle with salt and pepper. Put on top: grated Spam, chipped ham, bacon, bacon bits, or sausage. Sprinkle with 1 cup cheese. Bake at 350° for 30 minutes.

Linda's Pancakes

1 egg

1 cup all-purpose flour

¾ cup milk

1 tbsp. sugar

2 tbsp. shortening, melted, or vegetable oil

3 tsp. baking powder

½ tsp. salt

Beat egg with hand beater until fluffy. Beat in remaining ingredients just until smooth. For thinner pancakes, stir in additional ¼ cup milk. Grease heated griddle. To test griddle, sprinkle with a few drops of water. If bubbles skitter around, heat is just right. For each pancake, pour about 3 tbsp. batter from tip of spoon or pitcher onto hot griddle. Cook until puffed and dry around edges. Turn and cook other side until golden brown.

Once when I was making pancakes, I couldn't find the bottle of vegetable oil. I pulled the stepstool to the pantry shelf and was moving things around. Suddenly a mouse popped out and nearly ran into my face! It surprised and scared me so much that, according to my brothers who heard it from the barn, I made a sound like an Indian war whoop! It's good they didn't see me, or they'd have said I did an Indian war dance, too! The mouse got away, but we set several traps and caught it that night. Now when I need something from the pantry shelf, I send my younger sister, who isn't at all scared of mice and actually likes them!

chatting

This recipe *was handed down to me by my mother. After using it for twenty-four years, my recipe card shows signs of wear—worn and yellow. It's been a favorite of our family, mostly served for Sunday brunch. We like waffles with butter, jelly, honey, or maple syrup, or topped with chicken and gravy or ham and gravy. We also all like waffles for dessert, topped with vanilla ice cream and strawberry jam.*

Last time we had waffles, our twenty-three-year-old son suggested that we try warm apple pie filling with whipped cream on top. Mmm . . . it was delicious! (It was an idea he got from eating at a restaurant.) All the men of the family enjoy eating waffles, and even making them, which is a treat to Mom when she gets help in the kitchen!

Mom's Waffles

2 tsp. sugar

2 tsp. baking powder

3 eggs, well beaten

1½ cups buttermilk

1¾ cups all-purpose flour

1 tsp. baking soda

½ tsp. salt

½ cup oleo (margarine), melted and added last

Mix as for pancakes. Be sure to use a total of 3 eggs. Bake in waffle pan.

Whole-Wheat Muffins

2 cups whole-wheat pastry flour	$^2/_3$ cup honey
1 tsp. baking powder	$^1/_3$ cup vegetable oil
1 tsp. baking soda	1 egg
1½ tsp. cinnamon	1 cup water
¼ cup wheat germ	$^3/_4$ cup quick oats
$^1/_3$ cup molasses	¼ cup raisins

Combine dry ingredients, except oats, and separately combine liquid ingredients. Stir wet mixture into dry mixture, mixing very little; then mix oats in. Last, add wheat germ and raisins. Stir briefly; do not beat. Spoon batter into paper-lined or greased muffin cups. Bake in a preheated 350° oven for 15 minutes or until done. Makes 16.

Breads, Rolls, and Doughnuts

A Prayer

"Give us this day our daily bread."
How many times this prayer I've said.
Again this day I turn to you,
I'm trusting you to see us through.

I'm trusting that you will provide,
And all our needs will be supplied.
I'm thanking you once more, dear Lord,
For every promise in your Word.

The food that I prepare today,
Bless it, dear Lord, in every way.
And as about each task I go,
I pray your love to all I'll show.
Amen.

Author unknown

At school *we pupils and the teacher always repeated this little rhyming prayer before lunchtime:*

For health and strength and daily bread,
We praise thy name, O Lord.
We thank thee for this bountiful spread,
And for thy precious Word.

But at home we always just bowed our heads in silence to ask the blessing, and then after the meal was over, we bowed our heads again for a silent returning of thanks. Once when we had company for supper, I had been talking to my cousin and missed the reminder that it was time to pray. I heard a horse and buggy going past the house and turned my head to look out. "It's neighbor Amos driving his new saddlebred," I loudly announced. No one replied, and suddenly I noticed that everything was real quiet. To my embarrassment, they all had their heads bowed for prayer and were trying not to smile.

Honey Oatmeal Bread

3 cups white flour	½ cup honey
2 packages active dry yeast	2 eggs
1½ tsp. salt	2½ cups whole-wheat flour
1 cup water	½ cup regular rolled oats
1 cup cottage cheese	⅔ cup chopped nuts
4 tbsp. butter	

In a large bowl combine 2 cups white flour with yeast and salt. Heat water, cottage cheese, butter, and honey until quite warm. Add warm liquid and eggs to flour mixture. Mix well. Add whole-wheat flour, oats, and nuts. Stir in remaining white flour. Knead until smooth and elastic. Let rise until double. Punch down. Let rise again about 1 hour. Bake at 350° for 35 to 40 minutes. Makes 2 loaves.

This is our favorite bread recipe. I make it weekly for our family of four, sometimes twice a week. We use it for toast, sandwiches, jelly bread, etc. I sometimes keep a portion of the dough to make breadsticks, letting dough rise once; then I flatten dough with rolling pin to about a half inch thick. Put it on cookie sheets, cut it in one-inch strips, and let it rise a little. Bake until golden brown; then dip in melted butter and sprinkle with garlic powder and Italian seasoning. Serve with pizza sauce. Delicious! Since I use this bread recipe, my bread turns out nice. The only time it flops is when I let the yeast rise too long while it is dissolving—then at the last rising it doesn't rise much anymore. Since I've been making this bread, my husband doesn't care for white bread anymore, or even the store-bought brown bread. This recipe can also be used for dinner rolls.

100% Whole-Wheat Bread

3 tbsp. wheat germ
⅔ cup honey
4½ cups warm water
1½ tsp. salt
2 packages yeast (2 tbsp.)
3 beaten eggs
12 or 13 cups whole-wheat flour (fine)

Mix everything together except eggs, flour, and wheat germ. Leave undisturbed until yeast dissolves. Beat in eggs and 2 cups flour; then add enough flour to make a soft workable dough. Knead in wheat germ. Knead well and let rise twice. Shape into 4 loaves. Bake at 350°.

*These **are** our favorite bread recipes—the ones we always use. I'll always remember the time I had such a bad scare while I was making this bread. Our little boy was fifteen months old and loved to spend time outdoors. He needed supervision yet, and I would be constantly going to the window to check on his whereabouts as he played in the sandbox. I had often hinted to my husband how we needed a yard fence, but nothing had come of it. I was thinking about this as I kneaded the bread dough, and as I often did, I prayed for each member of the family with each punch, and tried to knead "love" into the dough.*

All at once I realized that it was high time to check on my little boy. My heart sank as I saw him way out in the field, headed for the pond. I outdid myself in running after him! When I reached him, I gratefully and with a prayer of thanks scooped him up in my arms. The next day my husband started digging holes for the fence posts.

Sarah's Wheat Bread

1½ cups milk, warm

1½ cups warm potato water

½ cup sugar

½ cup vegetable oil

1½ tbsp. instant yeast

1 tbsp. salt

about 5½ cups bread flour

2 cups whole-wheat flour

Stir sugar in milk and water. Add yeast and 2 cups flour. Stir well or beat with eggbeater. Let sit until it starts to rise a little. Add oil, salt, and rest of flour gradually until it doesn't stick. Knead about 10 minutes. Bake medium-sized loaves at 350° for 30 minutes.

Delicious Homemade Bread

5 to 6 cups flour
3 tbsp. sugar
2 tsp. salt
2 packages yeast
2 cups water
¼ cup vegetable oil

In large bowl, combine 2 cups flour, sugar, salt, and yeast. Blend well. In small saucepan, heat water and oil until very warm—120° to 130°. Add warm liquid to flour mixture. Blend until moistened, and then beat with beater or wire whip for 3 minutes. Stir in 2½ to 3 cups flour until dough pulls away from side of bowl. Knead 10 minutes, adding a little flour at a time if the dough feels sticky. Put in greased bowl. Makes 2 loaves.

chatting

My hobby *is browsing through cookbooks and trying new recipes. I must have handed down this trait to my son, for it's nothing new to see him page through a cookbook and hear him say, "Mom, make this for supper." He has already given me five cookbooks for Mother's Day, birthdays, etc.*

This onion braid is especially good served with a hot soup. Most of our family likes onions, but even those who don't still enjoy this onion braid.

It is also quite good to use for sandwiches. Spread slices with onion butter; then bologna, cheese, and lettuce. Our teenage boys that carry lunches really enjoy this for something different. It takes ideas to keep their meals interesting!

Sesame Onion Braid

1 (1/4-ounce) package active dry yeast

1 1/4 cups warm water (110° to 115°), divided

1 cup warm sour cream (110° to 115°)

3 eggs

1/2 cup (1 envelope) onion soup mix

2 tbsp. butter or margarine, softened

2 tbsp. sugar

2 tsp. salt

1/4 tsp. baking soda

6 1/2 to 6 3/4 cups all-purpose flour

1 tbsp. cold water

3 tbsp. sesame seeds

Caramelized Onion Butter

1 tbsp. diced onion

6 tbsp. butter (no substitutes), softened, divided

1 garlic clove, minced

1 package (3 ounces) cream cheese, cubed

½ tsp. minced fresh parsley

In a mixing bowl, dissolve yeast in ¼ cup warm water; let stand for 5 minutes. Add sour cream, 2 eggs, onion soup mix, butter, sugar, salt, baking soda, and remaining warm water; mix well. Stir in enough flour to form a soft dough. Turn onto a floured surface; knead until smooth and elastic, about 6 to 8 minutes. Place dough in a greased bowl, turning once to grease top. Cover and let rise in a warm place until doubled, about 1 hour.

Punch dough down. Turn onto a lightly floured surface; divide into six portions. Shape each into a 15-inch rope. Place three ropes on a greased baking sheet; braid. Pinch ends to seal; tuck under. Repeat. Cover and let rise until doubled, about 1 hour. Beat cold water and remaining egg; brush over dough. Sprinkle with sesame seeds. Bake at 350° for 35 to 40 minutes or until golden brown.

In skillet over low heat, sauté onion in 1 tbsp. butter until golden brown. Add garlic; cook 1 to 2 minutes longer or until golden. In a mixing bowl, beat the cream cheese, onion mixture, parsley, and remaining butter until creamy. Serve with bread. Yields ⅔ cup butter, enough to butter slices from 2 loaves.

This is *a recipe that my mother-in-law gave to me when we were just married. It is a good recipe to get girls started on bread making and most always makes bread nice and light.*

An amusing incident once happened when my husband offered to work bread dough. We had planned on going on a trip, and I knew we needed more bread for the chore boys. I had mixed in everything except the flour, so I instructed him to work in fourteen cups of it. (I used a two-cup measuring cup.) I then left the kitchen to put the little ones in for their naps.

Later, as I worked down the bread dough, I was puzzled by the texture. This was soon explained when Dad remarked, "You women sure work hard to get flour in your bread dough!" He just couldn't get fourteen cups in! Thinking the two-cup measuring cup was only one cup, he had put almost twenty-eight cups of flour in! As the truth dawned on us, we both had a good laugh. (And we've often laughed about it since, too!) The bread was edible, but rather crumbly and dry.

White Bread

Mix together and let rise 10 minutes:

1 cup warm water	2 tbsp. yeast
1 tbsp. sugar	

In a big bowl mix:

4 cups warm water	⅔ cups sugar
6 tbsp. oil or melted shortening	2 tbsp. salt

Add yeast mixture and stir well.
Mix in 14 cups Occident flour (See p. 6).

Knead 10 minutes. Bake in a 350° oven for 30 minutes. Makes 6 loaves.

English Muffin Loaves

Makes 2 loaves.

5½ to 6 cups flour (measure by spooning flour lightly into cup)	
2 packages Fleischmann's active dry yeast	
1 tbsp. sugar	2 cups milk
2 tsp. salt	¼ tsp. baking soda
½ cup water	cornmeal

Combine 3 cups flour, yeast, sugar, salt, and baking soda. Heat liquids until quite warm (120° to 130°). Add to dry mixture; beat well. Stir in more flour to make a stiff batter. Grease 8½ x 4½ inch pans, sprinkle cornmeal in them; then spoon in the batter. Sprinkle tops with cornmeal. Cover; let rise in warm place for 45 minutes. Bake at 400° for 25 minutes. Remove from pans immediately and cool.

chatting

Time *and again over the years we've been glad for this recipe. It's easier and takes less time than our usual bread recipe. So sometimes when we need bread quickly, we go for this. It's also good for gifts, or for a token of appreciation when someone does you a favor, such as the man who brought our dog back.*

For seven years now we've had two dogs, Holly and Heidi. One evening a truck driver brought us a piece of machinery. Holly apparently got on the trailer without anyone noticing. Later we became aware that she was no longer around and didn't know what happened. A week later Dad met the man again and asked him about Holly. Sure enough, he told us she raced off his trailer when he opened it about 100 miles from home. He said he'd bring her back to us if anyone found her. We also put an ad in Die Botschaft.

Later we received a letter informing us that someone is keeping her. She came to them when it was thundering. (She's afraid of thunder.) About five to six weeks after she left, the same man brought her back. We sure rejoiced to have our dog back!

One day *a salesman came to make supper for us, to demonstrate water-less cooking in the Towncraft cookware he was selling. He said he usually doesn't stay to eat with the family, but since I was baking this almost sugar-free whole-wheat bread, and he wanted to taste it, he asked to stay. He really liked it, and to my surprise, he even asked for the recipe!*

Almost Sugar-Free Whole-Wheat Bread

1 egg, beaten	1 heaping tbsp. dry yeast
2 tbsp. honey	1 tsp. sugar
2 tbsp. blackstrap molasses	1 tbsp. lecithin powder
4 tbsp. butter	1 heaping tsp. salt
1⅓ cups milk	1 cup water
3 cups 100% whole-wheat flour and 3¼ cups Occident bread flour	

Heat 1⅓ cups milk; add butter. Dissolve yeast in 1 cup warm water; add sugar. In another bowl, combine egg, salt, honey, and molasses. Add lecithin into milk and butter to dissolve; after it has cooled a little, add it to the rest and add yeast. Then add 3 cups whole-wheat flour. Mix until lumps are done. Add 1½ cups Occident mix. Then add the rest occasionally. Mix with hands until it isn't sticky. Bake at 375° for ½ hour. Makes 2 loaves.

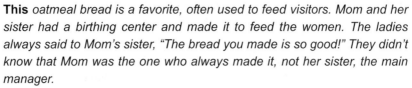

This oatmeal bread is a favorite, often used to feed visitors. Mom and her sister had a birthing center and made it to feed the women. The ladies always said to Mom's sister, "The bread you made is so good!" They didn't know that Mom was the one who always made it, not her sister, the main manager.

Once she let it rise too far, and seeing the dough ballooning out over the bowl and onto the floor frightened one of the helpers. She grabbed it, and wrapped it in a shawl, and threw it out! That was the last of that bread!

Mother's Oatmeal Bread

3½ cups boiling water
2 cups quick oats
1 cup honey
2 tbsp. salt

Let set ¼ hour

Soak: *2 tbsp. bread yeast in 1 cup warm water*

4 eggs

Add to first mixture

Then add ½ whole-wheat and ½ white flour until thick enough. Let rise. Then knead and put in pans. Let rise again. Knead. Let rise; then bake ½ hour at 350°.

Makes 4 loaves.

My job *is to feed our thirty calves their milk replacer every morning and evening. My three-year-old daughter always wants to run along, unless she oversleeps in the morning. Oft-times she comes out to the barn when I'm about half done. One morning she didn't show up at all, and I was kind of worried. After I was done, I hurried to the house and was amused to find her on a chair by the table, up to her elbows in the bread dough I had start-ed before I left for the barn.*

"You don't need to help. I can do this by myself," she quickly said, sounding quite out of breath from punching the dough so energetically. "Won't Daddy be surprised when he finds out I can knead bread, too?" She was so happy and enthused that I didn't have the heart to reprimand her. Her bread even turned out lighter and better than mine usually does, and she got the praise she wanted from Daddy!

Here's one of our favorite recipes:

Whole-Wheat Oatmeal Bread

2½ cups boiling water	2 tbsp. salt
2 cups oatmeal	¾ cup vegetable oil
2 tbsp. yeast	4 eggs, beaten
1 cup lukewarm water	2 cups whole-wheat flour
1 cup honey (part Karo may be used)	white flour

Dissolve yeast in lukewarm water. Pour boiling water over oatmeal and cool to lukewarm. Beat together with remaining ingredients, except white flour. Work in enough white flour to make dough workable, not sticky. Knead well. Grease top of dough and let rise. Punch down and let rise again. Shape into loaves. Let rise. Bake at 400° for 10 minutes; then 350° for 25 to 30 minutes more. Makes about 6 loaves.

Mary's Filled Doughnuts

2 packages yeast

1 cup lukewarm water

1 cup milk, scalded and cooled

½ cup shortening or butter

½ cup sugar

1½ tsp. salt

4 egg yolks or whole eggs

5 cups flour

Dissolve the yeast in lukewarm water and let it set for 10 minutes. Mix in the rest of the ingredients, except for flour, then add yeast mixture. Stir well, then stir in flour and knead for 10 minutes.

Work like bread dough and let rise until double. Roll out and cut. Let rise again; then drop in hot lard until brown. In place of lard, you can use Crisco oil, 3 inches deep in the kettle.

Filling

4 tbsp. milk

½ cup Crisco shortening

2 tbsp. vanilla

4 cups confectioners' sugar

Measure the confectioners' sugar into a bowl and add the rest of ingredients. Stir well.

To fill, cut the dough when cool into 3-inch squares. With a sharp knife, make a slash in one side and insert the filling with a spoon.

Crème-Filled Doughnuts

2 cups water (lukewarm)	2 eggs, well beaten
1 tbsp. yeast	2 tsp. salt
½ cup vegetable oil	about 6 cups flour
½ cup sugar	

Soften yeast in water. If it is instant yeast, mix it right in and add the rest of the ingredients. Add just enough flour so that dough is still a little sticky but smooth. Knead with hands. Let rise until double. Then roll out or lay out. I like to pat it out, and then use the rolling pin lightly and sparingly. Let rise again. Fry in hot fat or oil deep enough so doughnuts float (don't have oil too hot or doughnuts will have doughy centers). Makes 30 doughnuts. This recipe also works for sticky buns, which I make with scraps.

EZ frosting for filling

½ cup Crisco shortening	7 tbsp. flour
½ cup butter	1 tsp. vanilla
¾ cup sugar	½ cup milk

Put all ingredients in a bowl and let set a ½ hour. Then beat 5 minutes (do not cook).

Doughnuts *always bring back a bittersweet memory of when pride came before a fall. I believe I was nineteen, and my sister was one-and-a-half years younger. I was the older, and I felt myself the wiser and superior one. The day I became humbled was a big day in our life—we were going to have the youth for a singing. Living in Lancaster County, that could be quite a number of people. We decided on doughnuts as a treat, or rather, I decided it. And I also decided that to be sure they were good enough, I'd make them all myself.*

Mom decided differently—my sister and I would each make a portion. I relented rather reluctantly, for our reputation was at stake! What if she would goof it up? Before we were finished, we discovered that I had for-

chatting

gotten the salt in my portion! Oh dear! They tasted flat, and hers were good. The singing turned out to be a big one; we served hers, but mine were needed, too.

Every time I make doughnuts, I remember when the older, wiser, superior sister became humbled!

Delicious Doughnuts

2 tbsp. yeast	¼ cup warm water
1 tbsp. sugar	1 cup shortening
2 eggs	½ cup sugar
2 tsp. salt	2 cups warm water
1 cup warm potato water	7 to 8 cups flour

Dissolve yeast in lukewarm water; add 1 tbsp. sugar. Let stand 10 minutes. In large bowl, combine shortening, eggs, sugar, and salt. Add water and potato water. (If potato water isn't available, just use total of 3 cups water.) Mix well; then add yeast and mix again.

Add flour, stirring after every 2 cups until dough is soft but not sticky. Let rise in a warm place until double in size, about 1 hour. Knead well. Roll and cut into doughnuts. Cover and let rise about an hour. Fry.

Shortly *after our marriage, I invited the neighbors over for Sunday dinner. Wanting to get an early start with Saturday cleaning and baking, I prepared the doughnut dough Friday evening—something I had never done before. I was a little uneasy about going into the kitchen the next morning, wondering if the towel covering the dough would be on top of a bowl of risen dough or drooping into the bowl, meaning my dough was a flop. Imagine my surprise to find the towel neatly folded on the kitchen table! A more pleasant surprise awaited me on the cupboard—the dough had risen, making a nice heap on top of the bowl despite me forgetting to cover it.*

chatting

Potato Doughnuts

2 packages dry yeast	2 tsp. salt
½ cup warm water	1½ to 2 cups mashed potatoes
2 cups scalded milk	4 eggs, beaten
½ cup shortening	10 to 12 cups flour
½ cup sugar	

Knead until smooth and satiny. Place in lightly greased bowl. Turn over to grease top. Cover. Let rise until doubled. Roll and cut with cutter or floured scissors. Don't let them rise too long until you start frying them, since they do still rise while frying. Always fry them with the top turned down. Fill doughnuts with filling and roll in doughnut sugar.

Doughnut filling

2 egg whites, beaten	4 tbsp. flour
4 cups confectioners' sugar	4 tbsp. milk
2 tsp. vanilla	1½ cups Crisco

Beat egg whites, sugar, and vanilla. Add rest of ingredients and beat well.

My mother *used to think that she couldn't make nice doughnuts. She used to go and help her sister make some every now and then. Finally, she decided she'd try to make some herself. And sure enough, she could. Ever since, she makes these yummy doughnuts every now and then.*

Every year in April our church people go together and have a big yard-and-bake sale to help with hospital expenses. My mother usually has some of her cream-filled doughnuts there. The people just snatch them up in no time and there are never any leftover. She is also asked to make some for food stands at sales. And every year, my dad has sale days in his shop, for three days. Those days we are always busy making doughnuts; we have free coffee and doughnuts for the customers. The people often remark about the good doughnuts. We usually make six hundred or more for three sale days.

chatting

This is an old recipe of mine. When our six children were little, I'd get up at 4:00 a.m., cut and fry them, and be done by 7:00 a.m. in time for our neighbors' annual yard sale. Every year people would come, just for these doughnuts. One man bought six and ate them right away!
Now our children have left home and make doughnuts themselves.

Overnight Doughnuts

1 cup mashed potatoes

4 tbsp. sugar

2 tsp. salt

4 cups potato water

2 tbsp. yeast, dissolved in ½ cup warm water

Set this at 5:00 p.m. Let rise until bedtime. Then add:

8 eggs, room temperature

4 cups warm potato water

3 cups sugar

3 cups shortening (I use oil)

flour to stiffen (knead until elastic)

In the morning, knead and roll, cut. Let rise and fry.

Sisters Day Doughnuts

(and Glaze)

1 cup warm water	1 cup shortening
4 tbsp. yeast	4 eggs
1 quart warm milk	3 tsp. salt
1 cup sugar	12 cups bread flour

Combine water and yeast. Let set 15 minutes. Add remaining ingredients. For extra softness, you may add a pack of instant mashed potatoes (prepared as on box) before adding all the flour. Dough will be a little sticky and does not need much kneading. Use plenty of flour to roll out. Fry in hot oil until golden brown on each side.

Glaze for doughnuts

1 pound confectioners' sugar	2 tbsp. vanilla
2 tbsp. cornstarch	4 tbsp. milk
2 tbsp. butter	

Add water (by tablespoon) until the desired consistency. Warning: Don't hold the bowl under the faucet to add water; before you know it, you have too much water added.

Doughnut day! *A day looked forward to during the long winter days and weeks. On Mom's birthday in December every year, my sisters bring their supplies to our basement—at the sink down there. Dinner is carry-in.*

We like having lunch upstairs in the kitchen so we can stay out of the doughnuts' way during dinner (as the doughnuts stay out of our way). It's usually a crowd with six mothers and Mom and I, plus two mothers in Kentucky who have to miss out. Boo hoo! At least twelve children and babies are running around putting fingerprints (unwanted) in the rising doughnuts. Some of the ones at the outer edge of the table have funny shapes sometimes!

Precious memories! Each sister and sis-in-law makes at least two to

chatting

three hundred doughnuts, some filled and some glazed. We like to mix pie filling with the icing for the filled ones for a different flavor.

Of course, a lot of doughnuts get eaten while at their best—fresh and warm. Mmm . . . At the end of the day no one wants to see or eat another doughnut for a day or two. But each heads home with sleepy children and lots of yummy doughnuts—and memories, of course—because work goes faster when you have your sisters to talk with.

Egg Rusks

| 1 tbsp. or package yeast |
| 1 cup warm water |
| 1 cup mashed potatoes |
| 4 eggs |
| 1 cup sugar |

Mix ingredients in evening. Next morning add bread flour to make dough just dry enough to handle and knead. Form into buns and place in pan to rise. Bake at 350° for 30 minutes or until done.

These were *a childhood favorite of mine. The buns were bigger than a slice of bread, and very delicious with butter and molasses spread over them. Food was a magnet to my childhood appetite. Whenever I walked past food, I always had an urge to sample some. Once when Mom saw me eating, she exclaimed, "You'll get to be as fat as Grandma!" Since I desperately hoped I wouldn't become that fat, I guess then already I knew girls want to be slim. Thus I started to think before eating food at my fingertips and before stuffing myself at the table. Later I learned that some foods are less fattening than others, and healthier, too.*

We had *these pecan rolls at a skating party at my uncle's place last winter, and everyone liked them, especially my brothers, who ate the most! So I got the recipe from my cousin, who is my age. We were probably all extra hungry from all that exercise in the frosty, cold air, which made them taste better. That night we played crack the whip and prisoner's base, for the ice was super smooth and didn't have a bit of snow on it. It was a full moon, too, and we had so much fun! That evening a boy asked my eighteen-year-old cousin for a date, so the evening was extra special for her, too. They were skating togeth-er for awhile, and got teased and whistled at. Those pecan rolls, along with mugs of Ovaltine, sure tasted good when we got back to the warm kitchen.*

Pecan Rolls

1⅓ cups flour	½ cup water
1½ cups flour	¼ cup oleo
2 packages yeast	¼ cup sugar
¾ cup milk	1 egg

Place in bowl 1½ cups flour. Add yeast and stir. In saucepan, measure milk, water, oleo, and sugar. Stir just until oleo is melted. Add rest of flour. Let rise until double.

Bottom portion

¾ cup oleo, melted	1 cup brown sugar
1 tbsp. Karo syrup	1 tbsp. water
1 tsp. cinnamon	½ cup chopped pecans

Mix and spread into a 9 x 13 inch pan. Lay rolls on top and let rise again. Bake at 350° for 25 minutes.

Here's another favorite:

Hot Cross Buns

2 cups milk	1 cup butter or oleo
2 cups water	2 tsp. salt
1 cup sugar	2 tbsp. yeast
4 eggs	enough flour for a stiff dough

Mix all together as for bread and knead 10 minutes. Divide into 48 rolls and arrange in 4 cake pans. With a sharp knife, slash an X on top of each roll. Let rise until double and bake 25 minutes at 350°. Frost and enjoy!

Katie's Corn Bread

¾ cup yellow cornmeal	1 tsp. salt
1 cup white flour	3 tsp. baking powder (rounded)
2 tbsp. sugar	2 eggs
2 tbsp. vegetable oil	1 cup milk

Beat eggs; add oil and milk. Stir in dry ingredients. Mix well. Pour into greased 8 x 10 inch pan. Bake at 375° for 25 to 30 minutes.

This is *my favorite sticky bun recipe. I like to use it for giving to the neighbors at Christmas. We live in a small town, so we have close neighbors on all four sides of us. One year for my buddies' Christmas cookie exchange, I baked each a pan of these instead of a plateful of cookies, for something different. I have also used raisins in place of the nuts in the sugar syrup, and those are good, too. Another thing we like is substituting whole-wheat flour for some of the flour; they turn out good that way, too. I enjoy making sticky buns with this recipe. They sure are delicious, especially when still warm. I usually substitute maple-flavored syrup for the molasses. Enjoy!*

Oatmeal Nut Sticky Buns

⅓ cup warm water	1 tsp. salt
1 package dry yeast	2 eggs, beaten
1 tsp. sugar	1 cup quick oatmeal
1 cup milk, scalded	½ cup sugar
⅓ cup shortening	butter as desired
1 cup flour	
3 to 3½ cups more flour (use Occident flour)	

Combine water, yeast, and sugar; stir until dissolved. Set aside. Put shortening into the scalded milk and stir until melted. Add sugar, salt, and eggs; cool to lukewarm. Combine with yeast mixture. Add oatmeal and 1 cup flour; beat well with mixer. Add more flour and knead until smooth and elastic. Place in greased bowl and butter top of dough. Cover and let rise until double in bulk. Punch down, cover, and let rest 10 minutes. Then divide dough in half and roll out each half into a 12-inch square. Brush with melted butter and sprinkle each half with half of this filling mixed:

½ cup sugar	2 tsp. cinnamon.
½ cup brown sugar	

Roll up as for jelly roll and cut each roll into twelve 1-inch slices. Prepare three 8-inch or 9-inch round cake pans with this syrup mixed:

6 tbsp. melted butter	¾ cup sugar
2 tbsp. molasses	1 cup nuts

Sprinkle the nuts into the 3 pans. Mix butter, molasses, and sugar; pour over the nuts. Place 8 rolls on top of the syrup in each pan. Cover and let rise until double again. Bake at 350° for 18 to 20 minutes until lightly browned. Invert on plates soon after removing from oven so topping will not stick in pan. Yield: 24 buns.

No-Knead Refrigerator Rolls

2 cups boiling water	2 packages yeast
½ cup sugar	¼ cup water
1 tbsp. salt	1 tsp. sugar
2 tbsp. shortening	8 cups flour
2 beaten eggs	

Put together first four ingredients; let cool to lukewarm. Add 2 beaten eggs. Mix together yeast, water, and sugar. Add to first mixture. Add 4 cups flour and beat well. Add rest of flour and mix well. Form into balls and let rise until double. Bake at 400° until golden brown. This dough can be stored in refrigerator until needed. Delicious!

When put *in the refrigerator overnight or several days, I get nice soft rolls. One New Year's Day I had invited friends for dinner. I mixed these rolls the evening before, intending to bake them shortly before the guests came. I guess I didn't allow them enough time to warm up, for they didn't rise well and were tough. Guests were here and the meal was ready, so I served them without apologies, but it was one of my most embarrassing moments. I remember them glancing at me as they ate them, but no one said anything about them in my presence. After that I knew the rolls needed to rise until double in bulk, just like other yeast recipes.*

chatting

This recipe *was given to me by a dear niece who is seventeen years younger than I am but seems more like a sister. We often share recipes and ideas about cooking and baking. One day she came to our house and brought along these delicious fruit buns. From then on, our children clap and cheer when they come into the kitchen and mother is rolling out these fruit buns! We've tried them with different fruit toppings: cherry, strawberry, apple, and pineapple, all delicious. They've been made for many different occasions: frolics, quiltings, sister's day, and school get-togethers. I've also given them as Christmas gifts to the neighbors, or when there's a new baby in a home, and also for young folks' gathering. Results are often, "May I have your recipe?"*

Cinnamon Fruit Buns

Mix:

2 cups mashed potatoes	2 tbsp. salt
1 cup shortening or oil	1 quart scalded milk
1 cup sugar	

Cool this mixture to lukewarm.

½ cup warm water	soft butter
3 tbsp. dry yeast	brown sugar
2 eggs	cinnamon
15 cups flour	

Dissolve: 3 packages (3 tbsp.) dry yeast in ½ cup warm water. Add to milk mixture the dissolved yeast, 2 eggs, about 15 cups of flour (½ bread flour and ½ all-purpose flour). Mix well and knead.

Let rise until double in bulk. Roll out dough. Spread with soft butter; sprinkle brown sugar and cinnamon on dough. Roll up, slice ¾ inch thick, and place in greased pans. Let rise about ½ hour. Put fruit filling on top: 1 can of Lucky Leaf pie filling on each panful or make your own. Bake about 25 minutes or longer at 350°. Cool and put glaze on.

Glaze

Melt 1 cup butter	
Add: 6 cups confectioners' sugar	
4 tsp. vanilla	
6 to 8 tbsp. hot water	

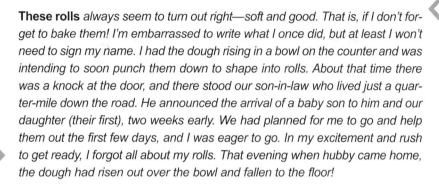

These rolls *always seem to turn out right—soft and good. That is, if I don't forget to bake them! I'm embarrassed to write what I once did, but at least I won't need to sign my name. I had the dough rising in a bowl on the counter and was intending to soon punch them down to shape into rolls. About that time there was a knock at the door, and there stood our son-in-law who lived just a quarter-mile down the road. He announced the arrival of a baby son to him and our daughter (their first), two weeks early. We had planned for me to go and help them out the first few days, and I was eager to go. In my excitement and rush to get ready, I forgot all about my rolls. That evening when hubby came home, the dough had risen out over the bowl and fallen to the floor!*

Soft Dinner Rolls

1 cup milk, scalded	1 cup warm water
½ cup butter	2 tbsp. yeast
2 eggs, beaten	2 tsp. salt
¾ cup sugar	6 cups bread flour (or more)

Mix as for bread dough and knead 10 minutes. Let rise 1 hour. Divide dough in half. Keep on dividing each portion in half until you have 32 pieces. Shape into rolls and put on cookie sheets. Let rise until double in bulk. Bake at 350° for 20-25 minutes.

Mama's cinnamon buns used to be one of my favorite comfort foods when I was a schoolgirl. When I came home from school and caught a whiff of the tantalizing aroma of freshly baked warm buns and cinnamon icing glaze, I would start to ransack the cupboards in search of them. My older sister, so good at making these buns (and even better at hiding them), didn't want me to sample any until supper. I remember how delighted I was once when I found them hidden on the top shelf in the fruit cellar!

Mama's Cinnamon Buns

3 tbsp. yeast	1 cup sugar
½ cup warm water	2 tsp. salt
1 cup margarine	11 to 12 cups flour
3 cups milk, scalded	1 tsp. cinnamon
5 eggs	

Dissolve yeast in warm water. Put margarine in milk after it is scalded. Set aside until lukewarm. Beat eggs and sugar. Add salt, yeast, and milk. Add the flour. It is quite sticky. Let rise until double in size. Make into cinnamon rolls. Bake at 350° for approximately 25 minutes.

Frosting

1 cup margarine	⅔ cup milk
2 cups brown sugar	powdered sugar

Melt margarine. Add brown sugar and milk. Heat just enough so sugar dissolves. Set aside until cool. Add confectioners' sugar. Do not stir while cooling.

Here's our favorite potato bun recipe:

Frosted Potato Buns

8 packages (tbsp.) yeast

2 cups warm potato water

5 cups milk, scalded

2 cups sugar

2 cups shortening

4 cups mashed potatoes

8 tsp. salt

about 28 cups flour (may substitute some whole-wheat flour)

8 eggs

Soften yeast in warm water. Combine milk, sugar, shortening, mashed potatoes, and salt. Cool to lukewarm. Add 10 to 23 cups flour and beat well. Add yeast and eggs. Gradually add remaining flour, kneading into a soft elastic dough. Cover and let rise until double in size. Divide dough into smaller portions; press out on greased and floured surface in a rectangular shape. Spread with melted butter and sugar-cinnamon mixture (1 tsp. cinnamon to 1 cup brown sugar). Roll up as jelly roll and cut in ¾ inch rolls. (Do not have dough rolled too tightly or centers will pop up when baking.) Place in greased pans. I drizzle a mixture of butter, brown sugar, and corn syrup that has been heated together in bottoms of pans first. Let rise until about double in size and bake in 350° oven until golden brown (approximately 25 minutes). Remove from pans and cool. Drizzle with icing. This recipe can be cut in half for a smaller batch.

Before *I got married ten years ago, I gave my friends each a recipe card to fill out and give back to me. Thus, I had a nice variety of recipes when I got married. Now this roll recipe is one of my favorites and often brings compliments on how delicious they are. My friend died at the young age of thirty-five due to leukemia. But I like to remember her every time I make these rolls. On the recipe card, she also wrote this verse:*

It's the little things we do and say
That mean so much as we go our way.
A kindly deed can lift a load
From weary shoulders on the road.

And that is exactly as I remember her. Always doing a kind deed or giving someone a friendly word.

Delicious Rolls

1 cup hot water	2 tbsp. yeast
½ cup sugar	1 cup lukewarm water
1½ tsp. salt	2 eggs, well beaten
8 tbsp. oleo	7 cups flour (scant)

Pour hot water over sugar, salt, and oleo. Dissolve yeast in lukewarm water. Add yeast and eggs. Beat well; gradually add flour. Knead into soft elastic dough (a softer dough than for bread). Let rise in a warm place until double in size; knead and let rise again. Roll out and spread generously with butter. Sprinkle cinnamon to your liking. Let rise for about 1 hour. Bake at 350° for only 15 to 20 minutes, just so they start to brown slightly.

Easy Penuche Icing

Melt ½ cup butter in saucepan. Add ½ cup white and ½ cup brown sugar (packed). Boil and stir over low heat for 2 minutes. Add ¼ cup milk. Bring to a boil, stirring constantly. Cool to lukewarm. Gradually add 1¾ to 2 cups sifted confectioners' sugar. Add vanilla if desired. Place in ice water and stir until thick enough to spread.

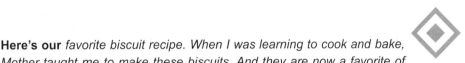

Here's our *favorite biscuit recipe. When I was learning to cook and bake, Mother taught me to make these biscuits. And they are now a favorite of our six children. We use them for biscuits and gravy, and sometimes for pizza crust. Sometimes I make a filling of chicken and gravy with diced potatoes, carrots, and peas and top it with these biscuits and bake it in a casserole. Once I added chopped parsley to the biscuits when two of our cousins ate supper with us. One of the men told his wife to be sure to get the recipe. She said, "I have a biscuit recipe." He said, "You don't have this one," and so she copied my recipe!*

chatting

Drop Biscuits

2 cups flour	
4 tbsp. butter	
1 cup milk	
4 tsp. baking powder	
½ tsp. salt	

Put dry ingredients together. Add shortening and mix with fork. Add milk to make a soft dough. Drop by teaspoonfuls in a buttered cake pan. Bake at 475° for 12 to 15 minutes.

Breadsticks

1½ cups warm water	
1 tbsp. yeast	

Let stand a few minutes until yeast is dissolved.

Add:

1 tbsp. oil	2 tbsp. parsley
1 tbsp. sugar	2 tbsp. oregano
1¼ tsp. salt	1 tsp. garlic powder
4 cups bread flour	
3 cups mozzarella or cheddar cheese	

Mix and let rise until double, or if in a hurry, use it before it rises that much. Roll out ¼ to ½ inch thick. Cut into 1-inch wide strips. Twist 2 to 3 times. Roll in 1 cup melted butter. Then put on greased pan 2 inches apart. Bake at 400° for 15 to 20 minutes. Best when baked to crusty brown. Brush with butter. Serve with warm pizza sauce and cheese sauce.

A favorite *meal at our house is breadsticks and potato soup. I usually serve our family a special Christmas supper, eaten by candlelight, and I enjoy trying a new dish or something different to surprise them. One year I made cheese sticks, but they turned out a bit on the dry side and a big disappointment for this mother, who thought she was making something fancy! So after hearing folks talk about delicious breadsticks eaten at Pizza Hut, I decided to try my hand at making my own recipe. I searched my cookbooks and combined three recipes into one. The results were cheers from everyone! One of my favorite hobbies is collecting recipes and trying out new ones. I really enjoy baking and cooking for our family of ten: six boys and four girls. We live on a three-fourths-acre farmette.*

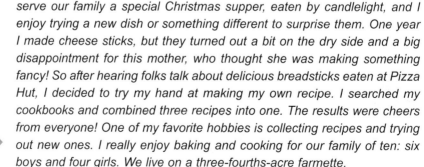

chatting

Mae's Soft Pretzels

1¼ cups warm water	
1 tbsp. sugar	
1 tbsp. or packet yeast	
3½ to 4 cups flour	
pinch of salt	

Work dough and shape into pretzels. Let rise 10 to 15 minutes. Boil for 1 minute in the following solution:

4 cups boiling water	4 tsp. baking soda

Drop pretzel in boiling water. Wait 1 minute; then remove with metal spatula. Dab with a dishcloth to remove excess moisture. Slide it from spatula onto a greased cookie sheet. Sprinkle with pretzel salt. Bake at 375° for 20 minutes.

 My brother *was making soft pretzels as a treat for his wife and several of her friends. It gave quite a chuckle when he used tapioca to sprinkle on the top, thinking he had coarse pretzel salt! (If you're not sure, I'd advise you to taste before using!) (Smiles.)*

chatting

This is *a favorite for our family of six children. It is often our Sunday evening supper or snack. Served with cheese and chocolate milk, it's a real treat any time!*

Sometimes I use part whole-wheat flour, also sour cream and onion, or cheddar cheese powder sprinkled on them after they are dipped in butter also gives them a different taste. Hope you will enjoy them.

Favorite Soft Pretzels

1 tbsp. yeast

1 tbsp. brown sugar

¾ cup warm water

2½ cups flour

¼ tsp. salt

Dissolve yeast in warm water and let stand 5 minutes. Add rest of ingredients. Mix and knead until soft dough is formed. Shape into pretzels and dip in solution of 1 cup water and 1 tsp. baking soda.

Place on a greased baking sheet; sprinkle with coarse salt. Bake at 475° for 10 to 12 minutes. Brush with melted butter.

This recipe *tastes more like Auntie Anne's soft pretzels than any other I've ever tasted! Our daughters have often made these for get-togethers, and they sure do bring smiles! Telling our neighbors we're making soft pretzels is a good way of making them show up on our doorstep.*

Elizabeth's Soft Pretzels

1 cup warm water
1 tbsp. yeast
1 tbsp. brown sugar
1 cup Softasilk flour
1 cup all purpose flour
1 cup Occident flour
4 tbsp. baking soda in 4 cups water

Combine first 6 ingredients and shape into pretzels. Dip pretzels into baking soda water. Then put on baking sheets. Sprinkle with salt. Bake at 450°. Occasionally brush with butter.

Vegetables and Side Dishes

Friendship Is a Recipe

Take a heap of joy, blend well with trust,
And measure the dreams you share;
Add minds more than willing to understand,
And hearts more than ready to care.

Fold in a generous fluff of forgiving nature,
Kindly words and thoughtful deeds,
A pinch of humor and a dash of spice
Whipped in with loving speed.

A recipe as old as time itself,
Yet always delightfully new. . . .
They call it simply friendship,
Beloved, tried, and true!

Author unknown

One summer *evening my two daughters and I drove to the neighbors to pick string beans. They had extra that year, and we needed more, so they kindly offered to share with us. We tied the horse to the white barnyard fence and took our baskets to the garden. We had each picked a full basket already and set it on the wagon and were starting on the second when we heard a clattering sound. Something must have scared the horse, and he tore loose and took off running home without us. The baskets upset and there were beans scattered over the road. A neighbor man was coming down the road on a scooter and managed to stop the horse. All's well that ends well, but there for a while we were pretty worried that the horse would run into a car or upset the wagon. We had enough beans left to can thirty quarts and make barbecued string beans (our favorite).*

Barbecued Green Beans

3 quarts green beans, cooked, salted, and drained
1 onion
1 cup ketchup
1 cup brown sugar
6 slices bacon

Put beans in baking dish. Mix onion, ketchup, and brown sugar; pour over beans. Bacon slices may be placed on top or chopped and mixed in. Cover. Bake at 275° for 4 hours.

Note: Beans may be canned with this recipe, too.

Two-Bean Bake

2 cups cooked string beans	1 cup chopped celery
2 cups of canned kidney beans	2 tbsp. vinegar
1 medium onion, chopped	2 tsp. mustard
½ cup ketchup	1 tsp. salt
3 tbsp. brown sugar	4 strips bacon

Combine beans and onions. Combine remaining ingredients except bacon and add to beans. Pour into baking dish and lay bacon on top (I like to fry it first). Bake at 375° for 45 minutes. Serves 6 to 8.

Simple, quick, and delicious!

Carrot and Celery Bake

3 cups chopped carrots
3 cups 1-inch celery slices
1½ cups shredded processed cheese
1 can cream of chicken soup, not diluted
⅓ cup slivered or sliced almonds
1 tbsp. butter or margarine

Cook carrots and celery in boiling water 8 minutes; drain. Alternate layers of celery, carrots, cheese, and soup in greased casserole, ending with soup. Lightly brown almonds in butter and sprinkle over celery mixture. Bake at 350° for 20 to 30 minutes or until hot all the way through. Serves 6.

Copying these *lima bean recipes made me think of the pole limas we had in our garden when we were children. Four bean poles were set up like a teepee, and the beans climbed up these poles so vigorously that they formed a little playhouse inside. My sister and I took our little benches and sat inside the leafy house to play with our dolls, tell stories, or have a little snack. We had a litter of playful kittens, and they liked to play there, too, pouncing on grasshoppers or playing tag with each other's tails. Our favorite story was about the city mouse that lost its tail when a cat pounced on it. We decided we'd rather be a country mouse and live on garden vegetables than to be at the house cat's mercy.*

Easy Creamed Limas

4 cups fresh lima beans

1 tsp. sugar

2 tsp. salt

2 tbsp. butter

$\frac{1}{8}$ tsp. pepper

$\frac{3}{4}$ cup milk

$\frac{1}{4}$ cup cream

1 tsp. cornstarch

Cool beans in water until tender and almost dry. Add seasoning and butter, milk, and cream. Bring to a boil and thicken with cornstarch.

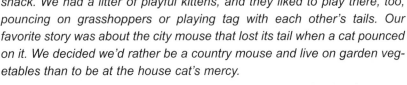

Lima Bean Bake

2 cups dried lima beans
4 slices bacon or 2-inch cube of salt pork
1 small onion
1 green pepper
1 cup canned tomatoes
2 tsp. salt
1 tsp. mustard
2 tbsp. brown sugar

Wash beans and soak overnight in cold water. In the morning drain and add 2 quarts fresh water. Cook until almost tender. Pour beans in a buttered casserole. Add minced pepper, onion, tomato, and seasoning; mix together. Place bacon or salt pork on top and bake with cover on casserole. Add more liquid as necessary. Bake 2 hours at 325°; leave uncovered the last 30 minutes. Serves 6.

One year *we had a cousin quilting in November. We served platters of fresh tomatoes. One of our cousins jokingly remarked that this is evidence that we live further north and have a late growing season. But this is a special method of preserving them, which I recommend to anyone who enjoys tomatoes as much as we do. One year I actually had them last until January.*

Garden Tomatoes in December

Just before frost pick green, unblemished tomatoes. Wrap individually in newspaper and store in a cool, dry place (not freezing). These will ripen slowly, and you will have fresh tomatoes until Christmas.

Living in *a new settlement with no church house yet, the people having the church services at their home would often invite the families to stay for dinner. When our turn came to have church at our house, I wracked my brain, trying to think of something simple and easy to serve, so there wouldn't be much work to do on a Sunday.*

As I was trying to plan the menu, I thought about all the canned string beans and tomato juice we had in the cellar. I thought about making a sauce with the tomatoes, adding to it browned ground beef, and pouring it over string beans. That would do for the meat and the vegetable, and I wouldn't need gravy. I could also make creamed potatoes to go with it, and that would be a complete meal. So I devised my own recipe for the bean dish and hoped people would like it.

I was quite surprised and pleased when, after our church meal was over, a proper Indiana lady asked me for the recipe of my meat and string bean dish. I had to tell her there was no recipe; I had made it up myself! But I did try to write it out then, as I had made it.

Green Beans in Tomato Sauce

1 quart tomato juice

1 tsp. salt

2 tbsp. sugar

dash of baking soda

Bring this to a boil in saucepan and thicken with a flour paste.

1 pound hamburger

1 small onion

season to taste

Brown the meat and onion in a frying pan; then drain and add to the tomato sauce. Pour over 2 quarts of canned string beans, in a large baking dish. Bake at 325° for 25 minutes.

Baked Tomatoes

Slice raw tomatoes in a cake pan or casserole. Over this arrange pepper and onion rings. Season with sugar, salt, and pepper. Cover with bread crumbs toasted in melted butter and seasoned with salt and pepper, as for filling. Bake in moderate oven for 1 hour or until browned.

Note: This is quite a delicious dish for hungry farmers (or anyone). It's good with fresh tomatoes and onions. Mom often makes this recipe.

This is *a simple recipe. Mom can't make these often enough to suit us. They're better than McDonald's or store-bought onion rings. I'm a ten-year-old girl who likes to help Mom cook. And it's so much fun to dip these onion rings and fry them. I really like to cook!*

Onion Rings

Cut onions into rings. Dip in the following mixture and fry in deep fat or oil:

$\frac{1}{2}$ *cup flour*

$\frac{1}{4}$ *tsp. salt*

$\frac{1}{2}$ *tsp. baking powder*

1 egg, beaten lightly

2 tbsp. oil

$\frac{1}{4}$ *cup milk*

We never *sprayed our sweet corn, and so sometimes the fall corn was a bit wormy. Those ugly grubs gave me the shivers, and I always handed the suspicious-looking ones to Mom to do. It was fun, though, having a corn day with my two single aunts coming over to help. They knew such interesting stories—the work never got boring or tedious when they were here. I remember one aunt asking me, "What has two ears but can't hear, white, silky hair, but never combs it, grows delicious and sweet and we love it?" (meaning cornstalk and roasting ears.) Without thinking, I burst out, "My baby brother!" She laughed heartily at my guess and told me it was a clever answer. We like dried corn almost better than the canned and frozen.*

Dried Corn

2 cups dried corn	2 tsp. sugar
1 tsp. of salt	½ cup cream
⅛ tsp. pepper	1 cup milk

Grind dried corn before cooking. Cook in water until nearly tender. Add milk and cream and simmer another 15 minutes.

How to dry corn

Cook corn for 10 minutes as for roasting ears. Cut from cob. To each gallon of cut corn add ¾ cup sweet cream, ½ cup white sugar, and salt to taste. Pour into flat pans and place into the oven to dry. Stir often so the corn will dry more evenly. One may omit cream and sugar. Don't forget to leave the oven door partly open when using the oven for drying.

Favorite Scalloped Corn

2 cups corn	1 cup milk
1/2 tsp. salt	2/3 cup cracker crumbs
1/8 tsp. pepper	3 tbsp. melted butter
1 tbsp. sugar	2 eggs, beaten
1 tsp. minced onion	

Mix all together and pour in a greased casserole. Bake at 350° for 30 minutes. Serves 6.

Baked Beans

1 quart cooked beans	1/2 cup ketchup
1/3 cup brown sugar	salt and pepper to taste
2 tbsp. lard or shortening	
1/4 pound bacon, fried and crumbled	

Mix and bake at 350° for 45 minutes.

Years ago *we had a pet raccoon that could open the screen door by himself and come into the kitchen whenever he wanted to. He knew he wasn't allowed up on the kitchen table, but we soon found out that if there were ears of fresh sweet corn on the table, he didn't have a conscience anymore, or else forgot the rules! He didn't need to wash his corn before he ate it, either! He looked so cute and comical when attacking a roasting ear that we couldn't help but laugh and laugh! We had an electric fence around our corn patch in the garden, and so this was his only chance at his favorite snack.*

Kansas Corn Pie

1¼ cup fine cracker crumbs

⅓ cup butter, melted

2 tbsp. butter

1¼ cup milk, divided

1½ cups fresh raw corn

½ tsp. salt

2 tbsp. flour

½ tsp. onion salt or plain salt

2 eggs, beaten

Combine crumbs and ⅓ cup butter. Line 9-inch pie pan with ¾ cup buttered crumbs (reserve ½ cup for topping). Combine 2 tbsp. butter, 1 cup milk, corn, and ½ tsp. salt. Bring to boil; reduce heat and cook 3 minutes. Add flour to remaining ¼ cup milk; mix to smooth paste. Add slowly to corn, stirring constantly. Cook 2 to 3 minutes or until thick. Cool slightly; add onion salt. Add eggs slowly, stirring constantly. Pour into crumb-lined pan. Sprinkle ½ cup buttered crumbs on top. Bake 20 minutes at 400°.

Here's our favorite broccoli dish:

Broccoli Bonanza

2 eggs

⅔ cup mayonnaise

1 (10¾-ounce) can cream of mushroom soup

2 (10-ounce) packages frozen chopped broccoli

1 medium onion, finely chopped

1 cup cheese, grated, loosely packed

½ cup fine dry bread crumbs

2 tbsp. butter, melted

paprika

Cook broccoli according to package directions and drain well. Whisk eggs slightly; add mayonnaise and soup and whisk to blend. Stir in broccoli, onion, and cheese. Turn into oblong 1½-quart baking dish. Mix bread crumbs and butter and sprinkle on top. Sprinkle with paprika. Bake in pre-heated 350° oven about 35 minutes or until sides begin to bubble. Serves 8.

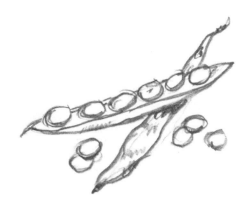

Vegetable Loaf

1 cup chopped cabbage

1 cup diced potatoes

1 cup diced carrots

1 cup bread crumbs

1 cup milk

1 egg

1 onion, chopped fine

1½ pound hamburger

1 tsp. salt

¼ tsp. pepper

1 tbsp. butter

Mix all ingredients together like meat loaf. Bake at 350° for 2 hours. Sometimes I like to put a glaze over the top made with ½ cup brown sugar, 1½ tsp. prepared mustard, 1 tbsp. Worcestershire sauce, and 1 tbsp. vinegar. Spread over top and bake. Delicious! This makes a nice one-dish meal: you have your meat and vegetables all in one, it is handy and quick for a busy mother to mix it up and put in oven, and it will be ready for dinner. It could also be served with noodles or elbow macaroni and a salad to go with it. Mmm!

To my *way of thinking, no corn is as delicious as when it's eaten fresh from the cob! Dripping with melted butter and sprinkled with salt—yum! When I was a youngster, we children didn't like the job of hoeing corn, especially not when the sun was beating down mercilessly on the corn patch, and the creek that flowed through the nearby meadow looked so very inviting!*

One Sunday when our parents were away visiting elderly friends, we children decided to have a corn party down at our picnic spot in the meadow. We made a campfire on our stone hearth with the old grate over top; then we boiled ears of corn in the old cast-iron pot. As I remember it, we didn't have much else to eat besides roasting ears, but they were about the most delicious we'd ever tasted. Maybe it was the flavor of the wood smoke, or the tangy scent of the pines that did it. Scalloped corn is also a favorite of our family, and we make it often.

Corn Croquettes

2 cups fresh corn	1 tsp. salt
2 eggs	1/8 tsp. pepper
1 tbsp. melted butter	1 tsp. baking powder
1/4 cup flour	1 tbsp. cream

Mix all together. Drop by spoonfuls into hot fat in a frying pan and brown on both sides.

Cornmeal

Dry nice selected ears of field corn or sweet corn in slow, open-door oven for several days, or until the corn shells easily by hand. The cornmeal is tasty when the corn has been slightly browned. Shell; then take to a mill to have it ground. Put into oblong pan and bake in a slow oven (275°) for a more toasted flavor. Stir occasionally. Place in a tight container when cool.

Cornhusking time, *with its memories of bantering and visiting (and racing), is here again, only we don't do it by hand anymore like we used to. I always thought it such a nice time of year when most of the cornfields are bare again, and only the corn stubble remains. Now we can see the neighboring farms again (instead of only the windmills) and also the creek valley. I always liked working in the fields, especially at cornhusking time when the heat of the summer is past and a person has more energy. When the weather gets cool, we start to cook cornmeal mush again regularly, and always have fried mush for breakfast over the winter. We like it with eggs and homemade ketchup, but Grandpa likes to eat his topped with molasses. Once we had out-of-state guests here for breakfast, and they poured milk over the mush and ate it with peach slices. We always cook our fresh batch of cornmeal mush before supper, and have hot mush with milk for supper, but when we fry the molded mush for breakfast, we never eat it with milk. It's an economical dish and probably healthier fare than most other recipes.*

Cornmeal Mush

Bring 3 cups of water to a boil. Make a thickening with 1 cup cornmeal, 1 tsp. salt, and 1 cup milk. Add to the boiling water. Stir until it has reached the boiling point, and then stir occasionally. Cook for 15 to 20 minutes; then pour into a deep baking dish. Cool. Slice and fry.

Note: To clean the mush kettle after the mush has been poured out, put a cup or two of water into the kettle. Add 1 tsp. baking soda. Cover and bring to boiling point. Set kettle aside, but keep covered until dishwashing time.

California Potatoes

6 medium potatoes
¼ cup butter or margarine
1 (10½-ounce) can cream of chicken soup
1 pint sour cream
⅓ cup chopped onion
1½ cups shredded cheese
2 cups crushed cornflakes
2 tbsp. butter

Boil and slice potatoes; set aside. Heat ¼ cup butter or margarine and add undiluted soup, onion, sour cream, and cheese. Stir mixture into potatoes and place in a greased baking dish. Mix together cornflakes and 2 tbsp. melted butter. Place on top of potatoes. Bake at 350° for 45 minutes. Yummy!

The three *years since we're married, we planted our own potatoes but somehow never had enough to last through the winter. Every time my sister-in-law shared so generously, but this spring we decided we'll make sure we have plenty. So we planted fifty pounds. Our friends and family thought we would find out that we're going to the other extreme! Not knowing that we'd have a wet summer, we planted them in the lowest part of the garden. How wise a God we serve! He is too wise for us to know his plans. Anyway, he sent us plenty of "showers of blessings" this summer, and we don't want to complain. We have plenty to eat, but have even less potatoes for the winter than other years because they rotted in the wet ground! My kind sister-in-law is sharing potatoes again. She says she's just glad to share, and she knows we tried. I guess it is a real lesson for us so we don't take too much pride in being able to manage well.*

chatting

On my *fifteenth birthday, I was home alone for the day. Before the others had left for their various appointments, no one had even thought of or mentioned my birthday. It was a rainy day, but when the mail carrier went, I splashed through the downpour to see if a card had come for me. When none was there, I felt a bit forgotten and blue. I tried to do some sewing that afternoon, but after sewing a seam wrong and breaking two needles, I gave up in frustration. I didn't feel like cooking much for supper and decided that we'd all have to be satisfied with tomato soup. A little later a carriage drove in, and it was my married sister, her husband, and baby. She had brought a complete supper for us, including party potatoes, baked beans, sauerkraut balls, and a birthday cake with candles for me. It turned out to be the best birthday I'd ever had.*

Party Potatoes

4 cups mashed potatoes

1 cup sour cream

1 package cream cheese, softened

1 tsp. dried chives or parsley flakes

¼ tsp. garlic powder

¼ cup dry bread crumbs

1 tbsp. butter or margarine, melted

½ cup shredded cheese

Turn into a 2-quart casserole. Combine bread crumbs with butter. Sprinkle over potatoes. Bake at 350° for 50 to 60 minutes. Top with cheese and serve.

Sauerkraut Balls

4 tbsp. oleo

1 medium onion, chopped

1½ cups ham, cooked and chopped

½ cloves garlic, minced

4 tbsp. flour

½ cup liquid from sauerkraut

3 cups sauerkraut, drained and chopped

1 tbsp. chopped parsley

1 egg

2 cups milk

flour

fine bread crumbs

Melt oleo in skillet. Add onion and brown lightly. Add ham and garlic and brown lightly. Stir in flour and cook thoroughly. Add sauerkraut, liquid, and parsley. Cook and stir a few more minutes. Mixture should form a thick paste. Remove from heat and chill. Form into 1-inch balls. At serving time, beat eggs and milk together. Dip balls in additional flour, next into egg mixture, and last into fine bread crumbs. Fry in deep-well fryer until brown. Serve hot. Makes about 50 balls.

Hot-pepper rings *are our favorite recipe for hot peppers. We got it from my cousin Becky. We also like it for relishes. We like to can them once they have turned orange and red. My married sister doesn't like to wait that long and always cans them green and yellow. I remember so well when my little brother didn't know what hot-pepper rings were, and we told him to eat some, which he did. Oh my! Tears came to his eyes, and he spit and spat and actually cried. The poor thing didn't eat them right away again. But now that he's bigger, he likes them better. Once when he was sick with flu, he ate about a pint just out of the can, and they were hot, too. He sure got better in a hurry! They shouldn't be cut without plastic gloves, though, or your hands will burn for hours. Eat them while hunting to keep warm.*

Hot-Pepper Rings

1 peck hot peppers

1 quart vinegar

$^3/_4$ quart water

1 pint oil

2 handfuls salt

2 cloves garlic, minced and chopped

$^1/_2$ cup oregano

Wear rubber gloves to chop peppers. Slice the peppers. Mix other ingredients together and pour over the peppers. Let set at least 4 hours; longer is okay. Put in jars and boil 5 minutes. Yummy if you like hot stuff!

One snowy *New Year's Day over thirty years ago, when my two sisters and I were home alone, each of us decided to try out a recipe we'd never made before. We thought it was a special meal, and I'll include three recipes we used.*

That afternoon, we went for a walk in the snow, along the creek that winds through the meadow. We tried to identify the tracks we saw of all the little woodland folks and birds. When we came back, we felt famished again, and with the help of our brothers polished off the leftovers! Whenever I feel twinges of homesickness for those long past days, I relive all the memories and make our special recipes again.

Spinach Supreme

1 (10-ounce) package frozen spinach
2 pounds ground beef
2 eggs
¼ cup ketchup
¼ cup milk
¾ cup soft bread crumbs
½ tsp. salt
¼ tsp. pepper
¼ tsp. oregano
1 (3-ounce) package smoked sliced ham
3 slices mozzarella cheese, sliced diagonally in half
1 tsp. salt

Thaw spinach quickly by rinsing with running hot water. Mix next 8 ingredients. Pat into 10 x 12 inch rectangle on a piece of tin foil. Arrange spinach evenly on top of meat, leaving a ½-inch margin around edge. Sprinkle with 1 tsp. salt. Arrange ham on top. Carefully roll up, beginning at narrow end and using foil to lift meat. Press edges and ends of roll to seal. Place on ungreased 9 x 13 inch pan. Bake at 350° for 1 hour and 15 minutes. Overlap cheese triangles on roll. Bake 5 minutes more.

Ham and Potatoes

½ pound smoked ham	1½ tsp. flour
6 large potatoes, sliced	½ cup thin cream
1 tsp. salt	

Cut ham into small cubes and cook until almost tender. Then add sliced potatoes and salt. When potatoes are soft and almost dry, add flour and cream that have been mixed together. Bring to a boil and serve. Serves 6.

Barb's Sweet Potatoes

3 cups sweet potatoes, cooked and mashed

2 eggs, well beaten

½ cup sugar

½ cup butter

Topping

1 cup brown sugar	1 cup chopped pecans
½ cup flour	1 cup miniature marshmallows
⅓ cup butter	

Place potato mixture in greased casserole dish. Crumble brown sugar topping over. Bake at 300° for 20 to 30 minutes. Spread marshmallows on after it's done and put in oven to melt.

Pineapple Sweet Potato Casserole

2 cups cubed sweet potatoes
¼ cup rice (cooked)
½ (12-ounce) can pineapple (chunked or crushed) with juice
1 tbsp. honey
1 tbsp. molasses
⅓ tsp. salt

Mix and bake 1 hour at 350° (if desired, add marshmallows on top after it's done and put in oven to melt). Delicious!

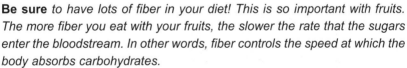

Be sure *to have lots of fiber in your diet! This is so important with fruits. The more fiber you eat with your fruits, the slower the rate that the sugars enter the bloodstream. In other words, fiber controls the speed at which the body absorbs carbohydrates.*

Foods high in fiber include beans, lentils, split peas, nuts, seeds, whole grains, vegetables, and fruits. Millet, bran, dried figs, sunflower seeds, and macadamia nuts have especially high amounts.

One tablespoon of oat bran with meals will dramatically slow down sugar absorption.

chatting

I don't think *we'll ever forget the first time we tried out this recipe! Our daughter had invited her special friend (who lived in another state) to our home as guest for a Sunday evening meal. She was anxious to have everything shipshape and the food tasty and appealing. "First impressions are so important," she declared. "I just wonder what he will think of my family, our home, and the meal."*

"It's you he is interested in, and he probably won't notice what he's eating," I teased. "Just relax and be yourself." But she was determined to have everything tip-top. She had gotten this delicious-sounding recipe from a friend and wanted to try it out for the special occasion. It turned out beautifully! To add a decorative touch, she garnished it with sprigs of parsley and halved cherry tomatoes around the rim. Everything went as planned until it was time to serve her fancy dish. As she was carrying it to the table, it somehow slipped out of her hands and flopped upside down on the floor! She was terribly embarrassed and disappointed, and later said she was close to tears, sure that her boyfriend would think her awkward and dappich *(clumsy). But apparently he didn't, for that very evening he asked for her hand in marriage, and they chose a wedding date.*

Ham, Cheese, and Broccoli Bake

6 strips bacon, fried and crumbled	7 cups milk
12 slices frozen bread	4 tsp. minced onion
20 ounces frozen broccoli	1 tsp. salt
4 cups diced ham	½ tsp. dry mustard
10 eggs	
1 pound grated cheese	

Layer bread, bacon, cheese, broccoli, and ham in a 9 x 12 inch pan. Beat eggs; add milk, onion, salt, and dry mustard. Pour milk and egg mixture over all. Refrigerate 6 hours. Bake at 325° for 60 minutes. Lay Velveeta cheese slices on top and allow to melt before serving.

My husband *just loves this casserole. Someone served us this casserole when my in-laws came to see our new baby boy (sixteen years ago). We both liked it so much. Since then I have given recipes to friends who ate at our table. It's a full-course meal all in one dish.*

Yummasetti

1 large package noodles (cook in salt water; drain)

3 pounds hamburger (fry in butter with an onion)

1 pint peas, slightly cooked

2 cans mushroom soup

1 can cream of chicken soup (I made my own; just a white sauce)

1 cup sour cream

Toast ½ loaf of bread in butter. Mix all the soup and cream together. Add to the other ingredients, which have been in a large container. Mix. Pour into a roast pan and bake 1 hour at 350°.

I got *this recipe from a friend of mine who hosted a mystery dinner one Sunday. We girls were all seated at the table, but there was no food or plates and utensils on it. We each got a list and could choose three items from it. Some of the things listed were Shimmering Silk, Mountain Sauce, Tangled Topiary, Dazzling Delight, Sculptor's Scheme, and Splendid Creation. I don't remember the rest, but for most of them, we hadn't a clue as to what we were getting. One girl got a chocolate cupcake, a mound of mashed potatoes, and a pickle, with no utensils! She ate the mashed potatoes with her pickle! I was lucky; I got this lasagna, potato salad, and a fork. For my next course, I got ice-cream dessert, apricot jam, and a knife! The lasagna was the Splendid Creation, and I liked it so well that I copied off the recipe.*

Lisa's Lasagna

1 pound hamburger

10 ounces lasagna noodles

spaghetti sauce

2 eggs

3 ounces cottage cheese

½ cup Parmesan cheese

1 pound mozzarella cheese

2 tbsp. parsley flakes

1 tsp. salt

½ tsp. pepper

Brown meat and remove fat. Add sauce. Cook noodles and drain. Beat eggs. Add remaining ingredients except mozzarella cheese. In 9 x 13 inch pan layer these: noodles, cottage cheese mixture, meat sauce, mozzarella cheese. Bake at 375° for 45 minutes.

I remember *the first time I tasted these Spatzlein (Little Sparrows) when I was a little girl at grandmother's house. I was staying for a few days while my parents were visiting in Michigan. Because of the name, I didn't want to taste them at first (I thought they were boiled sparrows), but my uncle really bragged them up and smacked his lips as he ate them to prove that they really were delicious. Finally I got up the courage to taste them, and to my surprise, they were quite good! I ate a big serving and later told my mother she ought to make them, too.*

On that visit Grandmother gave me a little butter plate with pink flowers on it, which I still have, and value as a remembrance of her. Later we moved to another state, and I didn't see my grandmother much anymore. I often think about it, that the children privileged to grow up close to their grandparents really have a blessing. My other grandparents weren't close either, so I don't have many memories of being at their house. At least we could write to them and were thankful for the letters we received in return.

Spatzlein (Little Sparrows)

1 egg or 2 egg yolks	dash of black pepper
1½ tsp. salt	1 cup water
¼ tsp. turmeric	2½ cups flour
¼ tsp. saffron	1 tbsp. butter
1 tsp. dried parsley (optional)	2 quarts boiling water

Beat the egg with a fork in a bowl, add the 1 cup of water, and continue beating until well blended. Work in the flour to make a soft batter. In a large kettle bring the seasonings and 2 quarts water and the butter to a boil and drop the Spatzlein into it. (Tilt the bowl of batter over the kettle and cut with a spoon as it pours over, to make Spatzlein about 1 x ½ inch). Cook for 3 minutes after all the batter is in the water. Drain and top with plenty of browned butter.

One winter day *we were notified that school was canceled for the day because something was wrong with the heater. Hurrah! Mother decided that since she had us girls at home to help, it would be a good day to make noodles. We mixed a double portion of dough, and soon filled our long table and the countertops with rolled-out noodle dough, cut noodles, and noodles in various stages. We planned to eat dinner at the laundry room table, because the kitchen table was filled with noodles.*

At 11:00 someone fetched the mail, and here was a card saying that our two uncles and aunts and their families were coming for dinner on Thursday, a whole vanload of them. What? Thursday was today! A few minutes later the van was coming in the lane already! The postcard had been delayed for some reason, and we were unprepared.

Our company (the women) pitched in and helped with the noodles, and the men and children patiently waited until we cleared the table. They were satisfied with a meal of canned vegetable soup with plenty of fresh noodles in it!

Noodle Dough

6 egg yolks	
6 tbsp. water	
about 3 cups flour	
1 tsp. salt	

Beat egg yolks and water thoroughly. Work in flour. Divide in 4 balls, roll out very thin or put through noodle maker. Lay separately on a cloth to dry. They're ready to cut when they're dry enough not to stick together.

Noodle Cheese Bake

3 tbsp. margarine	1 tsp. salt
1 (8-ounce) package homemade noodles	¼ tsp. black pepper
½ pound Velveeta cheese	1 quart cold milk

Melt margarine in a 9 x 11 inch baking pan. Pour noodles in and stir until well coated. Cover with sliced cheese, each slice cut in fourths. Add salt, pepper, and milk. Bake, uncovered, at 325° for 1½ hours. Do not stir while baking. This comes out of the oven golden and creamy. Cold sliced hot dogs and well-drained canned peas can be added.

Noodles and Cheddar Cheese

½ pound hamburger, browned

2 cups uncooked noodles

2 cups shredded cheddar cheese, divided

1 can cream of mushroom soup

½ cup milk

½ cup chopped, canned tomatoes

¼ cup chopped celery

Cook noodles in boiling, salted water until tender. Drain. In shallow baking dish, combine 1½ cups cheese with remaining ingredients. Top with ½ cup cheese. Bake at 350° for 30 minutes.

Gathering *the eggs was my task when I was a schoolgirl, and how I hated the biddies that stayed on the nests and defended their rights to the eggs! I would try to reach in to yank them off, but they sure were quick with their sharp beaks. And such a fuss and cackling when I managed to steal their eggs! Once when I was gathering eggs at my uncle's place, there was a saucy rooster in the pen. He came after me, and I, with a basket of about ten eggs, tripped over a waterer, fell, and smashed all the eggs. The chickens came running and gobbled them all up! I shed tears of frustration and thought they were mighty greedy and stupid.*

Oriental Egg Rolls

Filling

1 pound ground turkey

¼ cup butter

4 cups finely shredded, partially cooked cabbage

¼ cup green onion, chopped fine

¼ cup grated carrots

1½ cups finely diced celery

2 cups bean sprouts

¼ cup soy sauce

1 tsp. salt

2 tbsp. sugar

Batter

2 cups flour	1 tsp. sugar
2 tbsp. cornstarch	2 cups water
1 tsp. salt	vegetable oil to deep fry
1 egg, beaten	

Brown turkey lightly in butter. Add vegetables and seasonings and cook 5 minutes. Drain and cool. Prepare batter by combining dry ingredients and adding the egg and sugar. Gradually beat in water until smooth batter is formed. Grease a 6-inch skillet lightly with oil. Pour ¼ cup of batter in the center; then tilt pan to spread evenly. Cook over low heat until edges pull from sides. Carefully turn pancake with fingers and cook other side. Cool. Put 1 heaping tbsp. filling in center of pancake and spread filling to within ½ inch of edges. Roll, folding in sides, and seal with a mixture of 1 tbsp. flour and 2 tbsp. water. Deep-fry egg rolls in 360° oil until golden brown.

Easy Cheesy Egg Bake

6 hard cooked eggs

1 cup grated cheese

2 cups bread crumbs

½ tsp. salt

⅛ tsp. pepper

½ cup cream

Slice eggs and arrange alternate layers of eggs, cheese, and crumbs in a buttered casserole. Season with salt and pepper. Pour cream over mixture and sprinkle with additional crumbs. Bake at 350° for 30 minutes.

On Thanksgiving Day *a few years ago, our cousins who lived nine miles away invited us for Thanksgiving dinner. When we woke up that morning, the ground was covered with several inches of snow, and it was still snowing. Everyone in our family would have been so disappointed if we'd have had to miss the gathering (the other cousins all lived much closer). So Dad borrowed the neighbor's two-seated sleigh and quickly reinforced and repaired it at some places. We loaded plenty of carriage blankets for covering the little ones, and we tucked them in up to their noses. I think I enjoyed that ride as much as I did the food, fun, and fellowship. The snow was so beautiful, with big flakes drifting down softly and tapering off.*

I got these filling or stuffing recipes from my aunt, and they've been favorites of ours since.

Filling Balls

2 (20-ounce) loaves white bread

½ pound melted butter

1 tsp. salt (rounded)

⅛ tsp. pepper

4 eggs, beaten

2½ cups milk

Shape into balls and arrange on cookie sheets. Bake at 350° on upper rack for 20 to 25 minutes. Do not preheat. Top with giblet gravy.

Aunt Ida's Stuffing

5 eggs
1 quart milk
1 tsp. salt
½ tsp. pepper
½ tsp. poultry seasoning
½ cup melted butter
1 cup chopped celery
½ cup minced onion
1 loaf bread, cubed

Beat eggs well. Add remaining ingredients, adding bread last. Pour into greased baking dish. Bake at 350°, covered until set. When almost done, uncover to brown top.

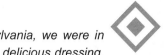

In 2003 *when Hurricane Isabel went through Pennsylvania, we were in Indiana attending a friend's wedding. They served this delicious dressing, a new dish for us.*

After we came home to Pennsylvania, I tried it on my family, and it immediately became a favorite. There are nine of us to cook for, and this is the right amount for our family. A handy one-dish meal!

Chicken Dressing

1 (20-ounce) loaf white bread

4 potatoes

1 carrot

1 stalk celery (leaves and all)

¼ cup chicken soup base

3 eggs, beaten

¼ tsp. black pepper

1 pint chicken broth and chicken pieces

¼ cup melted butter

¼ tsp. poultry seasoning

¼ cup onions

3 cups milk

Toast bread and cube. Dice veggies and cook until tender in 2 cups water and soup base. When veggies are done, mix with broth, milk, and bread. Add butter and seasonings. Dressing should be moist. Grease a 9 x 13 inch cake pan and bake the dressing in it at 400° for 45 to 60 minutes, or until firm and lightly browned.

Meats and Casseroles

A Recipe for a Happy Life

A heaping cup of Kindness,
Two cups of Love and Caring,
One cup of Understanding,
One cup of Joyful Sharing.

A level cup of Patience,
One cup of Thoughtful Insight,
One cup of Gracious Listening,
One cup of Sweet Forgiveness.

Mix ingredients together,
Toss in Smiles and Laughter,
Serve to everyone you know,
With Love forever after.

A Storm to Remember

Years ago when we were farming, and had three little girls, we lived with my husband's parents. One Sunday morning, it was cold but not stormy. So we hurried and milked our thirteen cows, and got ready for church. His parents stayed home, so we left one girl with them. By the time we got to church, it was really blowing and snowing. It got colder and colder and by the time we wanted to go home, it was a real blizzard. The men got ready to go, then didn't trust it to take women and children along. So some of us women and children stayed overnight. On Monday some then went home, but my husband was snowed in, and it was twenty below zero (F). It really drifts where we lived, and roads were completely closed. Tuesday noon they finally opened the road with high lifts, so my husband came and got me and two little girls. Was it ever good to be home and all together again!

Stormy Day One-Dish Meal

In a cake pan, put:

1 quart carrots

1 quart beans

some cut-up potatoes

a quart of canned beef chunks

Cover with cut-up cabbage. Cover with foil and bake. Thicken broth with flour when ready.

Stir up biscuits (see recipe on next page) and drop by spoonfuls on top and bake.

Biscuits

2 cups flour	4 tsp. baking powder
½ tsp. salt	½ tsp. cream of tartar
2 tsp. sugar	⅔ cup milk
½ cup shortening	

Corned Beef

25 pounds meat (steak preferred)

Rub with 1½ pounds salt. Let stand 24 hours; then rinse well and put in brine, using the following:

1½ pounds brown sugar

2 ounces baking soda

1½ tbsp. liquid smoke

2 ounces saltpeter (scant)

Water enough to make brine; then add enough brine to cover meat in a crock or plastic pail or what you have. Let stand 2 weeks; it is ready to use. Or keep it in a cool place up to 3 months. One can also can it after 2 weeks of being brine cured.

chatting

We often *serve this dish when we are busy working outside and have little time to prepare a full-course meal. I put this in the oven a few days ago before we left for our back woodlot to pick up shellbarks. We hitched Bob to the spring wagon and drove out the rutted back lane, enjoying the brightly colored leaves on the trees, and the fall breezes and mists along the creek. The squirrels were busy gathering nuts, too, and scolded us plenty for invading their territory. The two preschoolers each had their little sacks to fill, too, and thought it was great fun watching the squirrels. I always enjoy this time of year when the summer harvest is in the barns and granary, and in jars on the cellar shelves. We have so much to be thankful for, and we must remember Whom to thank.*

Seven-Layer Dinner

3 cups sliced raw potatoes	2 tsp. salt
2 cups sliced raw sweet potatoes	¼ tsp. pepper
2 cups chopped celery	1 tbsp. butter
½ cup minced onion	2 cups canned tomato juice
1 pound hamburger, browned	1 cup water
2 cups frozen peas, thawed	

Slice potatoes and sweet potatoes in bottom of greased casserole. Add celery, onions, peas, and hamburger. Sprinkle salt and pepper over all. Mix the tomato juice with 1 cup water and pour over mixture in dish. Dot with butter. Bake at 350° for 2 hours.

Here's a similar dish that we often make on washday, letting it bake for several hours:

Poor Man's Dinner

1 quart diced raw potatoes	
1 medium head cabbage	
2 cups diced carrots	
1 cup white rice	
1 tbsp. minced parsley	
1½ pounds ground beef	
2 tsp. salt	
¼ tsp. pepper	
¼ cup butter, melted	
½ cup minced onion	
3 cups tomato juice	
3 cups water	

Chop cabbage and put half of it in a greased roaster. Sprinkle rice over it. Add the carrots, potatoes, onions, parsley, and seasonings. Add the rest of the cabbage and melted butter; spread ground beef over top. Pour tomato juice and water over all and bake at 350° for 2 hours or more.

I often *make this one-dish meal when I'm in a hurry. It's a favorite of our family. It can also be made with sausage, which goes well with cabbage. We live on a farm, so it's a quick dish for dinner or supper when we're busy outside. It satisfies the hunger of the chore boys! I got the recipe from a lady I worked for as hired girl (in a bakery) and now make it for my family and pass it on to others.*

chatting

We have *several guinea hens wandering around on our farm, and they sometimes can become quite noisy. Our pet peeve is when they make a nuisance of themselves in the garden. When they do, we run and shoo them out by flapping our aprons. When they see us coming, they retreat and raise a racket that sounds like they're squawking, "Get back! Get back!" to each other. They do make delicious stews, though, and their fresh eggs are good hard boiled.*

One day I tried out a new dish and happened to add too much chili powder. I threw it out behind the manure pile, and the guinea hens came running for their share. But they didn't like it either, which hurt my feelings still more. Since then I've gotten some good meat recipes, and I'll share a few with you.

Guinea Patties

½ cup chopped onion

½ cup minced green pepper, optional

⅓ cup chopped celery

4 tbsp. butter

2 pounds ground guinea fowl

2 tbsp. minced chives or onion tops

1 tbsp. minced parsley

1 tsp. salt

½ tsp. pepper

½ tsp. dry mustard

dash of each: marjoram, thyme, and paprika, if desired

Sauté onion, peppers, and celery in 2 tbsp. butter. Add to remaining ingredients and mix well. Shape into 6 patties about 1 inch thick. Fry in remaining butter on both sides until done.

Poor Man's Steak

3 pounds ground turkey

1 cup soda cracker crumbs

1 cup cold water or milk

1 tbsp. salt

¼ tsp. pepper

1 onion, finely chopped

1 can mushroom soup

oregano and sage, optional

Mix all ingredients, except mushroom soup, and press onto cookie sheet: make it ½ inch thick or shape into balls. Refrigerate several hours or overnight. Roll in flour and brown on both sides. Put into roaster; top with a mixture of 1 can mushroom soup and 1 soup can water, or top with undiluted soup. Bake 1½ hours at 325°.

Variation: Use 2 cups cracker crumbs and 2 cups cold milk.

Last fall our neighbors' young feeder steers got out and ran off—into the surrounding fields and woods. Our fourteen-year-old son jumped on his pony, and along with other neighbors on horseback, went to help round them up. One steer, seeing his chance for escape, charged the pony. The pony stood his ground, but our son was thrown off. He hurt his elbow and couldn't work for a few days. He became interested in helping to make chicken croquettes and could still crank the meat grinder with his good arm.

Chicken Croquettes

2 tbsp. butter	1/8 tsp. pepper
2½ tbsp. flour	2 tbsp. minced parsley or celery
1 cup milk	2 eggs, beaten
2 cups minced cooked chicken	1 cup dried bread crumbs
1 tsp. salt	
¼ tsp. onion juice or ¼ cup minced onion	

Make a white sauce: Melt fat; add flour, and stir in milk. Add finely chopped chicken and seasoning. Cool thoroughly; then shape into balls. Dip into crumbs, next into beaten eggs, and again into crumbs. Fry in deep fat for 3 to 5 minutes. Serves 6.

Quick method: Omit cooling; drop in skillet and fry like pancakes. Good with ketchup.

Freezes well. Put in a tight container. When ready to use, place on cookie sheets and cover with aluminum foil. Bake at 350° until hot.

Variation: Mix 2 cups cooked chopped chicken, 2 cups bread crumbs, 2 beaten eggs, ¼ cup chopped onion; salt and pepper to taste. Shape into balls and follow the directions above.

Creamed Chicken

1 chicken, cooked and deboned, or 2 quarts chicken with broth

4 to 6 cups macaroni, cooked in chicken broth

2 cans cream of chicken soup

2 cans cream of celery soup

2 packages frozen peas

2 cups Velveeta cheese

1 onion

Placed in greased casserole and add 2 cups buttered bread crumbs. Bake at 350° for 1 hour.

Delicious! Our family never gets tired of this. We have it every Saturday evening for supper.

One *Thanksgiving Day we were having this Amish roast when* Mamm *(Mother) had invited our grandparents, aunts, uncles, and cousins for dinner.* Mamm *had also made a molded cranberry-apple salad. When my six-year-old cousin was trying to lift the dish of cranberry salad, it slipped out of his hands and flipped upside down into the Amish roast. As a result, the roast had a somewhat different color and taste, but Dad remarked, "That's okay; it would all have ended up at the same place anyway." (Smiles.) Some people grind up the chicken or turkey giblets and add it to the roast, but* Mamm *always adds it to the gravy. We think no meal would be complete without gravy.*

Original Amish Roast

3 large chickens
3 gallons cubed bread
8 eggs
1 pound butter
⅓ gallon celery, finely blended
2 tbsp. salt
1 tsp. pepper

Roast chicken in oven until done; remove meat from bones and cube. Set aside. Mix butter and celery; cook until butter is brown. Set aside. Beat eggs and seasonings; pour this and butter mixture over bread. Mix with meat. Place in a greased pan; cover and bake at 250° for 1 hour. Stir a few times so sides don't dry out.

One can make it a day before and refrigerate it. Excellent for a wedding dinner.

Here's the recipe our cousins use:

Modified Amish Roast

4 quarts soft bread crumbs

12 eggs

8 cups milk

4 tbsp. parsley

4 tsp. onions

4 tsp. salt

4 tsp. sage or poultry seasoning

7 tbsp. butter or chicken fat

4 to 6 cups chicken or turkey meat

Beat eggs and add milk. Pour liquid over bread crumbs. Add melted fat, parsley, onions, and seasoning. Mix well. Add chicken or turkey meat. Bake at 350° until done, approximately 45 minutes.

On our farm we have a big pond, with plenty of ducks always on it, so duck is what I usually serve when I invite the family to our place for dinner. I always make two plump ones and stuff them with bread filling. Last Thanksgiving Day I invited the family, and they were on their way here. My sister told me that as soon as they could see our farm, their little four-year-old piped up, "Oh look, that's where the duck people live!"

Here are two recipes I changed into duck dishes:

Duck and Herb Stuffing

3 cups duck, chopped
1 can celery soup
1 can cream of mushroom soup
⅔ cups milk
1 stick margarine
1 package herb stuffing or croutons

Stew duck and remove bones. Reserve ½ cup broth. Cube or chop duck and place in bottom of greased casserole dish. Mix soups with milk and pour over duck. Melt margarine and mix with broth. Mix this with stuffing. Place on top of soup and duck. Bake at 350° for 30 minutes. Serves 6 to 8.

Variation: Add 2 cups cooked macaroni and 1 cup grated cheese before baking.

Duck-in-a-Nest

Crumbs

5 to 6 cups soft bread crumbs	⅛ tsp. pepper
¼ cup minced onion	½ cup butter or margarine, melted
1 tsp. celery salt	½ tsp. poultry seasoning, optional

Filling

⅓ cup butter or margarine

⅓ cup flour

½ cup light cream

1½ cups milk

½ tsp. salt

½ tsp. pepper

1 tsp. Worcestershire sauce, optional

3 cups cooked duck, chopped

1 cup peas, optional

For nests, combine first 5 ingredients. Line 6 greased individual casseroles with crumb mixture. Press into place and bake at 375° for 15 minutes or until crumbs are brown.

Filling: Melt butter; blend in flour. Add cream, duck, broth, and seasonings. Cook until thickened, stirring constantly. Add duck and peas. Serve in crumb nests.

When copying *this chicken recipe, I thought about the rooster we had the first year we were married. We lived in a little house on the outskirts of a small town. Having such close neighbors was new for us, but we wanted to do our part in getting along with them. We had a horse, a few cats, a dog, and three banty hens and a rooster, which we kept in a big wire pen. We would have preferred to let them roam but knew that it wouldn't work in town. The rooster always started to crow at the crack of dawn, and to us it was a pleasant sound. It reminded me of home and the farm.*

One morning when the rooster started crowing, I got up and stood at the window for a few minutes to check the weather. Just then I saw a movement—the neighbor's teenage boy was sneaking over to the chicken pen! He picked up a stone, aimed for the rooster, and let it fly! The rooster fell over as if dead, and the boy turned and fled. I told hubby and quickly put a kettle of water on the stove to heat, for plucking the feathers. He went to behead the rooster only to find that it had revived and was strutting around again. But he got the ax and chopped off its head anyway, and I made fried rooster for supper. We considered inviting the boy and his family over for supper, but we didn't quite have the spunk.

Crisp and Tender Chicken

1 frying chicken, cut up	*¼ tsp. pepper*
1 cup flour	*1½ tbsp. paprika*
1 tbsp. salt	*2 tbsp. melted butter*
½ tsp. seasoned salt	*2 tbsp. milk*

Combine flour, salt, seasoned salt, pepper, and paprika. Work mixture into chicken pieces, leaving no moist spots. Brown chicken in ½ inch hot fat; then place in pan. Do not stack pieces. Drizzle melted butter and milk over pieces. Bake uncovered at 350° for 30 to 40 minutes or until tender. Pour extra milk over chicken during baking if chicken looks dry.

Oven-Baked Chicken

2 frying chickens, cut in serving pieces

½ cup butter, melted

2 tsp. salt

1½ cups cornflakes, crushed

¼ cup Parmesan cheese

¼ tsp. pepper

Dip chicken pieces into butter, then into mixture of remaining ingredients. Arrange in two 9 x 13 inch baking dishes, allowing space between pieces. Bake uncovered at 350° for 1½ hours or until tender. Serves 6 to 8.

Variation: Brush chicken with ¾ cup Miracle Whip instead of melted butter and increase Parmesan cheese to ½ cup.

We like this chicken served with pepper cabbage.

Tender Quick Chicken Breast

Coating mix

1 cup flour

4 tsp. seasoned salt (Tender Quick)

1 tsp. paprika

1 tsp. poultry seasoning

1 tsp. ground mustard

½ tsp. pepper

Rub 5 pounds chicken breasts with Tender Quick. Put in a plastic bag or container overnight (in refrigerator). Next day, rinse and cut raw meat into thin strips. Coat with coating mix. Fry in ¼ cup oil until brown (it only takes a few minutes).

I used to *make this recipe without the Tender Quick—until one hot week in July when I was preparing for my third set of travelers in one week. This is a special blessing one has when living in a new Midwest settlement!*

I decided on this meat because it was simple and I could make it on the stove top instead of in the oven. In my tiny kitchen I knew I'd roast us and the company if I turned the oven on.

My husband came in and wrinkled up his nose at the idea of meat for company. He stated, "Meat usually takes a lot of heat to make it tender." I didn't want to serve meat to company if it was even a little bit tough! So in desperation, I decided to rub it with Tender Quick, which made something good taste even better! I had two big platters full that the visitors polished off, with compliments, which is something every cook basks in!

chatting

Greetings *from the Midwest! With a new baby in the house, who is very braav (good) and sleeps almost from one feeding to the next, I believe I'll have time to copy a few recipes and comments. She was born on my birthday, and the next evening our neighbors sent over a full-course meal for supper, including a decorated birthday cake! How thoughtful! It certainly is nice to have good neighbors. I later got her chicken dish recipe. We thought it was simply delicious, and I intend to make it often. We have around thirty broilers, which will soon be ready to butcher, with the help of my sisters. I'm looking for different ways to serve chicken, besides roasting and frying it. It's our three-year-old's favorite meat, and I believe he would eat chicken croquettes at every meal.*

Yummy Chicken Dish

¼ cup onion, finely chopped

¼ cup celery, finely chopped

¼ cup butter

1 can cream of chicken soup

1 can cream of mushroom soup

3 cups chicken or turkey, cooked

1 cup long-grain rice

½ tsp. poultry seasoning

1 tsp. salt

2 cups milk

2 cups chicken broth

Sauté onion and celery in butter. Add all other ingredients; mix well. Bake in large 9 x 13 inch pan, uncovered, for 2 hours at 325°. Stir occasionally.

This is our favorite fried chicken:

Golden Fried Chicken

3 pounds frying chicken	
1 cup flour	
¼ tsp. paprika	
1 tbsp. salt	
½ tsp. pepper	
1 cup shortening or oil	

Cut chicken into serving pieces. Combine flour, salt, and pepper. Roll chicken in flour mixture (or put flour mixture into paper bag and shake one piece of chicken at a time). Heat oil in skillet and brown chicken 5 minutes per side. Reduce heat to low and remove all but 3 tbsp. oil from skillet. Cook, covered, for 30 minutes. Uncover and cook for 15 more minutes. Serves 4 to 6.

We raise *our own chickens for meat and eggs, so it's good we're fond of chicken dishes. I have already served this to company because, with two little girls, it's handy to take it out of the oven and put it onto the table.*

One year we decided to kill the rest of the flock to can for the winter. We were almost done and thought we'd gotten them all. To our surprise, one lone rooster strutted by, and by all appearances he realized how lucky he was to have slipped past unseen! We decided to let him go for now and enjoy a roast later.

Huntington Chicken

1 hen, cooked and boned

2 cups macaroni, cooked and drained

4 cups chicken broth

1 cup grated cheese

Thickening for broth

8 tbsp. flour

¾ to 1 cup milk

1 tbsp. chicken seasoning

salt and pepper to taste

Combine flour, milk, and seasonings; use it to thicken the chicken broth. Melt cheese into the gravy. Pour over chicken and macaroni. Do not over stir or meat will get stringy. Pour into casserole dish and top with buttered bread crumbs. Bake at 350° for 30 minutes or until bubbly. Serves 8 to 10.

My husband *used to go with the neighborhood silo-fillers when he was a teenager. It was a job he enjoyed, even though it had its dangers. He liked the good meals he got at the places where they were filling and even remembers some of the dishes. One of them was this casserole, and I later got the recipe from the lady of the house. I often make it now, and his eyes light up when he sees it on the table.*

I'm always glad when the silo-filling and harvesting season is over and the fields are ready for snow. We neighbors get together for a carry-in dinner every fall after the harvest, and I usually bring this casserole.

Aunt Anna's Chicken Casserole

12 cups chicken
12 cups bread cubes
12 tbsp. parsley or celery leaves
6 tsp. pepper
12 eggs
8 cups chicken broth
8 cups milk

Place a layer of bread cubes in a greased casserole; add a layer of chicken, parsley, and seasonings. Continue in alternate layers, with bread cubes on top. Beat eggs and add milk and broth; pour over mixture. Bake at 350° for 1 hour. Serves 40.

Here's a smaller, family-sized casserole recipe:

Savory Chicken and Corn

⅓ cup margarine

¾ tsp. salt

½ tsp. celery salt

1 whole small chicken, cooked and cut up

1 tbsp. butter

⅓ cup flour

¼ tsp. pepper

2 cups milk

1 pint creamed corn

¼ cup bread crumbs

Melt margarine over low heat. Stir in flour, salt, pepper, and celery salt.
Cook until smooth. Remove from heat; add milk and bring to a boil for
1 minute. Combine sauce, chicken, and corn. Pour into 1½-quart casserole. Top with crumbs. Dot with butter. Bake at 350° for 25 to 30 minutes
or until brown on top. Serves 8.

Chicken Bologna

25 pounds ground chicken meat	
½ cup salt	
½ cup Tender Quick	
3 tbsp. black pepper	
¼ cup brown sugar	
2 tbsp. liquid smoke	
2 tsp. saltpeter	
2 tsp. coriander	
2 tsp. garlic powder	
¼ tsp. mace	

Mix well, put in jars, let set 24 hours, and process at 10 pounds pressure for 1 hour.

This is *our favorite recipe for chicken. We like to freeze it and use it freshly thawed. Often I add a bit of onion, several eggs, a handful of crushed crackers, and a dash of milk; then I bake it for meat loaf. Everyone seems to like it. I have received many requests for the recipe. We also like to use this recipe and substitute turkey or beef for chicken.*

But when the rooster gets to be quite mean, this is a good ending for him!

chatting

Marinated Turkey Tenderloins

1 cup lemon lime soda or pineapple juice

¼ cup ketchup

2 tbsp. lemon juice

2 pieces garlic cloves, minced if desired

1 tsp. prepared horseradish or liquid mustard

½ tsp. lemon pepper seasoning

¼ tsp. curry powder

¼ tsp. ground ginger

¼ tsp. paprika

¼ tsp. red pepper flakes

2 pounds turkey tenderloins or beefsteak

In a bowl, combine the first 10 ingredients. Mix well. Pour 1 cup into a large container. Add turkey. Refrigerate 8 hours or overnight, for grilling. Drain and discard marinade from turkey. Grill it covered over medium to hot heat for 20 to 25 minutes or until a meat thermometer reads 170°, turning it every 6 minutes. Serve with remaining marinade.

This is a delicious recipe. Instead of grilling it, we bake it in a roaster at 375° to 400° for three hours. We all like it.

Barbecued Meatballs

6 pounds ground beef	¼ tsp. pepper
2 cups oatmeal	½ tsp. garlic powder
4 eggs	2 small onions, chopped
2 cups cracker crumbs	2 cups evaporated milk
4 tsp. salt	

Sauce

4 cups ketchup	½ tsp. garlic powder
2 tsp. liquid smoke	½ cup chopped onion
2 cups brown sugar	

Shape into balls. Pour sauce over balls. Bake uncovered at 225° for 1 to 2 hours. Makes 60 small balls.

"These meatballs are delicious!" I exclaimed as I tasted a crumb. I was one of the cooks at a wedding where they were serving them for dinner. The two stoves standing side by side had their ovens full with cake pans of meatballs. All forenoon the delicious aroma kept tempting us. Just before noon, the head cook began checking them for doneness, taking a meatball from the center of each pan. We each had a bite. Mmm! How delicious! When the time came to plan who would dish up what, we all jumped for the meatballs. For the first sitting we carefully placed only the nice ones on the platters as we nibbled on the broken pieces. For the second sitting, we did likewise. We kept chiding each other about picking at the meatballs. Some commented on how hungry they were becoming, and how good those meatballs would taste with mashed potatoes, salad, and so on.

While filling the platters for the third sitting, someone remarked that there weren't a lot left anymore! We asked the table waitresses how many were left to serve this last sitting of guests. We counted the meatballs and discovered there just might not be enough, especially if some of the men each take two!

Sure enough, by the time the cooks sat down to eat (we were last to be served) and the platters reached us, only crumbs and sauce were left!

chatting

My family's *favorite meat is hamburger, and there are so many different and delicious ways you can prepare it. We like to do our butchering in the winter, so the meat stays cold while we're preparing it for the cans and the freezer. Once we had to butcher in the middle of the summer, though, and this is why: Our neighbors were away on a trip. Their hired boy was alone with the milking and the chores. Our tame bull got out of his pen and ran into the neighbor's barnyard. The hired boy was exasperated, tied a paper feed sack to his tail, and slapped him on the rump. This rattly sack scared the bull, and he galloped for home at top speed. Coming out of the neighbors' lane, a car nipped him and broke his front leg. So we had to butcher him right away and had a bill to pay for fixing the car, too!*

Marian's Meatballs

3 pounds ground beef	½ cup onions
1 (12-ounce) can evaporated milk	½ tsp. garlic powder
1 cup oatmeal	½ tsp. pepper
1 cup cracker crumbs	2 tsp. salt
2 eggs (optional)	1 tsp. chili powder

Mix meatball ingredients and shape into 1½- to 2-inch balls. Freeze on cookie sheets. Store frozen meatballs in freezer bags until ready to use.

Sauce for baking meatballs

2 cups ketchup	1 tsp. Worcestershire sauce
1 cup brown sugar	¼ cup onions

Bake at 350° for about 1 hour.

Best-Ever Meatloaf

2 eggs

⅔ cups milk

3 slices torn bread

1½ to 2 pounds ground beef

½ cup chopped onion

½ cup grated carrot

1 cup shredded cheese

1 tbsp. fresh parsley or 1 tsp. dried

1 tsp. salt

1 tsp. dried basil

¼ tsp. pepper

1 tsp. red pepper

Topping

½ cup ketchup

½ cup brown sugar

1 tsp. mustard

Beat eggs; add milk and bread. Let stand. Mix rest of ingredients with beef; add bread mixture. Mix well and shape in a shallow pan. Pour topping over all and bake at 350° for approximately 45 minutes.

I well *remember butchering days from my childhood, watching Dad sharpening the knives and getting down the sausage grinder. Mom scrubbed the big furnace kettle and prepared a lot of jars for the canning. I didn't like to watch them hang up the carcass, but I liked to be along for the storytelling and visiting while the meat was being cut up and put through the grinder. One year when we were butchering a pig, my teenage uncle put on an apron to help with the meat and was acting a somewhat silly and cocky. One of my married uncles decided to play a trick on him and tied a pig's tail behind him, to his apron string. He didn't know why the others thought he was so funny, thought he was really "it," and began to show off still more. It earned him a nickname for awhile, with the teasing all in good humor.*

It's easy making meals when you have a fresh supply of meat on hand. Bacon is one of my favorites; there are so many dishes you can improve with it. Happy cooking!

Bacon Spaghetti Casserole

6 slices bacon
1½ pounds ground beef
½ cup minced onion
1½ cups diced raw potatoes
1½ cups diced celery
2 cups peas
1 can mushroom soup
¾ quart tomato juice
1½ cups carrots, diced
1½ cups cooked spaghetti

Cut up bacon and fry with ground beef and onion until brown. Drain off fat. Layer with rest of ingredients in casserole and season to taste. Bake at 350° for 2 hours. Lay Velveeta cheese slices on top before serving (let it melt).

Bacon Beef Balls

3 strips bacon, cooked and crumbled

½ cup rice

½ cup water

⅓ cup chopped onion

1 tsp. salt

½ tsp. celery salt

⅛ tsp. pepper

⅛ tsp. garlic powder

1 pound ground beef

2 tbsp. cooking oil

1 (15-ounce) can tomato sauce and 1 cup water (or 2 cups tomato juice)

2 tbsp. brown sugar

2 tsp. Worcestershire sauce

Combine first 8 ingredients. Add beef; mix well. Shape into 1½-inch balls. In a large skillet, brown meatballs in oil; drain. Combine tomato sauce, water, sugar, and Worcestershire sauce; pour over meatballs. Reduce heat; cover and simmer 1 hour.

Note: I usually bake these for 1 hour at 350° instead of simmering them 1 hour.

Our *first baby was so fussy that my husband and I took turns walking the floor with him, sometimes night and day. Other people, kind neighbors and friends, sent in casseroles and soups and even complete meals. When he became three months old, his colic mysteriously disappeared, and he became a contented baby. What a blessed relief and joy! I got some recipes from those who had sent meals and will share a few of them here. I wouldn't want to live those hard weeks over again, but it was a learning experience, too. It taught me to try to help others more when they are in need, and to really appreciate our baby's sunny smiles and contented cooing!*

Beef and Cheese Casserole

8 to 10 boiled potatoes

¼ pound dried beef

2 tbsp. butter

2 tbsp. flour

2 cups milk

1 cup cheese (any kind)

2 tbsp. buttered bread crumbs

¼ cup parsley, chopped

Slice half the potatoes into a 2½-quart casserole. Fry beef slightly in butter. Add flour and mix well. Add milk and cheese. Cool until thickened. Pour half of sauce over the potatoes. Add remaining potatoes, then the rest of the sauce. Sprinkle bread crumbs on top. Bake at 350° for 30 minutes. Garnish with parsley.

Spaghetti Chicken Casserole

1 (8-ounce) package spaghetti, cooked and drained

4 cups chicken, cooked and chopped

¼ cup green pepper, chopped (optional)

1 cup chicken broth

¼ tsp. celery salt

½ cup celery, chopped

¼ tsp. pepper

¾ pound grated Velveeta cheese

2 (10½-ounce) cans cream of mushroom or cream of chicken soup

Reserve 1 cup cheese. Mix remaining ingredients. Put in baking dish and top with reserved cheese. Bake at 350° for 1 hour. Serves 8.

Sausage Zucchini Bake

1 pound sausage, fried	3 eggs, beaten
1 cup shredded cabbage	1½ cups cracker crumbs
⅓ cup butter, melted	½ tsp. salt
5 cups summer squash, shredded or cubed	
2 cups sharp cheese, shredded	

Mix all together and bake at 350° for 40 to 45 minutes.

My friend *shared this recipe with me. The first time I made it was on a Saturday. I put it in the refrigerator and made it Sunday to serve my special friend for supper. I made his favorite seven-layer salad to serve with it (if my memory is correct). He really liked the casserole and has asked me to make this many times since we were married. I always make it for his birthday in the summer and our anniversary in the fall, and many times in between. Our children like it, too, and they'll occasionally ask me to make "seashells"! We've tried other stuffed shell recipes, but never have we had any as good as this one. I'll often just open a jar of our canned beef and use that. Then I only need to bake it for one hour. I hope you'll like this as much as we do.*

Stuffed-Shell Casserole

15 jumbo pasta shells	1 tbsp. chopped onion
1 egg	½ tsp. salt
¾ cup bread crumbs	1 pound ground beef
2 cups mozzarella cheese, grated	
(reserve ½ cup of cheese for over top of casserole)	

Cook the shells until soft. Combine the rest of the ingredients and stuff the shells.

Sauce

1 quart tomato juice	¼ tsp. salt
¾ cup brown sugar	1 tbsp. oregano

Bring this to a boil and thicken it with ClearJel to consistency of gravy. Pour half of sauce into 9 x 13 inch baking pan (or 2-quart casserole). Place stuffed shells in sauce. Pour other half of sauce over top. Sprinkle with the last ½ cup of grated cheese (or more). Cover and bake in slow oven for 2 hours at 325°. Serve with lettuce salad for a complete meal. Serves 8.

Greetings *from Pennsylvania! We are a family of eight who live on an eighty-acre dairy farm. We all like this dish—especially our farm dogs! Let me tell you how we know. One evening in July we were planning to eat down by the Conestoga River, which flows through our meadow. We have a picnic table and a fireplace there in a grassy, shady spot that we keep mowed, especially for our picnics. My older brother went down first to start the campfire. He took the hot casserole along and set it on the picnic table. A short while later he came back for the hot dogs. Soon all of us were ready to go, too. Dad decided we'd better hitch the horse to the spring wagon; the younger children piled on back, and we started off. When we arrived at the campfire, two guilty-looking dogs were slinking shamefacedly away. They had knocked the lid off the casserole and eaten some of it. I hope they burned their tongues good and proper!*

Party Pizza Casserole

2 pounds hamburger	
1 pint pizza sauce	
8 ounces sour cream	
1 green pepper, chopped	
1 red pepper, chopped	
1 package onion soup mix	
3 cans Pillsbury biscuits	
2 cups shredded mozzarella cheese	

Brown hamburger and peppers. Add pizza sauce, sour cream, and onion soup mix. Bake the biscuits and place over the bottom of a big baking pan. Layer meat and cheese mixture over it. Bake at 350° just long enough to heat throughout. Excellent!

Here's another casserole we really like and make often:

Taco Beef Casserole

2 cups Bisquick mix

2 pounds hamburger

1 cup sour cream

⅔ cup milk

2 packages taco seasoning

1 cup mayonnaise

Knead Bisquick and milk. Press into 9 x 13 inch pan. Mix hamburger and taco seasoning and prepare according to directions. Layer on top of crust. Mix sour cream and mayo and spread on meat. Bake at 350° for 20 minutes. Melt cheese on top. Add lettuce, tomatoes, and taco sauce.

We usually double this casserole, and the family licks the pan clean!

On *Ascension Day our family usually gets together for a picnic if the weather permits. What better way to enjoy God's creation than to walk along nature's trails and see the beauties of his handiwork.*

I am always reminded to bring this dish (my specialty), and so far I've never had to carry any of it back home. After we repack the plates, cups, and empty dishes into the baskets, we women sit in a circle and visit. Meanwhile, the young fry run off to explore the woods and meadows. Sometimes we stay for supper, too, and the experience reminds me of a song: "Come home, . . . it's suppertime upon that Golden Shore" (Ira F. Stanphill).

Beef Noodle Casserole

1 pound noodles	4 tsp. salt
4 pounds ground beef	¼ tsp. pepper
1 cup chopped onion	1 pound grated cheese
2 cups cooked corn	white sauce (recipe follows)

Boil noodles in 2 quarts boiling water and 2 tsp. salt. Brown the beef, 2 tsp. salt, and onion. Drain off fat. In a big casserole or roast pan, layer the noodles, beef, and white sauce and cheese (half of it; then repeat with the other half). Bake at 350° for 1 hour.

White sauce

½ cup butter	3 tsp. salt
½ cup flour	6 cups milk

Melt the butter in a heavy saucepan. Add flour and salt and stir until well blended. Slowly add the milk, stirring and simmering until a smooth paste forms.

Sometimes I also take the following casserole, which they really like, too.

Beefy Tomato Shell Casserole

4 cups seashell macaroni (dry)
4 pounds ground beef
2 onions
2 green peppers, chopped
1 pound mushrooms
4 tbsp. Worcestershire sauce
4 tsp. salt
$\frac{1}{4}$ tsp. pepper
4 cups tomato soup
2 (12-ounce) cans tomato paste
$1\frac{1}{4}$ cups water
2 pounds grated cheese

Boil seashells in 2 quarts water with 2 tsp. salt. Brown beef, onions (chopped), green pepper, and mushrooms. Mix remaining ingredients (except cheese) for sauce. Put in layers half of seashells, meat, sauce, and cheese; then repeat with other half. Bake at 350° for one hour.

I am *the fourth girl in a family of seven children. My two oldest sisters are married. We often served this delicious casserole when their boyfriends came for supper. It's easy to make, and best of all, everyone likes it. Enjoy!*

Macaroni Casserole

4 cups dry macaroni

3 cups peas, cooked

1 pound of any kind of cubed meat

Cook macaroni; add peas and meat. Then mix with sauce.

Sauce

1 pound cubed Velveeta cheese

2 cups milk

2 cans cream of chicken soup

2 tsp. salt

Simmer sauce until cheese melts; add to macaroni. Bake at 300° for 1 hour. Serves 14 to 16. Delicious!

Note: For Sunday dinner, bring macaroni and peas to boiling, drain, and add other ingredients. Bake at 250° for 3 hours.

Years ago *we had a gray kitten with "thumbs." His front paws had extra toes that looked like thumbs. We liked our unusual kitty.*

One evening after dark, we heard funny noises outside. I went out to check, and what do you think I found? Tom Thumb (the kitten) had his head in a tin can! I helped him out. How did he manage that?

If you use tin cans in cooking, be sure to dispose of them properly!

We *seven sisters try to have Sisters Day every spring and fall. We often exchange recipes for the covered dishes we bring. We don't do any cleaning or other major work. Instead, we each bring some handwork of our own to do, such as crocheting, embroidering, or mending, and sit around visiting and reminiscing of our childhood and teen years, etc. One year we had a surprise for one of the sisters who had just had surgery—a comforter with embroidered patches from each of us, and also from friends and neighbors—made especially for her. She was really surprised and pleased.*

I'm including two of our favorite recipes, which I hope you'll all enjoy.

Sausage, Corn, and Potato Casserole

Crust

5 medium potatoes or leftover mashed potatoes

1 tsp. salt	½ cup cornflakes
1 egg, beaten	2 tsp. parsley flakes
½ cup onion	

Filling

1 pound sausage	1 can mushroom soup
½ cup green pepper strips	1 cup shredded cheese
2 tsp. cornstarch	

1 can corn, drained (frozen corn must be cooked)

Crust: Cook potatoes in boiling salted water until tender. Drain and mash. Stir in egg. Add onion, cornflakes, and parsley. Spread evenly in 10-inch pie plate.

Filling: Brown sausage in skillet; remove and drain on paper towel. Pour off all but 1 tbsp. of fat. Add pepper; sauté for 5 minutes or until crisp. Stir in sausage and cornstarch. Add soup and corn. Heat thoroughly. Put mixture into potato shell. Sprinkle cheese on top. Bake at 400° for 25 minutes.

Beef and Velveeta Casserole

½ cup milk

1 cup bread crumbs

1 egg

1 tsp. salt

1 tsp. dry mustard

¼ tsp. pepper

¼ tsp. thyme

⅓ cup minced onion

1 pound ground beef

Cheese-tato topping

4 slices Velveeta cheese

3 or more cups mashed potatoes

Mix milk with bread crumbs. Beat in next 6 ingredients. Mix in raw ground beef with fork. Turn into 9-inch pie plate. Bake at 350° for 30 minutes. Remove. Serves 4 to 6.

Topping: Season, cook, and mash potatoes; cover meat with cheese and swirl potatoes on top. Place under broiler for a few minutes.

Hello to all readers! I am an Amish girl, age sixteen, who likes to cook and try new recipes. My six brothers tease me about trying to make guinea pigs out of them, but I notice that they usually have a hearty appetite for anything I make. The first time I fixed this recipe, my fourteen-year-old brother decided to play a trick on me. The table was all set, with the big, double-portion casserole on hot pads in the middle. While I was out at the bulk tank in the milk house for a pitcher of milk, he sneaked into the kitchen and sliced some raw turnips (which I loathe) and stuck them here and there into the casserole; then he ran guiltily outside again. I knew right away he must have done something, but thought he'd just been sneaking a few bites. He just wanted to watch my face when I bit into a turnip slice while eating! Well, I got even with him later, but that's another story.

Holiday Ham Casserole

2 pounds cooked ham, cubed

4 cups cooked macaroni

2 (10½-ounce) cans cream of mushroom soup

½ pound Velveeta cheese

2 cups milk

1 tbsp. minced onion

1 tbsp. green pepper, chopped

1 tbsp. parsley, chopped

¼ tsp. black pepper

salt to taste

Combine soup, milk, pepper, onion, parsley, and seasonings. Place over low heat. Add cheese and stir until melted. Mix macaroni with the cheese sauce. Pour half of this in a 1½-quart casserole. Cover with half the ham cubes. Add remaining macaroni and sauce. Top with the rest of the ham. Bake at 325° or 30 minutes.

Here's another one they really go for, and so I always double the recipe:

Tip-Top Tater Tot Casserole

2 pounds ground chuck

½ cup chopped onion

2 cups baby carrots, cooked

2 cups peas, cooked

2 cups broccoli florets, cooked

2 cans cream of mushroom soup

2 cans cream of chicken soup

½ cup milk

1 (20-ounce) bag Tator Tots

½ pound Velveeta cheese

Brown meat with onion. Drain. Add soups and milk; stir until smooth.
Place in roaster. Distribute vegetables over top. Cube Velveeta cheese
and arrange on top of veggies. Put Tator Tots over all and cover with foil.
Bake for 45-50 minutes at 350° to 375°. Delicious!

This *is my favorite pizza casserole recipe. We clipped it from our weekly newspaper. It is a joy for me to try out new recipes, so when we receive our newspaper that has recipes in it, the first thing I do is check for a good and simple recipe. The whole family enjoys this recipe and especially on cold and stormy days! One of my friends was sick and had to be in the hospital for a few days. Then we put some quilt tops together and held a few quiltings for them, hoping that the quilts will sell to help them pay their hospital bill. We also planned a quilting at their house, so we decided to furnish a pizza casserole like this for lunch. At least one lady asked for the recipe. They thought it was so delicious!*

Pizza Casserole

Crust

1⅓ cup flour

2 tsp. baking powder

⅔ tsp. salt

¼ cup oil

½ cup milk

Mix and press batter for crust into bottom of 9 x 13 inch pan.

Fry together: 2½ pounds hamburger and one small diced onion. Cook ½ cup macaroni; then drain and add 1 pint pizza sauce; mix together hamburger and macaroni mixtures and put on the unbaked crust. If desired, top with 1 cup sour cream mixed with 3 cups grated cheese. Bake at 350° about 1 hour.

Some years ago my younger brother broke his leg in a mishap with a cow. He had been an active outdoor boy and was often bored while sitting there in the kitchen, with not much to do. We were all busy helping with the produce, so I decided to get him interested in helping with the cooking, telling him that his future wife would be quite pleased if he could give her a helping hand when necessary. He did take an interest in it. Soon he was learning to follow recipes and stir together the dishes he liked, making changes here and there to suit his fancy. He was never much for desserts and baked goods, so he chose casseroles and main dishes for his projects. I copied some of his favorite ones into a small booklet and illustrated it. I wrote "Dan's Own Cookbook" on the cover, and gave it to him for Christmas. Recently I asked his wife if he still has it, and she said, "Yes, indeed. He still cherishes it, too, and those dishes are still among his favorites." Maybe when this cookbook is finished I can give him a copy of it, too, with his recipes included.

Burrito Casserole

1 to 1½ pounds hamburger

1 onion, chopped

1 can cream of mushroom soup

16 ounces sour cream

1 package tortilla shells

1 can refried beans

1 package taco seasoning

4 cups shredded cheese

Brown meat and onions. Add taco seasoning and beans. Mix sour cream and soup together. Put some in bottom of dish. Put meat mixture in shells and layer on soup. Spread remaining soup mixture on top of shells and top with cheese. Bake at 350° until cheese is melted and burritos are hot. Serve with lettuce, tomato, and taco sauce.

Potato and Wiener Casserole

6 wieners, sliced thin

1 cup peas

¼ cup soft butter

1 tsp. mustard

4 medium potatoes, cooked and diced

2 tbsp. onion

1 can cream of mushroom soup

salt and pepper to taste

Mix and bake, covered, at 350° for 30 minutes.

Once *a year on a Saturday, our whole extended family of aunts, uncles, nieces, and nephews gets together for a carry-in dinner at my grandparents' farm. We're each supposed to bring one hot and one cold dish in the amount that would feed our own family. This works out fairly well, for there are never too many leftovers, yet no one goes away hungry (or if they do, it's their own fault). We never plan beforehand what each will bring, yet there's always a wide variety of interesting dishes. The others all remind me to bring my specialty, and so I'll share it with you.*

One year the children (ages four to twelve) went off by themselves for a walk in the woods and came back with several aprons full of good mushrooms. We are all mushroom lovers and have taught the children which are good ones and which are poisonous.

Midwestern Casserole

10 raw medium potatoes, shredded

1 quart peas or corn

4 cups uncooked macaroni

1 medium onion, shredded

6 tsp. salt

1 gallon milk

4 cups meat (hamburger is best), browned a little

1 can mushrooms

Mix all together and put in oven at 350° for 2 hours, or at 300° for 3 hours. This recipe is big enough for company dinner.

I'll also share our favorite weekday casserole with you:

Beefy Corn Casserole

1½ pounds ground beef

2 slightly beaten eggs

1 (8-ounce) can tomato sauce or 1 cup tomato juice

⅜ tsp. salt

dash of pepper

1 tsp. Worcestershire sauce

¼ tsp. sage, optional

1 (12-ounce) can corn or 1 pint frozen corn (if frozen, cook it first)

½ cup medium to coarse cracker crumbs

1 slightly beaten egg

¼ cup diced green pepper

¼ cup chopped onion

½ tsp. salt

2 ounces shredded cheese (½ cup)

1 (4-ounce) can mushrooms, optional

Combine beef with 2 eggs, tomato sauce, salt, pepper, Worcestershire sauce, and sage. Spread half of mixture in 8¼ x 1¾ inch round baking dish, or 8 x 8 x 2 inch pan. Combine remaining ingredients, except cheese, and spoon it over meat. Cover with remaining meat mixture and bake at 375° for 1 hour. At 5 minutes before it's done, sprinkle cheese on top. Serves 6.

Greetings *from Ohio! We live on a thirty-three-acre produce farm and have six daughters and four sons. This casserole came in handy during our busy season, when we're sometimes out in the fields picking produce from dawn to high noon. We must pick fresh berries and vegetables when they're ready, and this makes for quite busy spurts.*

We enjoy it but are thankful when the busy season is over and we can relax more and enjoy a slower pace. Our eleven-year-old son, Dan, broke his leg one summer, and he learned to put simple meals on the table when we womenfolk were too much on the run. I think one of our girls made a small cookbook for him, of easy recipes and hints. We try to make up for those hectic times later by cooking more elaborate and extra-special meals.

Make-Ahead Casserole

4 cups seashell macaroni, uncooked

4 cups cooked chicken, cubed

2 cans cream of mushroom soup

2 cans cream of chicken soup

½ pound shredded cheese

2 cups milk

½ cup minced onion

¼ cup butter

In the morning mix all ingredients well and put in a roaster. Refrigerate until the right time. Bake at 350° for 1 hour. Serve with a large lettuce-and-tomato salad.

Here's another one we really like, and it can be mixed a day ahead and refrigerated:

Turkey Casserole

12 slices of bread

3 cups turkey, cooked and diced

1 cup turkey broth

1 cup chopped celery

1 can cream of chicken soup

¼ cup melted butter

1 cup milk

4 eggs, beaten

2 cups grated cheese

salt and pepper to taste

2 cups crushed cracker crumbs

Place 12 slices of bread in 9 x 12 inch pan. Cover with cubed turkey and celery. Mix turkey broth, milk, eggs, butter, salt, and pepper. Pour the mix over turkey. Mix can of soup with one soup can of milk. Place a layer of grated cheese over the turkey and pour the diluted soup over it. Top with cracker crumbs and bake uncovered at 350° for 35 minutes or until bubbly. Serve with raw cabbage wedges.

About *a month ago, I prepared this recipe and popped it into the oven. Then I went out to paint the garden fence. As I worked I was thinking of the delicious meals we would be having. The closer it got to dinnertime, the more I looked forward to eating it.*

At 11:30 I quit, cleaned up for dinner, and called to my husband, who was working in the shop, that dinner would be ready in ten minutes. But alas! When I walked into the kitchen, no wonderful aroma greeted me—I had forgotten to turn on the oven! So instead of a scrumptious meal, we had tomato soup and crackers for dinner. I don't think I'll forget to turn on the oven right away again!

Baked Beef Casserole

2 pounds beef cut in cubes
¼ cup flour
¼ tsp. celery seed
1¼ tsp. salt
⅛ tsp. pepper
4 medium onions, sliced
6 medium potatoes, thinly sliced
2 medium carrots, thinly sliced
1½ cups hot water
4 tsp. beef bouillon
1 tsp. Worcestershire sauce
butter or margarine

Mix flour and seasonings and dredge meat in them. In a large casserole with tight-fitting cover, arrange meat, and vegetables in layers. Add bouillon to hot water and add Worcestershire sauce. Pour evenly over casserole. Dot with butter; cover, and bake at 325° for 3 hours. Leftover beef broth may be used instead of the water and bouillon.

chatting

Here are more of our favorites:

Mock Ham Balls

1 pound ground beef

1 pound ground hot dogs

2 eggs

⅓ cup sugar

salt and pepper

1½ cups cracker crumbs

Mix all together, shape into balls, and place in baking dish.

Sauce

1 cup brown sugar

1 tsp. mustard

⅓ cup vinegar

⅓ cup water

½ cup tomato juice

Bring sauce ingredients to a boil; pour over mock ham balls. Bake at 350° for 1½ hours.

Here's our favorite spaghetti casserole:

Supreme Spaghetti Casserole

5 tbsp. oil

1 onion, chopped

1 green pepper, chopped

1 clove garlic, chopped

1 medium can mushrooms

1 pound hamburger

1 large can tomatoes, chopped

½ cup olives

1½ tsp. salt

½ cup Velveeta cheese

½ pound spaghetti

1 can tomato soup

2 tsp. Worcestershire sauce

Sauté onion, pepper, garlic, and mushrooms in oil. Add hamburger and brown. Add tomatoes, olives, salt, and cheese. Cover and cook 30 minutes on low. Meanwhile, cook spaghetti. Add spaghetti, tomato soup, and Worcestershire sauce to meat sauce. Cover and keep in refrigerator 2 days. Bake at 350° for 1 hour.

Every spring and fall my teenage sisters and cousins get together to clean Grossdaadi's (Grandpa's) house. Grossmammi (Grandma) really appreciates our help and is still able to prepare a hearty dinner for us. We always remind her ahead of time not to forget that we want a roasted stuffed pig stomach that day, for that's about the only time we get that dish. She must stuff in some love, too, for I've never tasted any as good as what she makes. Nobody else has the knack of making it like she does. After dinner, Grossdaadi leans back in his favorite rocker and tells us stories of his childhood and rumschpringe (youthful running-around) days, and of when their children were still at home. (We've learned that our parents could get into Nixnutz (mischief), too, when they were little, and it's all so interesting.) Dad claims that Grossdaadi no doubt adds things to make his stories more interesting, but I'm sure he doesn't! We'll always have precious memories of cleaning for them and of that good roast pig stomach!

Roasted Pig Stomach

1 pig stomach, washed, inner lining removed
4 cups diced, raw potatoes
1 quart chosen filling
(using eggs, milk, and bread crumbs, as in favorite recipe)
1½ pounds loose sausage
2 cups chopped cabbage
salt, pepper, and onions to taste

Wash pig stomach and soak in salt water for several hours. Drain and fill it with the above ingredients mixed together. Sew the opening shut. Put in roaster and bake at 350° for 3 hours or more. If desired, make gravy with drippings.

Soup, Sandwiches, and Pizza

Sunshine Recipe

Two heaping cups of patience
One heart full of love
Two hands full of generosity
Dash of laughter

One head full of understanding
Sprinkle with kindness
Add plenty of faith and mix well
Spread over a period of a lifetime
Serve everyone you meet.

Author unknown

One *Saturday last winter I made a kettleful of chili soup and set it out on a shelf in the cold shanty to cool. We have a cat who tries to slip in the door every chance she gets; somehow that evening, unknown to us, she found her chance. She knocked the lid off the kettle. What a disappointment when we came home from church the next day, expecting to have our favorite soup, only to find it ruined by the cat! The cats got the rest of it, too, and we had tomato soup.*

Chili Soup

1 quart hamburger, canned or fresh

1 or 2 medium onions

Boil and fry together until onions are tender.

Add:

2 cans chili beans

2 cans kidney beans

2 cans cream of mushroom soup

small can of mushrooms

2 fresh peppers or 1 quart canned peppers

2 quarts chunked (no peelings) tomatoes

salt

chili powder

Simmer for 1 hour.

chatting

Chunky Beef Soup

2½ quarts water

⅓ cup beef base

1 can beef broth (optional)

1 quart tomato juice

½ cup sugar

1 tsp. salt

Bring to a boil and add:

1 small chopped onion, browned in ½ cup oleo

1 quart carrots, cooked and diced

1 quart potatoes, cooked and diced

3 cups frozen or fresh peas

2 cups navy beans, cooked

2½ pounds hamburger, browned and seasoned with salt and pepper

Simmer until the veggies are soft, approximately 30 minutes.

Grandma's Broccoli Soup

2 cups water

4 cups chopped, fresh broccoli (½ pound)

1 cup celery, chopped

1 cup carrots, chopped

½ cup onion, chopped

6 tbsp. butter

6 tbsp. flour

3 cups chicken broth

2 cups milk

1 tbsp. fresh parsley, minced

1 tsp. onion salt

½ tsp. garlic powder

In a Dutch oven or soup kettle, bring water to a boil. Add broccoli, celery, and carrots. Boil 2 to 3 minutes. Drain and set vegetables aside. In the same kettle, sauté onion in butter until tender. Stir in flour to form a smooth paste. Gradually add broth and milk, stirring constantly. Bring to a boil and stir for 1 minute. Add vegetables and remaining ingredients. Reduce heat. Cover and simmer for 30 to 40 minutes or until vegetables are tender. Makes 2 quarts.

This *is an original recipe I came up with to use my canned venison chunks. I have used beef chunks, but we preferred the venison over the beef. The recipe can be adjusted to the size of your family.*

We really like venison meat, so we're always glad when my husband gets a deer or two. Then I always like to can some chunks and make some ground venison. Every year at deer season, my husband and his brothers go hunting, so we wives go along, too, and enjoy being there doing winter things such as sewing and making Christmas cards. And of course, cooking food for our hungry men and listening to their deer stories of their close hits, etc. I'm glad they enjoy hunting and being out in the cold like that because I'm glad for the meat they get.

Venison Stew

1 quart venison chunks

1 sliced onion

1 tbsp. butter

1 quart broth or water

2 cups cubed potatoes

2 cups sliced carrots

2 cups peas

2 cups green beans

¼ cup chopped parsley

salt, pepper, and celery salt to taste

Brown venison chunks and onion in butter until nicely browned. Add broth or water and the vegetables and seasonings. Cook until tender, approximately one hour. Delicious!

Several years ago an English friend gave us a small donkey. He was cute but had a habit of braying at any time of the day or night. We hadn't realized how irksome this was to the neighbors a quarter mile down the road until one morning when we got up and saw a paper taped against the outside barn door. On someone had printed, "If you don't strangle that donkey, I will!"

That decided it. We sent the donkey to the sale barn the next Monday! A few days later the neighbor lady came and brought us a pot of soup. She probably felt guilty that her husband had put that on the barn door and wanted to make amends. I later got the soup recipe from her, and we're still good friends.

California Chowder

1 quart potatoes, cubed	5 shakes celery salt
1 medium onion	4 shakes paprika
3 sticks celery	4 shakes black pepper
3 medium carrots	3 shakes sage
1 cup home-canned beef	2 shakes seasoned salt
1 pint home-canned beef broth	1 pinch red pepper
2 tsp. salt	parsley, if desired
5 shakes oregano	
flour, water, and cream for thickening	

Fill a 6-quart kettle ¾ full of water. Add cubed and sliced vegetables, beef, and broth. Start cooking. Add seasonings. Cook an hour or two. Thicken like thin gravy, using flour, water, and a little cream.

Here's one of our old favorites: *tomato + milk*

Easy Hamburger Soup

2 tbsp. butter

1 pound ground beef

1 cup onion

2 cups tomato juice

1 cup sliced carrots

½ cup chopped celery or peppers

1 cup diced potatoes

1 tsp. seasoned salt

1 to 1½ tsp. salt

⅛ tsp. pepper

4 cups milk

⅓ cup flour

Melt butter in large skillet or kettle and brown meat and onion. Stir in next 7 ingredients. Cover and simmer until vegetables are tender, about 20 to 25 minutes. Combine flour with 1 cup milk. Stir into soup and boil. Add remaining milk and heat, stirring frequently. Heat until hot, but don't allow to boil.

Greetings *from our family on this beautiful autumn morning! This veg-etable soup recipe is our favorite. We try to have it every Saturday for the noon meal. It's best in the summertime when we have fresh garden veg-etables to put in—new sugar peas, little carrots, and fresh cabbage. Later in the summer, we have fresh limas, corn, and tomatoes, which make the soup especially delicious. When fresh tomatoes aren't in season, we use canned tomato juice.*

Last summer when I was at the birth center with our eleventh baby, our oldest daughter, age thirteen, made this soup because she thought it would be easier than making a full-course meal. As she found out, gathering the vegetables from the garden and preparing them took longer than she had planned. When Dad and the hired man came in for dinner, the vegetables weren't soft yet. They went back outside and worked for another half hour. But when they tasted the soup, they said it was well worth the wait!

Garden Vegetable Soup

2 to 3 pounds meaty soup bones

3 tsp. salt

pepper to taste

2 cubes bouillon

2 quarts water

1 cup shredded cabbage

2 potatoes, peeled and diced

¼ tsp. thyme or marjoram

2 stalks celery, sliced

2 carrots, sliced

1 small onion, chopped

2 cups fresh or canned tomatoes

Cover and simmer first 4 ingredients for 2½ to 3 hours. Remove bones; return meat to soup and add vegetables. Simmer about 30 minutes more.

Vegetable Soup to Can

1 quart potatoes, carrots, corn, green beans

1 quart chopped onions

1 pound soup beans or navy beans (3 cups),

   soaked in boiling water overnight

1 quart celery

3 pounds hamburger, baked in ¼ pound butter at 300° for a couple hours

1 quart spaghetti or 1½-ounce box Alpha-Bits

6 to 7 quarts tomato juice

½ cup brown sugar

12 beef cubes

1 to 1½ ounces George Washington beef broth powder

Put in jars, cold-pack, and put in boiling water for 2 hours.

Greetings *from our house to yours! On housecleaning days I don't like to take time off to fix big meals, so it's usually soup or casseroles for us then. After a forenoon of sweeping, moving furniture, scrubbing walls and floors, it's so nice to have a hot meal ready in the oven for the family. When you're working hard, a meal of sandwiches and snacks doesn't hit the spot and isn't as filling.*

A kettleful of bubbling cornmeal mush complements the one-dish meal and has never brought any complaints from our children. They like fresh things from our fall garden with it, too, such as sliced turnips, Chinese cabbage, and baby carrots. I'm looking forward to seeing this cookbook when it's finished.

Oven-Baked Stew

2 pounds chicken, cut in cubes	2 medium carrots, thinly sliced
¼ cup flour	1½ cups hot water
¼ tsp. celery seed	4 tsp. beef bouillon
1¼ tsp. salt	1 tsp. Worcestershire sauce
⅛ tsp. pepper	2 sliced turnips
4 medium onions, sliced	1 cup diced celery
2 cups peas	butter or margarine
6 medium potatoes, thinly sliced	

Mix flour and seasonings and dredge meat in them. In a large casserole with tight-fitting cover, arrange meat and vegetables in layers. Add bouillon to hot water and add Worcestershire sauce. Pour evenly over casserole. Dot with butter, cover, and bake at 325° for 3 hours. One may use leftover beef broth instead of water and bouillon.

Montana Chowder

2 pounds ground beef
2 tsp. salt
1/8 tsp. pepper
2 beaten eggs
1/4 cup chopped parsley
garlic salt (optional)
1/2 cup fine cracker or bread crumbs
2 tbsp. milk
3 to 5 tbsp. flour
1 tbsp. salad oil
2 bay leaves (optional)
4 to 6 small onions, cut up
2 or 3 cups diced celery
3 to 4 cups diced potatoes
1/4 cup long-grain rice
6 cups tomato juice
6 cups water
1 tbsp. sugar
1 tsp. salt
1 1/2 cups canned corn

Mix thoroughly meat, salt, pepper, eggs, crumbs, and milk. Form balls the size of a walnut. Dip in flour. Heat oil in large kettle. Lightly brown meatballs on all sides. Add remaining ingredients except corn. Bring to a boil. Cover and cook slowly until vegetables are tender. Add corn last. Cook 10 minutes. Serves 12. One can use carrots, peas, and celery leaves; or some V8 juice and less water.

When *I was ten years old, there was a really bad snowstorm in our valley. School was canceled for several days, which gave us a mini-vacation. We little girls worked on our embroidery patches and played with our dolls and games. But by midafternoon, we were bored and asked Mother what we could do. She told us we could make soup for supper and told us how to go about it. We added a little of this and a little of that and some leftovers, and we were amazed at how good it turned out! Homemade soups are delicious, nourishing, and warming on a cold, wintry day—far better than any you can buy in the tin cans. We often made some in the evening to put in our Thermos bottles for our school lunches. We felt sorry for those who had only dry sandwiches, pretzels, etc., in their lunch boxes.*

Cream of Potato Soup

4 medium potatoes

3 onions

1 stalk celery, chopped

boiling water

salt and pepper to taste

2 tbsp. flour

3 tbsp. butter, softened

4 cups hot milk

Pare and quarter potatoes. Combine onions and celery. Simmer until tender. Drain and reserve liquid. Mash potatoes with masher. Add potato liquid; season with salt and pepper. Blend flour with butter to a smooth paste. Add hot milk. Bring to a boil, stirring constantly. Add potatoes and heat.

Chilly Day Stew

In a kettle of rapidly boiling water, chop 1 large carrot. While it is cooking, clean and chop 3 onions. Add them to the stew kettle. Prepare 1 quart potatoes, peeled and diced. Add to the mixture. Add: 2 tbsp. rice, 2 tbsp. macaroni, 1 tsp. salt, and water to cover. Cook slowly until tender. When ready to serve, add 1 pint cream, or substitute butter and milk. Let mix thoroughly but do not boil again. Serve with crackers or hot toast.

Soups and stews *are very good in cold weather. A while ago I spent two and a-half months in Ontario, Canada, in the winter. Brrr! I found out what winter is like up there. The temperatures dropped quite a bit below zero, and it snowed time and again.*

At least one time in a storm the wind really blew and snow flew so thickly I couldn't see far. There was snow everywhere and high banks beside the roads. To me, those high banks were really something to look at. In that area, there are no warm spells in winter when all the snow melts, so you can imagine how it piles up!

I was getting quite tired of so much snow and always having to bundle up so warmly when going outside! Then, all at once it grew milder, and then it felt almost like summer. The sun was so warm, and there was no longer any need for all those warm clothes. In fact, the clothes I had with me were barely light enough. Those huge snow banks disappeared so fast it was almost unbelievable!

So I had the chance to see that Canada can have warm weather, and they do have spring. Such a memorable winter!

chatting

I am *a teenage Mennonite girl, the oldest of a family of ten children, and I like to cook and bake. A while ago I got a bunch of used* Taste of Home *magazines from a lady for whom I do cleaning. Oh wow! What lovely, elegant dishes and exotic recipes! I pored over them every spare moment, longing to try them out. But unfortunately, almost every recipe called for something we didn't have on hand. I complained to my mother that we had on hand only the basic staples, and that cooking the same old thing in the same old way was dull and boring. Mother looked pained, and then went to consult with Dad. That evening he gathered us all together to tell us stories of when our forefathers were refugees and nearly starved to death. He said there are many hungry, starving people in the world yet today, and that we have no right to fare sumptuously every day (like the rich man in the Bible) while closing our eyes to the needs of these people. Mother said if I want to try something new and different, I should try these lentil and barley recipes. They are family favorites now.*

Favorite Lentil Soup

1½ cups lentils, rinsed and drained	1 clove garlic, minced
6 cups water	1½ tsp. salt
2 slices bacon, diced	¼ tsp. pepper
1 medium onion, chopped	½ tsp. oregano
2 carrots, thinly sliced	2 tbsp. lemon juice
2 stalks celery with tops, sliced	
1 (16-ounce) can whole tomatoes	

Mix all ingredients together in a Crock-Pot and cook on low for 8 to 9 hours. Makes 2 quarts.

Beef Barley Soup

2 quarts beef and broth

1 quart tomatoes

1½ cups barley

1 cup carrots

1 cup potatoes

1 cup celery

½ cup onion

¼ cup parsley

½ tsp. thyme

1 tsp. basil

salt and pepper to taste

Cook together until barley is soft. Stir once in a while as barley thickens. Good for Crock-Pot.

This bean soup is a prizewinner! At a local shop's Christmas banquet, it was in a twelve-quart kettle beside someone else's bean soup, which was supposed to be the main attraction. But it wasn't touched until our twelve-quart kettle was completely empty.

Delicious Bean Soup

1 pound dried navy beans (soak overnight)

1 tbsp. salt

Cook until soft.

Fry in frying pan and add to beans:

1 onion

2 cups celery

½ cup butter

Add:

1 tsp. garlic salt

2 tbsp. brown sugar

2 tbsp. molasses

½ pound bacon, fried and crumbled

½ pound cheese

1 cup tomato juice

Mix and freeze in freezer boxes. When ready to eat, add a pinch of baking soda and some milk as desired.

Fresh Tomato Soup

Peel and cut up 3 medium tomatoes. Put into blender and chop; then puree into juice. Boil 3 to 5 minutes. Add ¼ to ½ tsp. baking soda. Add 3 cups milk, plus salt and pepper to taste. Heat.
Caution: Do not let it reach the boiling point after the milk is in!

Our *two girls, eleven and twelve years old, were making tomato soup for supper. They happened to let it boil, and it separated or curdled. Susie headed for other tomatoes, and Ellen picked up the boiling soup with intentions of pouring it away. They collided, and Ellen received first- and second-degree burns! Oh, the pain and suffering associated with burns. Use extreme caution: look both ways before carrying any boiling item.*

Hint: Dad immediately poured cold water over her, which kept the burns from going to the third degree.

chatting

Grandmother's Spaghetti Soup

1 basket tomatoes, or 10 to 12 quarts tomato juice
3 pounds spaghetti
4 pounds hamburger (browned)
3 stalks diced celery
1 quart shredded carrots
4 onions (chopped)
3 pounds dried Great Northern beans
salt and brown sugar to taste

Make tomatoes to juice; cook spaghetti. Fry or brown onions and hamburger in melted butter; chop celery and carrots. Cook until soft. Soak beans overnight; then cook until soft.

Mix ingredients together; put in jars, cold-pack, put in boiling water for two hours. We like it with some seasonings, such as hot pepper (sparingly) or seasoned salt.

This *spaghetti soup is a delicious, quick meal and is handy. Just heat it, and you have a tasty, healthy lunch! I have a sister and a brother living in Kentucky (we live in Pennsylvania). They both have large families of growing children. My sister and husband have seven children under age ten, including a set of twins, and she also has a fabric store to care for. My brother and wife have seven children, too. When some of the family from Pennsylvania visits them, we fill up a van and go to make precious memories. It naturally takes a lot of grub for the gang. So Mom makes some spaghetti soup and cans it in two-quart jars to take along. When we're visiting and suddenly it's mealtime, someone has to feed many people in a short order. So we use the spaghetti soup!*

chatting

Mom usually mixes the ingredients in a large Rubbermaid tub and then just scoops it into the jars. When serving, we sometimes make it like tomato soup, with baking soda and milk. Tastes like Hearty Hamburger soup then!

Clayton's Beef Stew

1 quart canned beef chunks and broth

4 medium carrots, diced

1 medium onion, diced

5 medium potatoes, diced

1 small pepper, diced

2 cups water

Cook together until the vegetables are tender; stir in the browned thickening. Cook over medium heat to desired thickness.

Thickening: Brown 4 tbsp. flour deeply in ½ cup vegetable oil. Flavor to taste with salt and pepper.

Variation: Any combination of vegetables may be used.

I am *twelve years old. One day my ten-year-old sister and I wanted to make a meal by ourselves. Mom said we could make any kind of sandwiches we want and also some soup. So we made pickled ham sandwiches, and they all liked it. I have three brothers and three sisters. We are Amish, live on a farm, and milk fifty cows.*

Pickled Ham Sandwiches

2 cups ham or bologna (shredded or ground)

1 cup grated white American cheese

½ cup onions, finely chopped

3 tbsp. ketchup

2 tbsp. mayonnaise

3 tbsp. milk

4 tbsp. chopped pickles (or use pickle relish, drained)

Put everything in a bowl and mix well. Put mixture between slices of bread or buns. Wrap in aluminum foil and bake at 350° for 30 minutes. Really delicious!

My husband's sister likes to tease him about the time he made himself a big Dagwood sandwich—two slices of homemade bread, with cheese, meat, tomato slices, and lots of lettuce in between. With a sigh of satisfaction, he leaned back in his chair and began to munch on his culinary creation. But he leaned too far back, and his chair tipped over, spilling him backward to the floor, with bits of lettuce, tomato, bread, and cheese flying into the air and landing all around him. He says he just opened the door and called the dog in; then he quickly made himself another sandwich just like it.

Hot Spam Sandwiches

1 can Spam, shredded	2 tbsp. green pepper, chopped
2 hard-boiled eggs	2 tbsp. minced onion
½ cup mayonnaise	2 tbsp. pickle relish
¼ pound cheese	8 kaiser rolls, split in half

Mix ingredients together; spread on buns; put top half back on. Wrap in foil; then bake at 250° for 35 minutes.

Easy Sloppy Joes

2 pounds hamburger	1 tbsp. vinegar
¼ cup minced onion	1 tsp. prepared mustard
½ cup ketchup	1 tsp. Worcestershire sauce
3 tbsp. brown sugar	1 tsp. salt

Fry beef and onion. Drain. Add other ingredients and simmer 12 minutes. Serve warm on buns.

When we make this recipe, I think of the hot-dog roast we had with our cousins in midwinter two years ago. The pond was frozen over solid, and our whole family (except Mom and the baby) decided to go skating that evening. The boys gathered plenty of firewood, and Dad made a big bonfire so we could keep warm while we rested. We wrapped potatoes in tinfoil and baked them in the fire. We roasted hot dogs on long, thin branches. Then we wrapped them in homemade bread to eat them, for we had no rolls. Dad let us skate as long as wanted to, and we made the most of it, staying until around ten o'clock. The weather wasn't as cold that night since there was no wind; hundreds of stars were twinkling overhead. We girls played tag, and the boys played hockey at the other end of the pond. I hope we'll have good skating weather again this winter.

Hot Dog Boats

8 hot dogs, diced	1 tbsp. ketchup
1 cup diced cheese	1 tbsp. minced onion
1 tsp. mustard	1 tbsp. pickle relish

Mix all ingredients and fill 8 wiener buns. Wrap in foil and bake 15 minutes or longer at 325°.

Egg Salad Sandwiches

4 hard-cooked eggs, mashed	½ tsp. salt
1 tbsp. minced onion	1 tbsp. mayonnaise
1 tbsp. chopped parsley	2 tsp. pickle relish
¼ cup chopped celery	

Combine all and mix well. Spread on bread and lay a slice of Velveeta cheese on top before putting top slice of bread on. Makes 1½ cups of sandwich filling.

A few years ago we had a sub-and-bake sale to help with the hospital bills of a family in our community. The evening before the sale, all the girls gathered at our house to make subs and wrap them. Many hands make light work: we had a lot of fun chatting and visiting while making a thousand subs! They sold well at the sale, and the baked goods went well, too. The family with the hospital bills could hardly believe it when we presented them with the check. They said they felt almost too unworthy to accept it. Here are a few of our favorite sandwich recipes.

chatting

Chicken Hoagies

2 cups cooked, diced chicken	2 tbsp. minced onion
½ cup diced celery	½ cup mayonnaise
½ cup diced cheese	salt and pepper to taste
2 hard-boiled eggs, chopped	3 hoagie buns

Combine ingredients. Butter the buns, fill them, and wrap in foil. Heat in 400° oven for 20 minutes. Top with tomato slices.

Hot Beef Subs

1 pound ground beef	½ cup ketchup
½ cup chopped onion	1 tsp. prepared mustard
1 tsp. salt	Velveeta cheese slices
1 (16-ounce) can baked beans	

Brown beef and onion; add remaining ingredients except cheese. Stir and heat thoroughly. Spoon into hoagie buns and top with Velveeta slices.

Popover Pizza

Layer in order given into 9 x 13 inch pan:

1½ pounds browned hamburger

1½ cups pizza sauce

½ pound grated cheese

4 cups macaroni (cooked) mixed with one can cream of mushroom soup

1½ cups pizza sauce

½ pound grated cheese

Cover with crust made by mixing:

2 eggs, beaten	1 cup Bisquick
1 tbsp. oil	2 tbsp. butter
1 cup milk	

Bake at 350° for 30 minutes or until crust is golden brown.

One of the first times I made supper for our family, I was thirteen or fourteen and made popover pizza. But as it turned out, it came to be called "flop over pizza"!

The preparing part went okay, although the sink was rather splattered. Eventually it was ready for the oven, though I was rather scared of this hot oven. So I timidly set the dish on the edge of the rack, but the bottom of the dish was wet. Since I did not hold it firmly, it slid with a clatter and ker-splash—onto the open oven door, over the edge, down on the floor, under the oven! Macaroni and meat and Bisquick were over everything. The stuff on the door was already sizzling. Yuck—what a mess! By the time we got it all cleaned up, the men were in for supper, and nothing was ready except some tomato soup Mom was heating so we would have something to feed these hungry farmers. It was a while before I tried to cook supper again. Right then I felt like crying, and Mom was grouchy with me, but now we both laugh about it. Since then, I have made popover pizza several times; it is a quick, easy, filling main dish, and we love it.

Years ago, when I was twelve, we school-age children were invited to our English neighbors for a pizza pie party. We had never heard of pizza before and laughed at the funny name! My brother declared that he wouldn't taste any, for it probably had hot peppers in it. At the party we helped to roll out the dough, spread on tomato sauce and ground meat, and then topped it with cheese. It sure smelled delicious while it was baking. To my brother's surprise, it tasted even better than it smelled. We sure make it often now since it's a favorite of our boys. None of us ever cared much for bought pizza, though, for that has a lot more zing in it—more than we care for. We like ours topped with mushrooms, or chopped green or red peppers (mild ones), and Muenster cheese.

Best-Ever Pizza

Dough

2½ cups flour	*1 tsp. garlic powder*
1 rounded tbsp. instant yeast	*1 tbsp. lard*
1 tsp. salt	*1 cup warm water*
½ tsp. oregano flakes	

Mix 1 cup flour, yeast, seasonings, lard, and water. Add remaining 1½ cups flour. Let rise and then press flat on pizza pan.

Add:

1½ cups pizza sauce

1 pound hamburger, fresh is best (browned), but canned is also good

1 medium onion, chopped

1 medium mango, chopped

1 can mushrooms

thin slices of ham on top

Bake until crust is slightly brown, about ½ hour at 350°. Add cheese and melt on top.

Pizza Crust

1 package dry yeast

1 cup warm water

1 tsp. each sugar, oil, and salt

2½ cups flour (whole-wheat flour is good)

Dissolve yeast in water. Stir in rest of ingredients. Beat about 20 to 30 strokes until it rolls in a ball. Let set 5 minutes. Spread with fingers on pan. Top as desired. Easy to make and not too dry!

Stovetop Pizza

Melt 2 tbsp. butter in skillet. Add 6 shredded potatoes, salt and pepper to taste. Fry 1 pound (1-quart can) ground beef with ½ onion and ½ green pepper, chopped. Drain off fat. Put on top of potatoes. Combine 3 eggs, beaten, and ⅓ cup milk. Pour over all. Cook uncovered until potatoes are done, about 30 minutes. Top with 2 cups shredded cheese. Heat until cheese is melted. A hearty, easy meal!

Mom's Pizza

Crust

2 tbsp. dry yeast	1 cup warm water
1 cup warm milk	2 tbsp. sugar
3 tsp. salt	¼ cup shortening
½ tsp. oregano	½ tsp. thyme
½ tsp. garlic powder	6 cups flour

Mix and let rise 15 minutes or until filling is prepared. This crust makes a good herbal breadlike crust with slightly crunchy edge. Makes crust for 2 cookie sheets. Put crust along edges to make deep-dish pizza.

Filling

3 pounds hamburger, browned

2 medium onions, chopped

2 small cans of mushrooms

2 quarts pizza sauce

2 bell peppers, chopped

Add hot sauce for zesty flavor

Mix hamburger and sauce and put on unbaked crust. Add toppings and cheese. Bake at 350° for 30 minutes.

Imitation Pizza

2 pounds hamburger

1 tsp. salt

1 tsp. pizza seasoning

1½ cups shredded cheese

1 quart pizza sauce

½ loaf bread

Crumble bread in a 9 x 13 inch cake pan; then toast in oven for 15 minutes at 300°. Fry hamburger in a pan, mix salt and pizza seasoning in, and fry a little longer. Spread the cheese over the toasted bread in pan, next the hamburger; finally, put the pizza sauce on top. Bake at 350° for 30 minutes.

I hope *you enjoy this recipe! This is the only pizza we make. It's easy and doesn't take long when one is in a hurry. It tastes just like real pizza, and can't easily be beat! Everyone in our family likes it greatly, even though it's the lazy way of making it. Pizza makes any meal special. We get a beef from my brother-in-law's farm, butcher it, and make our own meat products. Good luck everyone who tries this recipe!*

chatting

Stromboli

2 tbsp. yeast	2½ cups flour
1 tsp. sugar	1 cup warm water
2 tbsp. oil	mayonnaise to spread
1 tsp. salt	

Amounts as desired can also be used:

2 cups chipped ham (or salami)	1 cup shredded cheese
2 tbsp. minced onion	¼ cup diced peppers

Dissolve yeast in warm water. Stir in remaining ingredients. Add enough flour to make a medium stiff dough; work well. Let dough rest 5 minutes. Roll out dough to size you want. Spread with mayonnaise. Add ham (or salami), cheese, peppers, and onion on half of dough. Fold rest of the dough over the top and seal sides. Let rise ½ hour. Bake at 400° for 20 minutes.

A few years ago when I was a little girl, probably about five years ago, we used to farm produce. One man came for produce regularly and then sold it at his produce stand. This was a big hairy man. He called himself "Fat Albert." We liked when he came because sometimes he brought us things. One especially yummy thing he brought along was stromboli, which we had to pay for, though. We thought that was such a treat. Then over the years, my Dad's back just got too bad to farm produce anymore, so he started an implement business. Since we stopped selling produce, Albert stopped coming. From then on, we started to make our own stromboli; we still make it and still love it! Thanks to Albert, we learned what stromboli is.

chatting

To our boys, pizza is one of the major food groups. Luckily, they like it topped with lots of healthy veggies like cauliflower, broccoli florets, and green peppers. I don't think they'd grumble if I'd serve it every day, or even every meal!

Veggie Pizza

Dough

½ cup butter

1 cup flour

4 eggs

Mix 1 cup water with butter in pan and bring to a boil. Add flour all at once. Stir rapidly until mixture forms a ball. Remove from heat and cool. Beat in eggs, one at a time, beating well. Spread on ungreased cookie sheet and bake at 400° for 30 minutes. Top cool crust with following dressing:

2 (8-ounce) packages of cream cheese

½ cup sour cream

1 cup mayonnaise

1 package Hidden Valley dry ranch dressing

Top with vegetables of choice: lettuce, cauliflower, peppers, cucumbers, tomatoes, carrots, broccoli, and cheese.

Pepperoni Pizza

½ cup hot water	
½ tbsp. sugar	
½ cup milk	

Dissolve 1 tbsp. yeast in mixture and let stand for 5 minutes.

Add:

1 egg, beaten	
½ tbsp. sugar	
¾ tsp. salt	
2 tbsp. vegetable oil	

Mix together and add 3 cups flour. Knead until it is a little softer than bread dough. Let stand 20 minutes. Place on greased cookie sheet. Top with pizza sauce, seasoning, fried hamburger, onions, green peppers, mushroom stems, cheese, and pepperoni. Bake for 25 minutes at 350°. Delicious!

One *winter Mom was behind with making quilts for us girls (for our hope chests), so we decided to hold a quilting. We girls invited all our friends on a Saturday and pinned two quilts into borrowed frames in the big sitting room. We had made this fruit pizza for an afternoon treat, along with coffee and tea. With all the lively chattering and storytelling, it sure was a lot more fun than doing the quilts alone. Around midafternoon, Mom called us all out to the kitchen for the treat. My little two-year-old brother had already had his snack and wandered into the quilt room while we were eating. He climbed up on a chair and crawled onto the quilt—the naughty little chap! The frame held up, but the quilt sagged way down, nearly to the floor, and he slid to the middle. Our friends thought it was so funny and really laughed, but Mom and we sisters couldn't see anything amusing about it. I don't think he ever tried that trick again!*

chatting

Fruit Pizza

1½ cups flour
1½ tsp. baking powder
½ cup sugar
½ cup butter
1½ tsp. vanilla
1½ tbsp. milk
8 ounces cream cheese, softened
1 cup confectioners' sugar
½ cup milk
1 small box instant vanilla pudding
8 ounces whipped topping
mandarin orange slices
pineapple, blueberries, and kiwifruit
2 tbsp. strawberry-flavored gelatin
2 tbsp. sugar
1 tbsp. ClearJel

Combine flour, baking powder, ½ cup sugar, butter, vanilla, and 1½ tbsp. milk. Mix like a pie crust and press into a pizza pan. Bake at 350° for 10 minutes. Cool. Mix cream cheese, confectioners' sugar, ½ cup milk, and pudding mix. Add whipped topping and spread over cooled crust. Top with fruit. Combine gelatin, 2 tbsp. sugar, ClearJel, and ¼ cup water; cook just until thickened, stirring constantly. Cool and pour over fruit.
Note: fresh sliced strawberries may also be used with the glaze made with mashed strawberries, sugar, ClearJel, and water. Add a little strawberry-flavored gelatin for color.

Strawberry Pizza

1 cup flour

1 stick oleo

½ cup sugar

¼ cup confectioners' sugar

8 ounces cream cheese

1 quart strawberries, cut in half

Mix first 3 ingredients as for pie crumbs. Sprinkle evenly over 12 x 13 inch pizza pan. Press firmly. Bake at 325° for 12 to 15 minutes. Cool. Cream sugar and cream cheese together and spread over cooled crust. Chill.

Glaze

4 tbsp. sugar

4 tbsp. ClearJel

1 cup berry juice

Boil glaze together until thick. Spread over berries.

I sang *softly as I lifted a big, lush, tightly packed bunch of grapes from the leafy vine. Birds were singing in the sun-warmed vineyard. The distant lake shone a clear blue. Such a beautiful September day, just perfect to be outside picking grapes!*

As I lifted another branch, my eyes caught a movement in the vines. Oh! A bee! I waited until he had his fill of grape juice and flew away. Bees like grapes, too.

I knelt to pick some vines hanging close to the ground and observed a movement in the grass. Parting the blades disclosed a busy anthill. I watched for a moment, marveling at the busy tiny creatures.

chatting

As I moved on, I noticed a bird's nest built in the crook of a grapevine. Though empty now, earlier in the summer it probably had housed a family of birdies.

Trudging to the end of the row with my filled box, a rustle and a quick movement caused me to stop and peer under the leafy vines. Oh, oh! A woodchuck hole! They like the vineyard, too! While helping myself to more boxes, I breathed a prayer of thanks for the creation God has made!

Grape Pizza

Plain pastry dough for large cookie sheet

3 cups Concord grapes

1 cup sugar or ½ cup honey

½ tsp. grated lemon peel

3 tbsp. flour

dash of salt

Slip skins from grapes. Bring pulp to boiling. Press through sieve to remove seeds. Add skins. Mix sugar (or honey), flour, salt, and lemon peel; add to grapes. Cook until thick. Pour onto pastry.

Topping

¾ cup flour

½ cup sugar or ¼ cup honey

½ cup butter or oleo

Combine flour and sugar (or honey). Cut in butter until crumbly. Sprinkle on grape filling. Bake in hot oven at 450° for 20 to 25 minutes.

Salads and Pickles

Recipe for a Happy Marriage

1 cup of consideration

1 cup of courtesy

2 cupfuls of flattery carefully concealed

2 cupfuls milk of human kindness

1 gallon faith in God and each other

2 cupfuls of praise

1 small pinch of in-laws

1 reasonable budget

a generous dash of cooperation

3 teaspoons of pure extract of "I am sorry"

1 cup of contentment

1 cup each of confidence and encouragement

2 children, at least

1 large hobby or several small ones

1 cup of blindness to others' faults

Flavor with frequent portions of recreation and a dash of happy memories. Stir well and remove any specks of jealousy, temper, or criticism. Sweeten well with generous portions of love and keep warm with a steady flame of devotion. Never serve with a cold shoulder or hot tongue.

Author unknown

chatting

Tomatoes *are one of my favorite foods. I like them served in almost every way: pizza sauce, ketchup, soup, fried tomatoes, salads, and fresh in sandwiches—they're all delicious! We often sliced tomatoes on a plate, topped them with egg salad, and garnished them with bits of parsley or chopped celery. I've often wished for a greenhouse so we could have tomatoes almost all winter long! Store-bought tomatoes just aren't as flavorful as the homegrown ones. Cherry and grape tomatoes look nice in salads, but to my way of thinking, the big ones are better. The biggest tomato we ever grew just about filled a soup bowl!*

Egg and Tomato Salad

4 hard-cooked eggs

4 medium tomatoes

1 cup Miracle Whip

¼ cup chopped parsley

¼ cup celery

seasoning to taste

Mix and serve on lettuce leaves.

Luscious Layered Salad

3 cups tomatoes, chopped

1 head lettuce, shredded

1 cup celery, diced

1 cup carrots, shredded

4 hard-boiled eggs, chopped

2 cups slightly cooked peas

1 medium onion

8 slices bacon, fried and crumbled

2 cups mayonnaise or Miracle Whip

2 tbsp. sugar

4 ounces cheese, grated

Place first 8 ingredients in layers in the order given, using a 9 x 13 inch pan. Mix mayonnaise and sugar and spread on top. Top with cheese. Serve within one hour.

Red Beet and Apple Salad

2 cups cooked beets, diced

2 cups raw diced apples

2 hard-boiled eggs

½ cup chopped celery

¼ cup chopped nuts

¼ cup chopped parsley

1 tsp. vinegar

½ cup plain yogurt

Mix all together and serve on lettuce leaves.

Three-Bean Salad

1 cup cooked navy beans

1 cup cooked red kidney beans

1 cup cooked string beans

4 hard-boiled eggs

1 large sour pickle, chopped

¼ cup minced onion

2 tbsp. vinegar

1½ tsp. salt

⅔ cup diet margarine

Mix all together and serve with meat and mashed potatoes.

I'm seventeen, *and I love to cook, bake, and eat. I learned to make cookies and cakes when I was just in first or second grade, and soon I was making puddings and other desserts, too. I always had to sample everything I made while I was preparing it, and I loved to "lick the platter clean." The first year I was out of school, I noticed that my hips were getting wider and I was fatter. The pounds kept piling on, and I kept on making goodies like rich desserts and pies.*

Then a year ago, when I was lamenting to an older friend of mine about my increasing weight, she told me that with all the work I do and exercise I get, I could probably slim down by merely avoiding everything containing sugar and white flour. I really didn't believe her, but when I tried it, I found out it worked! I lost just a pound or so a week, but now I'm forty pounds lighter and feeling much better. I still cook and bake, but nothing with sugar, syrups, and white flour. And I try to make a salad at every meal.

Lettuce Bacon Salad

1 large head lettuce
1 large head cauliflower
1 small onion
2 cups mayonnaise
½ cup sugar
1⅓ cups Parmesan cheese
1 pound bacon, cut fine and fried

Wash and cut up lettuce in large bowl. Break up cauliflower into small pieces and put on lettuce. Add onions. Cover with mayonnaise. Add sugar and sprinkle with cheese. Add bacon and cover. Set in refrigerator overnight. Mix well when ready to eat.

Bacon Cauliflower Salad

1 head cauliflower

1 head broccoli

½ pound shredded cheese (cheddar or Muenster)

1 pound bacon

Fry bacon and break into small pieces. Cut cauliflower and broccoli into small pieces and mix together with bacon. Add cheese.

Dressing

1 cup Miracle Whip

¼ cup sour cream

1 package Hidden Valley Ranch mix

½ cup sugar

½ tsp. salt

Mix together and pour over salad.

Lettuce Carrot Salad

1 head lettuce

1 cup carrots, grated

2 cups shredded cheese

Dressing

2 cups sugar

1 cup vinegar

1 tbsp. mayonnaise

½ cup cream

pinch of salt

Place a layer of chopped lettuce on a flat dish. On that put a layer of shredded carrots. Top with grated cheese. Mix dressing ingredients. When ready to serve, pour dressing over salad.

We think *a meal is not complete without a good salad! One year we had trouble with a bunny nibbling on our lettuce plants in the garden. We set a trap for it, but it was too smart for that.*

Every evening I read a bedtime story to the children. Our four-year-old's favorite story was the one about Peter Cottontail and Mr. McGregor. When I mentioned to Daddy that something must be done about the rabbit in the garden, the four-year-old cried, "No! I won't let you hurt Peter Cottontail! I'm sure there's enough lettuce there for him and us both." He often sat out there beside the garden, hoping to catch a glimpse of his friend, the bunny. Well, Daddy did get rid of the bunny, but he also bought two tame bunnies in a cage for our boy, who happily feeds our extra loose-leaf lettuce to them.

chatting

Greetings *from Michigan! I am an eighteen-year-old girl from a family of eleven children (five girls, six boys). Cooking and baking are among my favorite hobbies, and I am anxious to see the other recipes and comments. We live on a sixty-acre dairy farm and milk fifty-six cows. Two years ago, I hurt my back and couldn't do heavy work for a while. I think that's when I acquired my love of cooking, when I was spending most of my time indoors anyway. But I am by no means an expert: our big Saint Bernard dog gets some flops to eat every now and then, when my experiments turn out to be failures! We like this salad with a meal of mashed potatoes, noodles, and peas.*

Hot Chicken Salad

1 cup diced celery

2 to 3 cups cooked chicken

1 can cream of chicken soup

2 to 3 hard-boiled eggs, chopped

1 tsp. minced onion

1 cup cooked rice

¾ cup Miracle Whip

salt and pepper to taste

Crush potato chips and put on top. Bake 25 minutes at 350°.

Here is our favorite coleslaw recipe:

Easy Coleslaw

1 medium head cabbage

1 green pepper, diced fine

1 cup celery, chopped

1 small onion, chopped fine

2 tsp. salt

1 tsp. celery seed

1 tsp. mustard seed

1½ cups sugar

½ cup white vinegar

Mix and refrigerate.

Frozen Coleslaw

1 medium shredded head of cabbage	
1 grated carrot	
1 tsp. salt	
1 red or green pepper, chopped	

Mix salt with cabbage. Let stand 1 hour and squeeze out excess moisture. Add carrot and pepper to cabbage; add syrup and mix well. Put in freezer containers and freeze. This is an easy and handy salad to serve year-round. It keeps awhile in the refrigerator, too.

Syrup

1 cup vinegar	1 tsp. mustard
2 cups sugar	1 tsp. celery seed
1 cup water	

Combine and boil 1 minute. Cool to lukewarm before pouring over coleslaw.

Cabbage *brings back memories of an exciting fall evening when Dad brought in corn he husked and unloaded by lantern light. We'd been helping Mother cover celery so it wouldn't freeze and carrying cabbages to the cellar for the winter. She never cooked cabbage; we ate it in coleslaw or the outer leaves in sandwiches. Sometime we took a chunk of cabbage in our school lunch boxes, and it was delicious raw! I didn't learn to enjoy cooked cabbage until I stayed at Aunt Martha's house. She added salt and butter and a bit of meat. Now I've also learned that topping cooked cabbage with cheese slices is really yummy, and a healthy food, too!*

chatting

When *I was a young girl, we had a dog that was fond of sweet things. He would sit up and beg nicely for treats and shake a paw. We pampered him and fed him so many goodies that he grew quite fat. One day my older sister declared that this must be stopped! She bought a sack of lean dog food and forbade us to feed him anything but that. I pitied him so much and fed him whatever he wanted when sis wasn't around. Then one day he got sick and lost his appetite entirely. Since he was a valuable dog, we took him to a vet, who gave him medication that soon had him feeling better. The vet told us in plain words to stop giving rich treats to our doggy if we want him to stay well.*

That should have taught me a lesson, but I apparently have to learn the hard way. I indulged too much, too, and now have to be on a reducing diet prescribed by my doctor. I'll include a few of my lean recipes here.

Carrot and Celery Salad

Shredded carrots (about 4 medium)

¼ cup finely chopped celery

1 tbsp. finely chopped onion

2 tbsp. diet mayonnaise

1 tbsp. sugar

2 tbsp. vinegar

Toss first 3 ingredients. Place in dish. Mix remaining and pour over vegetables. This is best made 12 hours or more before serving.

Sunshine Salad

1 (3-ounce) package orange Jell-O	1 tbsp. lemon juice
½ tsp. salt	1 cup grated carrots
1½ cups boiling water	⅓ cup chopped pecans
1 (8-ounce) can crushed pineapple	

Dissolve Jell-O and salt in boiling water. Add undrained pineapple and lemon juice. Chill until quite thick; fold in carrots and pecans. Serves 6.

Garden Salad

½ cup diced celery

2 pints peas, cooked (canned peas are also good)

2 hard-boiled eggs

1 to 2 tbsp. minced onion

½ cup diced or coarsely grated cheese

½ cup diced carrots

Dressing

½ cup salad dressing	3 tsp. lemon juice or vinegar
2 tbsp. sugar	1 tsp. prepared mustard

Mix first 4 ingredients. Stir together dressing and mix into pea mixture. This refrigerates well.

Greetings *from Wisconsin! We like to go picnicking in the woods every fall when the weather is golden and mellow and the sky is bright blue: as the poet Riley says, "When the frost is on the punkin and the fodder's in the shock." Our favorite picnic spot is by the creek, which is clear and shallow, and flowing over stones. There's a fire pit there, and an old picnic table and benches in the shade. We think a picnic wouldn't be complete without either potato salad or macaroni salad, so I'll include our recipes for both.*

One year our bull, which was on another meadow, broke through the fence and came running our way. We all ran screaming and splashed through the creek to get to safety. Although he had never hurt anyone or seemed dangerous, we knew that bulls can't be trusted. Luckily, our dog was able to herd him back to where he belonged, and we chased him into the barn until we could repair the fence.

Amish Macaroni Salad

2 cups dry macaroni	*1 carrot, grated*
½ cup celery, chopped	*6 hard-boiled eggs*
1 onion, chopped	*celery seed to taste*
1 tsp. parsley	

Dressing

1½ cups sugar

¼ cup flour

¼ tsp. salt

1½ cups water

½ cup vinegar (scant)

¼ cup mustard

1 cup Miracle Whip

Cook macaroni as directed and drain. Mix with remaining salad ingredients. Cook together the first 5 dressing ingredients. Cool. Add mustard and Miracle Whip. Stir into macaroni mixture.

Anna's Potato Salad

12 medium potatoes, cooked, peeled, and diced

Mix in another bowl:

1½ cups mayonnaise

1 cup cream

¼ cup sugar

¼ cup vinegar

4 tsp. mustard

1 tsp. salt

1 medium onion, chopped fine

1 cup fresh parsley, cut fine

Add to potatoes. Refrigerate before serving. One can make it the day before.

Egg Salad

6 hard-boiled eggs	*2 tbsp. milk or cream*
½ cup mayonnaise	*1 tbsp. vinegar*
salt and pepper to taste	*paprika (to taste)*

Peel eggs; then mash until fine. Add ingredients and mix.

After services one Ascension Day, some of us went for a picnic and a hike in the woods: my brother and his girlfriend, Malinda; I and Samuel, a boy who worked at our place. After going down a steep ravine, which scared me, we climbed up the other side. There, perched high on the bank, we ate our lunch and sang. Below us a beautiful stream flowed out to the creek.

We also stopped in at the neighbors' old barn and were looking closely at a hive of bees when the bees unexpectedly became angry! We quickly dashed out of the barn, but the bees did sting my brother, Malinda, and Samuel. My brother is a beekeeper, so he was used to bees, but Samuel, too, was familiar with bees. We thought it quite a story that my brother got his girlfriend stung! She got stung near her lip and my sister had to pull the "stinger" out for her.

Favorite Pickled Beets

beets, small and young	1 tsp. cloves
2 cups sugar	1 tsp. allspice
2 cups water	1 tbsp. cinnamon bark
2 cups apple cider vinegar	1 tbsp. salt

Cook beets until tender. Cool enough to peel off skin. Make syrup with remaining ingredients. Pour over beets and bring to a boil for 10 minutes. Pack in sterilized jars and seal. This is enough liquid for 3 to 4 quarts.

I'll never forget the day Mother and I were canning red beets last summer. I went to the garden with a knife, to fetch a bucketful of golf-ball sized beets and rinse them at the pump. I think I was daydreaming as I absentmindedly pulled the beets out and cut off the tops. I moved on to the next row and reached out for a beet. Suddenly, right where I was reaching, I saw a spotted, curled-up snake! It was such a shock that I screamed and leaped backward; with two mighty jumps I was out of the garden! My brother came running and killed the snake, and he had to get the rest of the red beets, too.

Plantation Pickles

cucumbers (choose them as long as quart jar)

2 cups vinegar

1 cup water

5 cups sugar

1 tsp. mustard

1 tsp. celery seed

1 tsp. turmeric

1 tsp. salt

Peel cucumbers. Slice in quarters lengthwise. Place in wide-mouth quart canning jars. Mix remaining ingredients. Fill jars. Cold pack 10 minutes. Good!

Dilly Pickled Green Beans

2½ cups vinegar

2½ cups water

¼ cup salt

green beans

4 cloves garlic or 1 tsp. minced garlic

1 head or 1 tsp. dill seed

Boil the first 3 ingredients together for brine. Remove ends of green beans; leave whole. Pack upright in wide-mouth quart jars. Add the last 3 ingredients to each quart. Process 40 minutes in boiling water.

I am *always hunting for new recipes to try because cooking is one of my hobbies; besides, they say, "Variety is the spice of life." I know my brothers are glad that I try new dishes (judging by how fast things disappear), but they pretend that I'm just trying to "roll" them! Once I unintentionally almost did, even though it wasn't a new dish. We have a container of cayenne red pepper in the cupboard, for when Grandpa comes. He always sprinkles it on his meat, saying it's good for his heart and circulation.*

I made a platter full of deviled eggs and wanted to sprinkle them with paprika. Instead, I accidentally (yes, it was accidental) sprinkled them liberally with Grandpa's red pepper! The boys crammed these egg halves into their mouths and were soon sputtering and choking and running outside with water tumblers in hand. I hadn't tasted one yet, but when I took a tiny nibble, I soon found out they weren't just play-acting!

Deviled Eggs

8 hard-boiled eggs	
½ tsp. salt	
½ tbsp. vinegar	
4 tbsp. mayonnaise	
⅛ tsp. pepper	
½ tsp. mustard	
2 tbsp. chopped parsley	
1 tbsp. cream	

Cut eggs in half, remove yolks, and mash them with the rest of the ingredients except the parsley. Refill the whites and sprinkle with paprika. Garnish with parsley.

Egg and Spinach Salad

6 hard-boiled eggs, chopped

5 cups chopped raw spinach

6 slices bacon, fried and crumbled

1 minced onion

1 cup bean sprouts

seasoning to taste

Mix ingredients and toss with the following dressing until spinach leaves are well coated.

Dressing

¾ cup sugar

¼ cup vinegar

¼ cup salad oil

⅓ cup ketchup

1 tsp. salt

1 tsp. Worcestershire sauce

Combine dressing ingredients and mix well.

I've always *been fond of corn relish, and every year we have a big corn patch. When I was of school age, we lived close to the woods and had trouble with little forest folks and blackbirds helping themselves to tasty morsels from our garden. So Dad and I decided that a scarecrow might solve the problem and spent some time in the shop making one. Dad sure had the knack for it; I almost wish I'd have gotten someone to snap Mr. Scarecrow's picture! Wearing Dad's old hat, shirt, and pants, he looked so lifelike. Our aged grandmother lived with us at the time. Her eyesight was poor, but she noticed the scarecrow and asked, "Is that one of the boys standing there in the garden?" Dad, grinning mischievously, told her, "No, that's Mr. Scarecrow. Shall I tell him to come in and visit with you?" (Smiles) Mr. Scarecrow did his duty well for several years, and we always had plenty of garden goodies left over for ourselves.*

Corn Relish

6 pints raw sweet corn
3 medium to large onions
1 bunch celery
4 sweet red peppers
1 pound sugar
2 tbsp. salt
1 tbsp. mustard seed
1 pint white vinegar
1 pint water

Boil all together until soft. Put into jars and seal. Or cold pack in a boiling water bath for 40 minutes.

Ella's Zucchini Relish

10 cups ground zucchini

4 onions, chopped

3 green peppers, chopped

3 red peppers, chopped

5 tbsp. salt

6 cups sugar

2½ cups vinegar

2 tbsp. cornstarch

2 tsp. celery seed

1 tsp. mustard seed

½ tsp. powdered alum

Cover first 5 ingredients with water and let stand overnight. Drain well. Mix together remaining ingredients and stir into zucchini mixture. Simmer ½ hour. Put into jars and seal. Delicious on hot dogs, hamburgers, eggs, and scrapple.

Gallon Jar Pickles

(This recipe is only for 1 gallon)

Take medium-sized whole pickles, wash, and pack into glass gallon jar.

Mix:

4 tbsp. salt	*1 tbsp. pickling spice*
3 tsp. alum powder	*4 cups vinegar*

Pour this over your pickles in the jar and fill the jar with water. Put cap on tight and let stand for 6 weeks (or you can let it stand for up to a year). When ready to eat your pickles, drain off all the juice and pour away. Slice pickles and put them back into jar. Put 5 or 6 cups of sugar over them. It forms its own juice. Shake jar once in a while to help dissolve the sugar. Have fun eating them in about 12 to 18 hours.

A young girl shared this recipe while working for me. She got it from an aunt. I tried it but put the pickles in two-quart jars for our small family, and we really liked it. I served them to company, and everyone tasting them wanted the recipe. Once at a family picnic I brought them, and everyone just loved them, so I had to copy a lot of recipes.

My sister-in-law usually does a lot of pickles, and she asked me for this recipe. One year she had these at a picnic. The folks ate a lot of pickles and asked about them. Folks have asked me many questions and wondered where I found such a good recipe. I've been copying this recipe for many people. I don't mind and hope everyone enjoys them as much as we do.

My husband's aunt recently told me she made lots of these pickles. She said she marked hers as first batch, second, and third. Her family eats many pickles, and she wants to use them in the order she made them. She was surprised when I told her she could keep them up to a year. So I keep sharing the recipe with others. This is the first time I've had a recipe that everyone wants. I wonder how many I copied already! Good luck!

chatting

Sweet Midget Pickles

7 pounds cucumbers, 1½ to 2 inches long	
½ cup salt	
8 cups sugar	
6 cups vinegar	
¾ tsp. turmeric	
2 tsp. celery seed	
2 tsp. mixed pickling spice	

First day: Place cucumbers in a glass, ceramic, or stainless steel container. Cover with boiling water in the morning. In the afternoon, drain and re-cover with boiling water.

Second day: Drain and cover with boiling water. In the afternoon, drain and cover with brine formed by adding salt to about 6 quarts of boiling water.

Third day: Drain, rinse, and prick cucumbers. Make syrup using 3 cups sugar, 3 cups vinegar, and all spices. Bring to a boil and pour over cucumbers. In afternoon, drain syrup into pan; to it add 2 cups sugar and 2 cups vinegar. Heat to boiling and pour over cucumbers.

Fourth day: Drain syrup into pan; add 2 cups sugar and 1 cup vinegar. Heat to boiling and pour over pickles. In afternoon, drain into pan, add remaining sugar and (if desired) either 2 tsp. vanilla or 1 tsp. chopped arrowroot and 1 tsp. nutmeg. Heat to boiling. Pour over pickles that have been packed in pint jars; add ½ stick cinnamon to each. Process 8 minutes.

These are very crisp and crunchy, well worth the fuss and not nearly as much time as the old 14-day sweet pickle.

I was having *an extra busy day, with lots of pickles to can, laundry to do, and also yard mowing on the list. After dinner I had a canner full of pickles ready on the stove in the shanty, intending to boil them for only a few minutes. After I put them on the stove, I stretched out on the kitchen couch to rest for a few minutes. You guessed it: I fell asleep and slept for about a half hour. When I awoke, I jumped up and looked guiltily at the clock. A thunderstorm seemed to be approaching, and I decided to quickly do some yard mowing before it rained. It wasn't until about an hour and a half later that I thought of my pickles. Oh no! I rushed into the shanty, dreading to see what I'd find. The jars were okay, but the pickles were far from crisp anymore, needless to say! I suppose we'll be able to eat them, but I certainly won't be putting them on the table when we have company!*

Bread and Butter Pickles

6 cups sliced cucumbers
1 pound onion, chopped or sliced thin
1 green pepper, chopped
¼ cup salt
2 cups brown or white sugar
½ tsp. turmeric
¼ tsp. cloves
1 tbsp. mustard seed
2 cups vinegar

Mix vegetables with salt. Let set 3 hours. Drain. Make a syrup with remaining ingredients. Bring to boil, add vegetable mixture, and bring to a boil again. Put in jars and seal.

Desserts and Yogurt

Friendship Is a Shining Gift

Friendship is a shining gift
That warms you with its glow,
Brightening life's pathway for you
No matter where you go.

Friendship is a priceless gift
That you can never buy,
Made of love and trust and care
That cannot fade or die.

Friendship is a priceless gift
That's always sweet and fair,
Bringing treasures bright as gold
And happiness to spare.

Author unknown

chatting

Fruit Cobbler

1 quart fruit (most any kind)

¼ cup sugar

1 tbsp. tapioca (if fruit is juicy)

2 cups unsifted all-purpose flour

1 cup sugar

2½ tsp. baking powder

½ tsp. salt

¼ cup oil

¾ cup milk

1 egg

Put first 3 ingredients in a large baking pan (greased). Sift together the next 4 ingredients and add the oil, milk, and egg. Stir well and pour over the fruit. If desired, dot with butter and sprinkle with cinnamon. Bake at 375° for 30 minutes. Serve warm with milk or ice cream. Delicious!

I learned *to make this while I was at my aunt and uncle's house after they had a new baby. My aunt was taking care of the baby and told me how to make it. Very simple!*

chatting

This recipe is easy for little girls to make. (I'm eight years old.) When the others come in from milking our fifty cows, they are so happy to see that I made this peach dessert. It's really yummy with ice cream!

Peach Delight

¾ cup oatmeal
½ cup brown sugar
1 tbsp. flour
1 tbsp. butter
5 fresh peaches

Slice peeled peaches in a greased casserole (9 x 9 inch) or a large pie plate. Mix oatmeal, brown sugar, flour, and butter into crumbs and sprinkle on top of peaches. Bake at 350° for 30 minutes or until top is nicely browned. Serve warm with milk or ice cream.

When we were married twenty-one years ago, a friend of my mother's gave me this recipe. Every spring when rhubarb is in season, we eat a lot of this dessert. It's simple to make and very delicious!

Rhubarb Dessert

4 cups cut rhubarb	2 cups sugar
4½ cups water	½ cup fine tapioca

Cook together until the tapioca is clear. Then add ¾ cup strawberry Jell-O. It will thicken in the refrigerator.

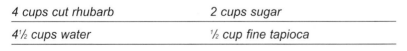

I used to *just guess when I canned my fruit salad. Then a friend gave me this recipe, and we loved it! When packing lunches, it's so handy to have the fruit salad ready to serve. Hubby and children love it! It's also a handy snack for preschoolers.*

Fruit Cocktail to Can

12 quarts water
2½ cups lemon juice
1 tsp. salt
8 cups sugar
3 cups Thermflo

Mix Thermflo with enough cold water to mix; then heat. Into the boiling water, stir lemon juice, salt, and sugar. Cook until it thickens.

Add:

1 basket peaches and 1 basket pears, peeled and cubed
19 pounds seedless grapes
3 gallons Mandarin oranges
3 gallons pineapple chunks

Don't cook it anymore after adding fruit. Put in canning jars (underfill a bit). Cold-pack and put in boiling water for 30 minutes.

Once *when I was making strawberry jam to can, I was just stirring in the Thermflo when my little daughter cried, "Mamm, come look; the birdies are hatched, the birdies are hatched! Oh! Just look!"*

There was a nest under the porch eaves, and I thought I'd join her at the window for just a moment. But I got caught up in the excitement and forgot the strawberry jam. It scorched a bit at the bottom. That winter, every time we opened a jar of the jam and could taste the scorch slightly, we thought of the little robins and wondered where they were—maybe down in the sunny south, enjoying summer-like weather.

Strawberry Jam

1 quart water	
1 package strawberry Kool-Aid	
½ cup ClearJel	
1 cup sugar	
2 quarts strawberries	

Bring water, sugar, and Kool-Aid to a boil. Thicken with ½ cup ClearJel mixed with a little water. Remove from heat. Wash, cap, and halve the berries. When jam is cold, add the berries to it.

Strawberry Grape-Nuts Dessert

Crust

2 cups finely crushed Grape-Nuts

3 tbsp. sugar

¾ cup melted margarine

Filling

8 ounces cream cheese, softened

½ cup confectioners' sugar

1 (8-ounce) carton Cool Whip

2 cups miniature marshmallows

Topping

1 (6-ounce) package strawberry Jell-O

2½ cups boiling water

1 (10-ounce) package strawberries

Mix sugar, Grape-Nuts, and margarine. Press into a 9 x 13 inch pan. Bake at 350° for 15 minutes. Cool. Cream together cream cheese and confectioners' sugar. Fold in Cool Whip. Add marshmallows and spread on cool crust. Dissolve Jell-O in warm water; stir in strawberries. Chill until slightly thickened. Spread over cream cheese layer. Chill overnight.

Fruit Cocktail

1 (20-ounce) can pineapple chunks	½ dozen bananas
1 dozen large marshmallows (2 cups minis)	
1 or 2 oranges	

Drain juice from pineapple chunks. Mix 1 tbsp. of flour with ½ cup of sugar in a 2-quart kettle. Stir in 1 beaten egg and mix until smooth, then add the pineapple juice. Cook until thickened and add 1 tbsp. butter. When cool, add 1 cup whipped cream. Pour over fruit.

Canned Fruit

6 quarts fruit	1¼ cup instant ClearJel
6 cups cold water	1½ cups Jell-O
4 cups sugar	

Mix sugar, ClearJel, and Jell-O. Add to fruit and water. Cold-pack 10 minutes. Do not fill jars too full.

I got *this recipe from my sister. We really like it for strawberries and peaches. Use flavored Jell-O according to your fruit. Our three school-age children really like it in their lunches. It is so handy to open a jar and have it ready to eat. If it seems too thick, I add some pineapples. We live on a dairy farm and have sixty cows and also a large garden, which is my hobby. This spring we planted a hundred strawberry plants, so I'm hoping for lots of berries next spring. Then I'll probably use this recipe to fill many jars. I hope you enjoy it.*

chatting

I got *this recipe from a friend of mine when I was a teenager. We had plans to go blueberry picking at a bog about ten miles away (five of us girls). Each of us was supposed to take along something to eat, and I decided to take raisin caramel dumplings, even though they are best eaten warm. We hitched two horses to the open market wagon and put our eats on back, along with a stack of buckets, leaving room for three of the girls to sit there since the seat had room for only two. I was to help with the driving, so I had the privilege to sit on the seat. The berries were big and the picking good. We didn't even mind the mosquitoes (much). By lunchtime our pails were nearly full, and we were famished. When I set out my dumplings, I noticed with dismay that some of them were squashed flat. One girl sheepishly admitted that she might have sat on them. We got a good laugh out of it and still had plenty else to eat. I'll include a few blueberry recipes, too.*

chatting

Raisin Caramel Dumplings

Bring to a boil:

1½ cups brown sugar	
1 cup raisins	
2 cups water	
dash of salt	

Mix for dumplings:

⅓ cup white sugar	
1 tbsp. oleo	
1 cup flour	
¾ cup milk	
1 tsp. baking powder	

Drop dumplings into syrup. Cook 15 minutes, covered. Don't peek!

Blueberry Buckle

³/₄ cup sugar	2 cups flour
¼ cup oleo or butter	2 tsp. baking powder
1 egg	½ tsp. salt
½ cup milk	2 cups fresh blueberries

Mix thoroughly sugar, oleo, and egg. Stir in milk. Sift together flour, baking powder, and salt. Add to batter and mix well. Toss blueberries in a little flour and add them. Spread into a greased and floured 9-inch square pan.

Topping

½ cup sugar	½ tsp. cinnamon
⅓ cup flour	¼ cup oleo or butter

Combine ingredients; then add softened butter. Sprinkle over batter. Bake at 375° for 45 to 50 minutes.

Blueberry Delight

2 cups graham cracker crumbs	8 ounces cream cheese
½ cup margarine, melted	1 package whipped topping
2 cups confectioners' sugar	blueberry filling

Mix cracker crumbs with margarine and press into a dish. Mix sugar with cream cheese and fold in topping. Pour mixture into cracker-lined dish. Top with blueberry filling.

Grandpa's Apple Dumplings

6 medium-sized apples

2 cups flour

2½ tsp. baking powder

½ tsp. salt

⅔ cup margarine

½ cup milk

Sauce

2 cups brown sugar

2 cups water

¼ tsp. cinnamon or nutmeg

¼ cup butter

Pare and core apples. Leave whole. Mix flour, baking powder, and salt together. Cut in margarine until crumbly. Add milk and mix together lightly, working dough together. Roll dough into 6 squares. Place an apple on each. Fill cavity in apple with sugar and cinnamon. Wrap dough around apple. Place dumplings in baking pan. Combine all sauce ingredients except butter. Cook 5 minutes. Add butter. Pour sauce over dumplings. Bake at 375° for 35 to 40 minutes. Serve hot with milk. One could also cut up apples, roll dough out in a piece ¼-inch thick, and then spread chopped apples over dough. Roll up as a jelly roll. Cut in slices 1¼-inch thick. Place slices on baking pan. Cover with sauce.

Cinnamon Apple Bake

6 large apples
1 cup pancake syrup
⅓ cup brown sugar
1 tsp. cinnamon
1 tbsp. butter, melted

Peel apples, cut in halves, and place in a flat baking dish. Combine rest of ingredients and pour over apples. Bake at 350° for about 45 minutes.

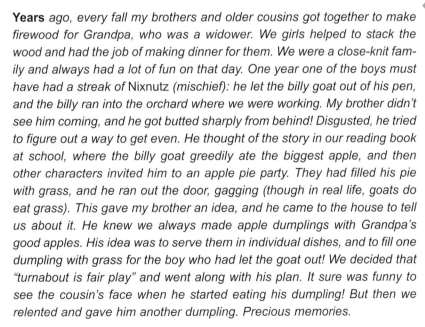

Years *ago, every fall my brothers and older cousins got together to make firewood for Grandpa, who was a widower. We girls helped to stack the wood and had the job of making dinner for them. We were a close-knit family and always had a lot of fun on that day. One year one of the boys must have had a streak of* Nixnutz *(mischief): he let the billy goat out of his pen, and the billy ran into the orchard where we were working. My brother didn't see him coming, and he got butted sharply from behind! Disgusted, he tried to figure out a way to get even. He thought of the story in our reading book at school, where the billy goat greedily ate the biggest apple, and then other characters invited him to an apple pie party. They had filled his pie with grass, and he ran out the door, gagging (though in real life, goats do eat grass). This gave my brother an idea, and he came to the house to tell us about it. He knew we always made apple dumplings with Grandpa's good apples. His idea was to serve them in individual dishes, and to fill one dumpling with grass for the boy who had let the goat out! We decided that "turnabout is fair play" and went along with his plan. It sure was funny to see the cousin's face when he started eating his dumpling! But then we relented and gave him another dumpling. Precious memories.*

chatting

Apple Crisp

4 cups apples, sliced and pared	1/2 cup oatmeal
3/4 cup packed brown sugar	3/4 tsp. nutmeg
1/2 cup all-purpose flour	1/3 cup oleo, softened
3/4 tsp. cinnamon	

Heat oven to 375°. Grease baking pan. Arrange apples in pan. Mix remaining ingredients with a fork. Sprinkle over apples. Bake until apples are tender and topping is golden brown—about 30 minutes. Serve with milk, cream, ice cream, or hard sauce as desired.

Ada's Apple Crunch

8 apples	1/8 tsp. salt
1 cup sugar	1/4 cup raisins
1 tsp. cinnamon	

Topping

3/4 cup rolled oats
3/4 cup brown sugar
1/4 cup melted butter

Peel and slice apples over raisins in casserole dish. Combine topping ingredients and pat on top of apples. Bake at 375° for 45 minutes.

Where we lived when we first married, we had a small apple orchard. My favorite apples were those big sweet ones we called Pound apples. I still get a longing to bite into one of those big, sweet, juicy, flavorful gems! The Yellow Delicious were best for canning apple pie filling and for drying. The flavor of the Red Delicious was hard to beat when they were at their peak, but all too soon they would turn slightly mealy. The Stayman Winesap were best for winter eating. For our year's supply of applesauce, we used the tart Early Harvest apples, and sometimes the Summer Rambos. The Early Harvest needed more sugar than any other kind, but they were worth it. They all have their good points, though, and apples have always been my favorite fruit.

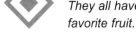

Cherry Dessert

1 can Eagle Brand condensed milk

1 (16-ounce) can crushed pineapple (well drained)

1 can cherry pie filling

¼ cup lemon juice

16 ounces Cool Whip

Mix together and chill overnight.

Cherry Cheesecake

Crust

2 cups graham cracker crumbs

1 stick butter

¼ cup sugar

Filling

2 (8-ounce) packages cream cheese

2 eggs

2 cups sugar

2 tsp. vanilla

dash of salt

2 cans cherry pie filling

Blend cream cheese, eggs, sugar, vanilla, and salt. Spread over crust and bake for 20 minutes at 350°. Cool. Top with cherry pie filling. Refrigerate 2 hours.

Copying *this recipe reminded me of when I was of preschool age and had a little table and two chairs just my size. I used to carry them out under the apple tree and have a little tea party with my dolls. Mother let me have tea to put in the cups, and animal crackers and raisins to put on the plates. What fun it was to pretend to be grown-up and having visitors! Once when it was my birthday, Mother made cherry dessert for the occasion. She helped me to wash and dry my tea set. Then she joined me for my tea party on the lawn. We ate the cherry dessert off my little plates with the tiny spoons. What fun that was! I remember pretending to be Aunt Lydia, and we had an interesting grown-up chat!*

chatting

Canned Rhubarb Dessert

| 10 quarts water in large kettle (take some out to mix with the Thermflo) |
| 10 quarts chopped rhubarb |
| 14 cups sugar |
| 2½ tsp. salt |
| 5 cups Thermflo |

Bring to a boil, stirring often. Mix 5 cups Thermflo with water. When the rhubarb mixture is boiling, stir in the Thermflo mixture. Cook until thick, stirring constantly. Stir in 5 packages strawberry Kool-Aid. Pour in canning jars, cold-pack, and put in boiling water for 5 minutes. Yields 19 to 20 quarts.

Every *old homestead seems to have at least a few rhubarb stalks thriving every spring. Most have thick green stalks, but I prefer the fine-textured, strawberry-colored stalks, which have a milder flavor and make pretty-colored jam and jelly.*

Many times when I make rhubarb jam, my mind goes back to when I was a teenager. In a busy spring season our neighbor came and wondered if I could help out a day or two until their regular maid would come. I was pleased to go! I felt quite grown-up when the Mrs. asked me to make a kettleful of rhubarb jam. All went well, and when it was done, she instructed me to set the kettle of jam out in the pump trough to cool while I put dinner on the table.

When the men came in, the Mr. brought this kettle along and set it on the gas stove burner. Thinking it must be water to heat for washing dishes, I quickly turned the burner on high before we sat down to eat.

After a while the Mrs. sniffed the air a little; then she calmly told her husband to turn off that burner! Oh! My jam! No harm was done, but we had to start over getting that jam cooled off!

chatting

Grape sponge *was one of my mother's favorites. She has gone on to that better land, and I miss her so. My first memories of her were of being rocked to sleep, and of sitting in church with my head resting in her lap. Sitting beside her in the carriage, on the way to church, I knew my face had better be clean, or she'd wet the corner of her hankie and scrub away!*

On Sunday evenings she'd stir us up to go for a walk. We'd gather bouquets of wildflowers, something I still love to do. We'd see if we could catch a glimpse of those tiny spring peepers.

In the winter she'd get out the boxes of fabric scraps, and we had many an evening of cutting and sewing. First she had me make a four-patch quilt, and then a nine-patch. When I sewed wrong, she taught me how to rip it open and try again. How I detested that, but I'm so glad now that she taught me!

How proud I was of the first cake she helped me to make. In cooking she taught me to keep it simple and healthy—something I still try to follow.

Every fall when the grapes were ripe, she would often make grape sponge. Mmm . . . maybe I should go make some today!

Grape Sponge

Soften one envelope unflavored gelatin in ½ cup cold water. Stir in 1 cup hot grape juice, ½ cup sugar, and 2 tbsp. lemon juice. Cool. Stir occasionally. When it begins to set, beat with a rotary beater until frothy. Beat in 1½ cups Cool Whip and continue beating until mixture holds its shape. Pile in sherbet glasses. Chill. Serve with soft custard as sauce.

• • •

I first *enjoyed this recipe at a friend's house. I never learned to drink coffee, but this (and coffee ice cream) gave me an appetite for it. Since I always have plenty of milk on hand, I mostly use milk instead of water to make it.*

Coffee Carnival

In heavy sauce pan, mix:

½ cup tapioca

½ tsp. salt

⅓ cup raisins

½ cup sugar

1½ cups water

Boil several minutes, stirring constantly. Remove from heat and add 1 cup strong coffee and 1 tsp. vanilla. Cool, stirring occasionally. Chill. Fold in 1 cup whipped cream.

I found *this recipe in the* Lancaster Farming *newspaper some years ago, and it sure is delicious. It looks quite good in most any color except purple! We once made it when we took hot lunch to school, and the milk in the purplish gelatin turned it into an unappetizing grayish color! It still tasted good, but how embarrassing!*

Whipped Milk Gelatin

1 (3-ounce) package flavored gelatin	1 cup milk
1 cup boiling water	

Add boiling water to gelatin. Cool until it begins to thicken. Add milk slowly, beating constantly. Beat well. Chill several hours in refrigerator before serving.

One day *in 2001, we were traveling home to Pennsylvania. As we stopped at a rest stop in Ohio, the bus driver told us that we could go no farther east than Akron. We heard that something serious happened but had no idea what. At Akron we finally heard the frightening news that terrorists had attacked the United States that morning. Oh! How scared and helpless we felt, but we knew God was in control.*

We had a long eight-hour wait in Akron. One of our traveling companions called his neighbor and asked if he would pick us up and take us home. We just didn't know if things would grow worse or what was in store for us. Instead of waiting until the buses were allowed to go, we wanted to find another way home.

While we waited, a woman came to talk to us and told us that she would call us later in the evening to see if we were still there. If we were, she would give us a bed for the night. Thankfully, by then we were on our way home in a pickup truck, but at a speed we did not appreciate! Our driver passed every vehicle we caught up with and really kept rolling.

So it was with grateful hearts that we arrived home safely to our children. We had been very concerned that they were worrying about us, but thankfully they had heard nothing of the tragedy yet. Yes! We were traveling home on September 11! How much more we should treasure our freedom since that day.

I don't know *how advisable it is to make this recipe anymore, with all the pollution from trucks, cars, and jets in the atmosphere. When I was a little girl, whenever we had a fresh snowfall, we'd grab our little bowls and fill them with fresh, clean snow. We'd add a bit of vanilla flavoring, a teaspoonful of sugar, some milk, and stir it a bit. We thought it was delicious and tasted even better than real ice cream, maybe because we could make it ourselves. Mother let us have as much as wanted, and we never tired of it. It brings back precious memories of us sitting around the table with our treats, each thinking our own was the best. To make various flavors, we could add whatever we liked to the snow, such as some strawberry or blueberry jam, or a teaspoonful of cocoa syrup.*

Snow Cream

1 cup milk	*⅓ cup sugar*
½ tsp. vanilla	*6 cups fresh snow*
⅓ cup strawberry or blueberry jam or 1 tbsp. fudge topping (optional)	

Mix all together and enjoy right away. It melts fast.

Here's another favorite:

Blueberry Delight

2 cups fresh or frozen blueberries	*2 cups cold milk*
⅓ cup sugar	*2 cups vanilla ice cream*

Mix together in blender. Pour into freezer trays and freeze. Stir often.
Serve partially frozen.

When I was a girl, I had a favorite spot to sit and read, or to go to when I just wanted to be alone. It was a wide branch up in an apple tree, between the chicken house and the meadow fence. From there I could see the back part of the house and the comings and goings of the others, yet I was within calling distance of the back door. One Saturday afternoon on a lovely spring day, the apple tree was in blossom and the robins were singing. I was sitting up there reading and enjoying the fragrance and beauty of the blossoms. The back door opened, and I heard my older sister call me. I didn't want to go to help finish the cleaning: there were just the porches and walks to do yet, and I figured she could do that. So I pretended I hadn't heard. After a while she went back inside, and I happily went on reading. About an hour later, I climbed down and sauntered back to the house, feeling a little guilty. What a disappointment I had when they told me that our favorite single aunt had been there (she came in the front door) and had brought homemade ice cream! I felt like crying (and did too, later). I was sorry I didn't get to taste the ice cream and sorrier yet that I didn't get to talk to my aunt. But I learned a good lesson from it, and later I got her ice-cream recipe. But nothing ever really tastes as special as when you eat it with loved ones.

Vanilla Ice Cream

5 eggs, slightly beaten	7 tbsp. cornstarch
¾ cup white sugar	1 tbsp. vanilla
1 cup brown sugar	dash salt
1¼ quarts milk	
2 cans evaporated milk	
1 can sweetened condensed milk	

Heat the milk and evaporated milk to boiling. Mix beaten eggs, sugars, cornstarch, and salt. Beat well. Add to the boiling milk and cook to boiling again. Remove from heat. Add sweetened condensed milk and 1 tbsp. vanilla. Cool and freeze.

Strawberry Ice Cream

2 cups crushed, sweetened strawberries	1 pint cream
¾ cup instant ClearJel	3 to 4 quarts milk
4 cups sugar (or less)	

Mix sugar and instant ClearJel; then mix it into the berries. Mix it with milk and cream in a 6- or 8-quart ice-cream freezer. Freeze and enjoy!

Several *folks were helping my sister and her husband with a building project. After supper, they enjoyed a bedtime snack of coffee ice cream, not realizing it's not a good bedtime snack for some people. Some of them could not relax to sleep when they wanted to! The outcome: Tired workers!*

chatting

Coffee Ice Cream

8 cups whole milk	1 cup strong cold coffee
4 eggs	1 cup sweet cream

Put 1 cup milk in a saucepan, add the 4 beaten eggs, and simmer for several minutes. Mix the rest of the above ingredients in a large bowl and add the egg mixture. Chill.

In a small bowl, mix:

1½ cups sugar	⅔ cups instant ClearJel

Mix well; then add to first mixture and beat well. Pour into ice-cream mixer and churn.

One day *we had a special valentine party at school. The teacher served pink iced heart-shaped cookies, strawberry-flavored and heart-shaped finger Jell-O, and valentine candies. Best of all, she brought the ingredients for peppermint twirl ice cream! Or rather, her brother brought it at the last recess—the custard, ice, rock salt, and the ice-cream freezer. The girls helped to get it ready, and the boys cranked the freezer. When it was ready, we girls dipped it into ice-cream cones. We all thought it was the most delicious we'd ever tasted, and we still make it often. We passed out the valentines then, which were much prettier than the ones they have nowadays, for they were homemade!*

Peppermint Twirl Ice Cream

4 cups milk

2 cups sugar

¼ tsp. salt

2 quarts cream

2 tsp. vanilla

3 cups finely crushed peppermint twirl candies

Scald milk; add sugar and salt. Stir until dissolved. Add cream and vanilla. Chill. Freeze in the ice-cream freezer. Crush candy in blender, a fourth at a time. Add after the ice cream is frozen but not hardened. Makes 4 quarts.

Raspberry Sherbet

1 cup water	1 tbsp. lemon juice
½ cup sugar	2½ cups milk
3 ounces raspberry Jell-O	

Boil water and sugar one minute. Add Jell-O. Cool. Stir in lemon juice and milk. Freeze 1 hour. Beat well and enjoy! It makes a refreshing treat on a warm summer evening.

 The *other week I baked pumpkin custard from the pumpkins I raise. My youngest brother (age six) declared right away, before he barely tasted it, that he doesn't like it. He was the only one, though; everyone else loved it!*

Pumpkin Custard

2 cups mashed pumpkin	¼ tsp. salt
1 cup bread crumbs	1 tsp. orange flavor
2 eggs, yolks and whites separated	1 cup brown sugar
1½ cups milk	1 tbsp. butter

Mix, but reserve egg whites for meringue on top. Or fold into the custard mixture last and bake with the custard. Bake at 360° until custard is set. Top with stiffly beaten eggs and return to oven to brown. Chill, then serve with whipped cream.

This ice cream is a favorite of ours. It doesn't have that floury burned taste that boiled ice cream often has. I remember noticing that as a child when we went to neighboring gatherings, etc. My mother always made Dairy Queen ice cream. After I married, my husband didn't like the Dairy Queen because of the gelatin effect that it had. So I felt extra fortunate to find this recipe, which calls for cornstarch instead of flour for thickening. We all enjoy our homemade ice cream. After all, what is more rewarding on a warm day? This recipe seems to make better ice cream if the pudding is more on the thin side. At times if it gets plenty thick, I add more milk to it before freezing. The can should be fairly full before starting to freeze it, since the cream and egg whites are beaten and/or whipped. Good luck and happy eating!

Velvet Ice Cream

2¼ quarts milk

2 cups white sugar (or brown)

4½ tbsp. cornstarch

7 egg yolks

½ tsp. salt

½ tsp. maple flavor

7 egg whites, stiffly beaten

3 cups heavy cream, whipped

Heat the milk to scalding. Mix sugar with cornstarch and egg yolks, using a bit of milk. Add to the hot milk. Stir until it thickens. Add egg whites and cook a bit longer. Remove from heat. Add salt and flavoring. Cool. Fold in the whipped cream. Makes 6 quarts.

We have *an apple and peach orchard and sell fruit at the roadside stand at the end of our lane. Another Amish woman bakes bread, pies, and other goodies for our stand, and still another family keeps it stocked with fresh vegetables.*

One day when I was waiting on the customers, an elderly man came up to me and handed me a ten-dollar bill. He said that about five years ago he had taken a $2.50 box of strawberries without paying, and now he wanted to return fourfold what he had taken. He apologized and asked for forgiveness, which I gladly granted. I had to think of the Bible verse, "If we confess our sins, he is faithful and just to forgive us our sins" (1 John 1:9). We should try to make restitution, too, for the wrongs we have done (as in Luke 19:8).

Peach Pudding Delight

1 quart hot vanilla pudding
½ cup peach flavor Jell-O
1 quart fresh peaches, diced
1 cup sugar
3 tbsp. instant ClearJel
12 ounces Cool Whip

Make your favorite vanilla pudding. Remove from heat; add Jell-O to 1 quart pudding. When cool, but not set, add Cool Whip. Put in dessert dish. Mix sugar and instant clear jell. Add to peaches and put on top of the pudding.

Peach Ice Cream

4 cups fresh peaches

1½ cups sugar

1 pint heavy cream

1 quart milk

1 tsp. vanilla

1 tsp. lemon juice

½ tsp. salt

Mix peaches and sugar and let set 30 minutes. Add remaining ingredients and freeze in 4-quart ice-cream freezer. Enjoy!

Peanut Butter Dessert

1 (8-ounce) package cream cheese

1 cup confectioners' sugar

½ cup peanut butter

½ cup milk

1 container Cool Whip

Oreo cookie crumbs

Mix first four ingredients together; then stir in Cool Whip. Line the bottom of the dessert dish with Oreo cookie crumbs. Add pudding mixture, putting some Oreo crumbs on top. Refrigerate to harden. Enjoy!

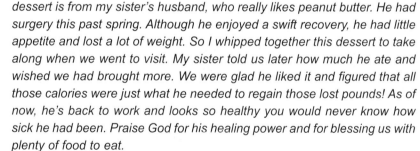

This *is a rich dessert for special occasions. One memory we have of this dessert is from my sister's husband, who really likes peanut butter. He had surgery this past spring. Although he enjoyed a swift recovery, he had little appetite and lost a lot of weight. So I whipped together this dessert to take along when we went to visit. My sister told us later how much he ate and wished we had brought more. We were glad he liked it and figured that all those calories were just what he needed to regain those lost pounds! As of now, he's back to work and looks so healthy you would never know how sick he had been. Praise God for his healing power and for blessing us with plenty of food to eat.*

chatting

Éclair Dessert

¾ to 1 pound graham crackers

2 (3-ounce) packages French vanilla or vanilla instant pudding

3½ cups milk, scalded and cooled

1 (8 or 9-ounce) container Cool Whip or 1 cup whipping cream

Topping

3 tbsp. cocoa

2 tbsp. oil

2 tsp. white Karo

2 tsp. vanilla

3 tbsp. soft margarine

1½ cups confectioners' sugar

3 tsp. milk

Line graham crackers in bottom of a 9 x 13 inch pan. Beat instant pudding and milk together. Blend well and add Cool Whip. Spread on crackers, and alternate graham crackers and pudding until crackers are all used. Put crackers on top (last), and then the topping.

Note: Don't use raw milk; bring to a boil and cool until cold!

Topping

Mix together as you do for frosting; then spread on top of pudding. Refrigerate for at least 1 day. For variety, top with cherry pie filling instead of chocolate.

When *I was a young girl going to school in our one-room country school with eight grades, the teacher presented the idea of a "guinea pig" dinner. We were all for it. Each older girl student would make a part of the meal, using a recipe they never made alone before; that was why we called it "guinea pig." I decided on éclair dessert, and I started off with high spirits and a clean sink. Mom helped me scald the milk because I was a little scared of trying that alone for my first time. Everything went fine, I thought, and I carefully transported it to school. When lunch was served to the excited pupils, some of them commented how "chocolaty" this dessert was! I gave it no thought until that evening when my family and I had the leftovers for supper. Mom exclaimed, "It's so strong! How much cocoa did you use?" "Three cups," I answered so assuredly. "Oh my!" she gasped. "Didn't you see that the recipe says three tablespoons?" My brothers nicknamed that dessert "Black Top" because they said it was so black!*

I hope you have just as much fun serving this delicious dessert. We like it especially well with the black cherry pie filling on top instead of chocolate.

Fancy Four-Layer Dessert

Crust

1½ cups flour

¾ cup butter

½ to 1 cup pecans, chopped

Second layer

8 ounces cream cheese, softened

1 small (8-ounce) container Cool Whip or 1 cup whipped cream

1 cup confectioners' sugar

Third layer

2 packages instant butterscotch, lemon, or chocolate pudding mix

3 cups cold milk

Fourth layer

Cool Whip or whipped cream

chopped nuts (optional)

Mix crust ingredients and press into the bottom of a 9 x 13 inch pan. Bake at 350° for 15 minutes. Combine cream cheese, Cool Whip, and confectioners' sugar; spread on cooled crust. Prepare pudding mix with cold milk and put on second layer. Top with more Cool Whip and sprinkle with chopped nuts.

This *is one of our favorite desserts now, but almost every time I serve it, I think of the proverb, "Pride goeth . . . before a fall." I was newly married and wanted to make something extra special for dessert. I believe I was trying to impress my husband that I'm a good cook. It turned out well, and I was "patting myself on the back," really pleased that I had something good to offer him. When hubby came in for a drink in midafternoon, he saw the dessert in the fridge and complimented me on it, saying it looks good enough to eat. Well, I*

chatting

believe I was already a bit proud of it and needed a comedown instead. His two little sisters, ages three and four, came over for supper that evening, and after we had finished our first course, I went to the refrigerator for my showpiece. I had piled it high with Cool Whip and sprinkled it with 5th Avenue candy. I don't know how it happened, but as I was lifting it out, it slipped out of my grasp and crashed to the floor, breaking the glass dish. Hubby was very sympathetic and helped to scoop it up into another dish, declaring that what hadn't touched the floor was still fit to eat. The dish had merely cracked in two, and we thought there were no glass chips. Imagine my horror when the three-year-old spat out a big glass chip when eating some of the dessert. We quickly removed the rest of it from the table, thankful she wasn't cut and hadn't swallowed the glass. I think I learned two lessons there: Pride goes before a fall, and never eat anything from a broken dish.

Graham Cracker Fluff

Soak ½ tbsp. gelatin in ⅓ cup cold water. Mix ½ cup sugar and ¾ cup rich milk; add 2 egg yolks.

Cook for 1 minute, stirring all the time. Remove from heat. Add gelatin and 1 tsp. vanilla. Chill until mixture begins to thicken. Then add stiffly beaten egg whites and 1 cup Cool Whip or whipped cream.

Crumbs: Melt 1½ tbsp. butter and 3 tbsp. brown sugar together. Mix with 12 crushed graham crackers. Line bottom of dish with half the crumbs and pour in pudding. Put remaining crumbs on top. Set in cool place to chill. Delicious!

You *will want to try the graham cracker fluff if you haven't yet. It's a very old recipe that everyone should like. When I was small, we children liked it so well. So one Christmas morning as we sat down to eat breakfast, my mother came with a bowl of the good yellow shimmering fluff for each of us. That sure was a treat. We each had a whole bowl to ourselves and could eat it whenever we wanted. Then when I grew up, I decided to make it myself. Boy, were my uncle and family surprised! It can also be made for special friends or dates, etc. If you wish to put fruit on top, that's good, too, I would think. (We never tried it with fruit since we like it this way.)*

chatting

Grandma's Caramel Pudding

¾ cup brown sugar

½ cup white sugar

¼ cup butter

2 heaping tbsp. cornstarch

1 tbsp. ClearJel

1½ quarts milk

1 egg

½ tsp. salt

1 tsp. vanilla

Melt brown sugar, white sugar, and butter; brown it to caramel color. Add milk, reserving 1 cup. Bring to almost boiling point. Combine cornstarch, ClearJel, egg, and salt in the reserved milk. Mix to a smooth paste and add to the hot mixture. Cook until thickened, and then add vanilla. Chill and serve.

This *recipe was a favorite while I was growing up. It brings back memories of going to Grandma's, for this was what she often served for dessert. When she passed this recipe on to my mom, she had no written recipe: she just told Mom the way she did it, and Mom wrote it down. That way it could be passed down to us girls, too.*

When we were little girls, and Mom was making this pudding, how we liked to eat a bit of the caramelized browned sugars and butter before she stirred in the milk. Of course, Mom didn't let us take too much or it would have spoiled the pudding. When Mom invited company for a meal, she was almost always sure to serve this pudding. We lived on a dairy farm, and she had all the milk she needed. We also served this pudding at our wedding—ten portions of it. Try it! It's delicious!

chatting

This eight-minute cheesecake is simply wonderful, so good, and easy to make. It's a favorite for our family. I got the recipe from a friend for whom I used to work. She served it once for a snack, and since our family has big eaters, it really pays to make it. Even our dog likes it. Once when my sister came to help, I decided to make extra and sent some along home with her. Her family likes it, too. It's different from the real kind because you don't have to bake it.

Yoder's Eight-Minute Cheesecake

8 ounces cream cheese

⅓ cup sugar

1 cup sour cream

2 tsp. vanilla

2 cups Cool Whip

graham cracker crust

Beat cream cheese until smooth. Gradually add sugar. Stir in sour cream. Blend in Cool Whip and vanilla. Spoon into cracker crust. Top with thickened strawberries, blackberries, raspberries, or cherries.

Tapioca Pudding

5 cups milk	1⅓ cups white sugar
¾ cup baby pearl tapioca	1 tsp. salt
2 eggs, well beaten	

Combine milk and tapioca and simmer 15 minutes, stirring often. If you soak it a while first, you don't have to boil it so long. Add eggs, sugar, and salt. Bring to a boil. Remove from heat. Cool and chill. Add whipped cream, cream cheese, fruit, or broken-up candy bars as desired.

Best Vanilla Pudding

4 cups milk

5 tbsp. cornstarch

1 cup sugar, divided

⅛ tsp. salt

2 eggs, separated

¼ cup sugar

1 tsp. vanilla

1 cup mini-marshmallows

In heavy kettle, heat milk to boiling. Add cornstarch, ½ cup sugar, and salt. Beat egg yolks with remaining ½ cup sugar. Remove pudding from heat and stir in egg yolk mixture. Beat egg whites stiff. Beat in ¼ cup sugar. Fold into pudding. Stir in vanilla and add mini-marshmallows.

Caramel Maple Pudding

¾ cup brown sugar
¼ cup water
¼ tsp. salt
1 quart milk
⅓ cup cornstarch
2 tbsp. butter
1 tsp. maple flavoring

Cook sugar, water, and salt until slightly browned. Stir together milk and cornstarch; pour into sugar mixture. Cook until thickened. Remove from heat and stir in butter and maple flavoring. Cool. Good served with sweetened whipped cream.

Greetings *from Pennsylvania! I decided to write about the time I made this pudding and scorched it so badly that we couldn't use it. I had everything added already and was cooking it in the Dutch oven on the stove top. All of a sudden, I heard a clattering sound and frightened "Whoa! Whoa! Whoa!" I ran to the window and saw our pony hitched to the cart, running out the lane. He was galloping at top speed, and the cart was bouncing up and down. He hit a rock by the roadside; the seat flew off and landed in the gutter. At the next bump, the pony cart overturned, and the pony was dragged it along. Our neighbor caught him at the end of his lane and brought him back. Not until the excitement was all over did I think of my pudding! The bottom was so scorched that the taste went all the way through it, and I had to make another go at it. I hope you have better luck!*

chatting

Easy Butterscotch Pudding

1½ to 2 quarts milk
1 cup molasses
1 cup brown sugar
1 cup flour
½ cup butter
1 tbsp. vanilla
5 eggs

In a heavy kettle, bring milk to boiling. Beat rest of ingredients together and add to hot milk. Stir constantly until pudding is thick. Cool and top with your favorite topping.

This *pudding is easy to make and our favorite (also our number one pudding for company dinners). We have goats for our milk supply. Friends who are accustomed to cows' milk find it a bit different tasting. But with this pudding, they take second helpings and afterward ask for the recipe!*

While going to school, we made a little recipe book for a Mother's Day gift. Everyone had to bring a recipe along to put in. That's where we got this recipe, and we have used it a lot since. That page is smeared with brown blotches and tattered, but it still serves the purpose. It was the beginner's pudding recipe for my sisters and me. Hope you enjoy it. Good luck!

chatting

Butterscotch Tapioca

6 cups boiling water	
1 tsp. salt	
1½ cups granulated or small pearl tapioca	
2 cups brown sugar	
2 beaten eggs	
1 cup milk	
½ cup white sugar	
1 stick butter	
1 tsp. vanilla	
2 cups whipped cream	
4 Snickers candy bars	

Boil water; add salt and tapioca. Cook for 15 minutes. Add 2 cups brown sugar and cook until clear. Stir often. Mix together 2 beaten eggs, ½ cup white sugar, and 1 cup milk. Add and cook until bubbly. Brown the butter and add vanilla. Cool; add cream and candy bars.

We *had company one day in the summer of 2001. Men were helping put new windows and siding on the house. The women were talking and helping with dinner. With all the sawing and hammering going on, it was hard to concentrate. The flies were coming in and were often a mess to sweep away. It was getting later, and the women asked me to cook some tapioca. After heating the stove, I stirred and waited for quite a while, and still nothing happened. Not knowing what else to do, I got Mom to check on it. Taking a close look, she asked where I got it and discovered I had fine coconut in there instead of minute tapioca! What embarrassment. So I had to start all over in making my pudding. "Haste makes waste" is what they say. To this day, I'm still being reminded of my "coconut tapioca."*

chatting

Cottage Puffs Dessert

⅔ cup white sugar	1 cup milk
¼ cup oil	2½ cups pastry flour
1 egg	4 tsp. baking powder
1 tsp. vanilla	½ tsp. salt

Mix all together and bake in 2 (12-cupcake) pans, well greased. While warm, take out and put in 2 deep bowls.

Sauce
In a saucepan, put:

½ cup cornstarch
½ cup cocoa
1 cup white sugar
a little vanilla and salt

Add enough cold water to mix; then add boiling water to make a nice sauce. Pour over the puffs and serve hot.

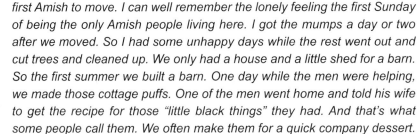

When *I was twelve years old, we moved to a new settlement. We were the first Amish to move. I can well remember the lonely feeling the first Sunday of being the only Amish people living here. I got the mumps a day or two after we moved. So I had some unhappy days while the rest went out and cut trees and cleaned up. We only had a house and a little shed for a barn. So the first summer we built a barn. One day while the men were helping, we made those cottage puffs. One of the men went home and told his wife to get the recipe for those "little black things" they had. And that's what some people call them. We often make them for a quick company dessert.*

chatting

Flavored Yogurt

1 gallon milk	
³/₄ cup sugar	
pinch of salt	
1 tsp. vanilla	
5 tbsp. flavored Jell-O	
1½ tbsp. Knox gelatin	
½ cup yogurt (plain)	

Put milk on low heat for one hour at 180°. Soak gelatin in ⅓ cup cold water. Add sugar, salt, vanilla, Jell-O, and gelatin (to warm milk). Let stand one hour; then add the plain yogurt. Put in jars. Put in bake oven (unlit, with only the pilot light on) overnight or 8 hours.

I find *this an easy and good yogurt recipe. I got it from my sister-in-law who lives in Indiana. We haven't seen yet where they have been living for almost five years. But I can use her recipe and think of them!*
We have a dairy farm with sixty cows, so there is always plenty of milk around! That is, if the milkman hasn't just picked it all up!
The first couple times I tried to make yogurt, it was a flop! It just stayed runny like sour milk. So I used it for making whoopie pies, and they turned out real good. I hope you enjoy this recipe and have good luck! "If at first you don't succeed, try, try again!"

chatting

We used *to buy our yogurt, but now since we have this recipe, we make our own, and all of us like it much better. You also can save money with it, especially if you live on a dairy farm.*

Sylvia's Favorite Yogurt

2 quarts milk

½ cup plain yogurt

½ cup sugar

1 tbsp. plus 1 tsp. unflavored gelatin

Heat milk in saucepan to 190°. Let cool to 130°. Meanwhile, soak gelatin in cold water; add to the 130° milk. Mix sugar and yogurt; also add to milk, mixing well. Put mixture in jars. Cover with lids but not rings. Put in gas oven with pilot light on for 8 hours. Serve with pie filling or dry Jell-O. Very delicious!

Note: If you have no pilot light in your oven, put a lamp with a 100-watt bulb in the oven, which works just as well.

Lena's Blueberry Cheesecake

Mix:

2 (5-ounce) packages graham crackers, crushed	
1½ sticks margarine, softened	

Combine and bake:

3 small eggs
½ cup honey
2 tbsp. ReaLemon juice
1 (8-ounce) package cream cheese
3 cups cottage cheese
2 tsp. vanilla

Combine and cook:

1 quart blueberries, fresh or frozen	½ cup ClearJel
2 cups water	2 tbsp. ReaLemon juice
1 cup sugar	2 cups blueberries
½ cup honey	

Mix crushed crackers with margarine and press firmly and evenly into a 9 x 13 inch baking pan. Combine eggs, honey, lemon juice, cream cheese, cottage cheese, and vanilla in blender. Blend. Pour this over crumbs. Bake at 300° for 35 to 40 minutes. When done, sprinkle with cinnamon. Cool. Combine 1 quart blueberries, water, sugar, and honey in saucepan. Cook 5 minutes. Add enough water to ClearJel to make a paste and add to blueberry mixture. Cook until thickened enough for bubbles to "pouff." Stir in remaining blueberries and cool. Pour over cheese mixture. Serve with sweetened, whipped cream. If you substitute cherries for blueberries, increase the sugar.

Party Cheesecake

14 graham crackers, crushed

¼ cup butter

6 ounces orange Jell-O

2 cups hot water

2 (8-ounce) packages cream cheese

1 cup sugar

1 tsp. vanilla

1 can evaporated milk

Mix cracker crumbs and butter; press into 9 x 13 inch pan. Bake at 350° for 15 minutes; cool. Dissolve Jell-O in hot water; set aside to cool. Beat cream cheese, sugar, and vanilla. Whip evaporated milk. Add cooled Jell-O and cream cheese mixture. Pour over crust. Chill.

Cakes and Pies

Grandma's Pies

When I sit back and close my eyes,
I still remember Grandma's pies,
All in a row on baking day,
Her handiwork there on display.

I still recall the spicy smell,
Her kitchen that I loved so well.
I wish I could go back once more
And see her standing at the door.

Then she would cut a slice for me,
And join me with her cup of tea.
Oh, how I long for days gone by,
For one more slice of Grandma's pie.

But cherished memories remain,
When I walk down memory's lane,
Of Grandma's pies and Grandma's love,
A blessing sent from God above.

Author unknown

Black Midnight Cake

2 cups flour

1 cup brown sugar

2 tsp. baking powder

¾ cup cocoa

1 tsp. salt

1 cup milk

2 eggs

1 tsp. vanilla

½ cup vegetable oil

1 cup black coffee

Stir dry ingredients together; add others in order as listed. Batter is very thin. Bake in a 9 x 13 inch pan at 350° for 35 minutes.

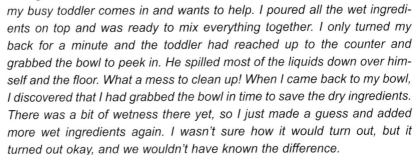

I often *make this cake since it is one of our favorites. One day as I was mixing it, I sure had a mess. I had just mixed all the dry ingredients when my busy toddler comes in and wants to help. I poured all the wet ingredients on top and was ready to mix everything together. I only turned my back for a minute and the toddler had reached up to the counter and grabbed the bowl to peek in. He spilled most of the liquids down over himself and the floor. What a mess to clean up! When I came back to my bowl, I discovered that I had grabbed the bowl in time to save the dry ingredients. There was a bit of wetness there yet, so I just made a guess and added more wet ingredients again. I wasn't sure how it would turn out, but it turned out okay, and we wouldn't have known the difference.*

chatting

In 1993, *when I was eleven years old, we lived in Pennsylvania. Mom and Dad went on a trip and left me in charge of the house and children. I had big plans for a perfect, clean house and perfect baked goods. So I got this simple recipe and baked this cake, which was a favorite with us all. But I had to make two, since one almost disappeared with a breakfast meal of warm oatmeal and this cake. You can imagine my proud feeling when Mom came home and saw this baked cake topped with a pudding-like frosting. In those years when eggs were scarce and we were still learning, we could easily make this cake without help.*

Moist Chocolate Cake

Mix:

3 cups flour

2 cups sugar

½ cup cocoa

2 tsp. baking soda

1 tsp. salt

Add:

2 tsp. vinegar

2 tsp. vanilla

2 cups water

1 cup oil

Mix well. Put in a 9 x 13 inch ungreased pan and bake at 350° for 30 to 40 minutes.

Richmond Chocolate Frosting

1 cup sugar	1 cup boiling water
3 tbsp. cornstarch	1 tsp. vanilla
⅓ cup cocoa	3 tbsp. butter
dash of salt	

Mix dry ingredients. Add boiling water and cook until thick. Remove from heat; add butter and vanilla.

I'm *a nine-year-old Amish girl who likes to help her mom bake and ice cakes. Licking the bowl is the fun part! This icing is very good on most any cake—especially good on carrot cake.*

Cream Cheese Frosting

1 tbsp. milk
1 tsp. vanilla
3 ounces (or ⅓ cup) cream cheese
6 tbsp. softened butter

Mix well and add:

1¾ cups confectioners' sugar

Beat until smooth.

chatting

This *is good in a sheet pan and topped with Cool Whip. We like to add a bit of mint flavor and a drop of green food coloring to the Cool Whip. My mother always used to bake it in a granite pan. When our parents' things were divided, I inherited the pan. I told my sisters I will try to have chocolate cake baked in Mother's pan when they come to visit. We always thought the cake tasted better baked in that pan!*

Elizabeth's Chocolate Cake

2½ cups flour

2 cups sugar

1 tsp. salt

1 tsp. baking soda

¾ cup cocoa

1 cup salad oil

1 cup milk

2 eggs

1 cup hot coffee

Mix ingredients in the given order, adding hot coffee last. Batter will be thin and the cake moist. Bake at 375° for 30 to 40 minutes. I like to mix a chocolate cake mix, mixed as directed on the box, with this batter.

When *I was teaching our oldest daughter how to bake, she made a chocolate cake. In the oven, the cake wouldn't rise. The cake seemed suspiciously runny. When I asked whether she put the flour in, she replied, "You didn't tell me to!" The birds benefited from this learning experience, as they got the cake.*

We got this recipe from our daughter-in-law; this cake is real nice and moist. However, be careful not to add a cup full of pure coffee grounds, as my daughter did! She couldn't understand why the cake did not taste good or get fluffy. The small girls had copied it, and she thought they made a mistake. But later she discovered the joke was on her: she added coffee grounds instead of brewed coffee!

Yummy, Yummy, Chocolate Cake

2 cups flour

2 cups white sugar

1 tsp. baking powder

2 tsp. baking soda

1 tsp. salt

⅔ cup cocoa

2 eggs

¾ cup salad oil

1 cup milk

1 tsp. vanilla

1 cup brewed coffee

In a large bowl, combine flour, sugar, baking powder, baking soda, salt, cocoa, oil, milk, eggs, and vanilla. Beat well; then add the coffee. Batter will be thin. While the cake is in the oven, take care. Even the slightest bump will ruin it. Bake at 350° for 35-45 minutes. (Good luck!)

Molasses Black Cake

1 egg

2 cups brown sugar (or 1 cup if using mild molasses)

1 cup lard

1 cup raisins

1 tsp. baking soda

1 cup baking (blackstrap) molasses

2⅔ cups flour

1 cup strong brewed coffee

½ tsp. cinnamon, cloves, and nutmeg

Mix and bake at 350° for 45 minutes or until toothpick inserted in center comes out clean.

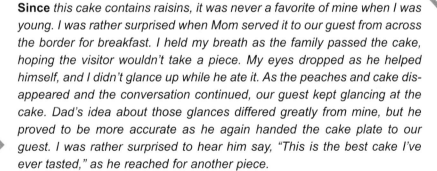

Since *this cake contains raisins, it was never a favorite of mine when I was young. I was rather surprised when Mom served it to our guest from across the border for breakfast. I held my breath as the family passed the cake, hoping the visitor wouldn't take a piece. My eyes dropped as he helped himself, and I didn't glance up while he ate it. As the peaches and cake disappeared and the conversation continued, our guest kept glancing at the cake. Dad's idea about those glances differed greatly from mine, but he proved to be more accurate as he again handed the cake plate to our guest. I was rather surprised to hear him say, "This is the best cake I've ever tasted," as he reached for another piece.*

chatting

Ruth's Chocolate Cake

In a big bowl, mix:

4 cups sugar	*1 cup lard*
½ cup cocoa	

Add:

1½ cups hot water	*2 cups sour milk*

Next add:

6 cups flour	*1 tsp. vanilla*
1 tbsp. baking soda	*1 tsp. salt*
3 tsp. baking powder	

Mix well. Bake at 350° for 1 hour. Delicious!

I tell *our children I almost grew up on Ruth's Chocolate Cake. Where or how it got the name, I don't know. It was a family favorite, partly because it was easy to make, but mostly because it doesn't need eggs. We didn't have our own laying hens and frequently ran out of eggs. If I let my memory go back to the time we all gathered around the big table as children, I recall often eating partly thawed chocolate cake, soaked up in milk, with a generous helping of applesauce on top.*

As time went on, I had a kitchen of my own with cake pans to keep filled. Since I was short of eggs, I went back to the old standby: Ruth's Chocolate Cake.

Once I was mixing a batch with two little children watching and "helping" (waiting to lick the bowl and spoon). The batter was mixed and ready for the cake pan. Not knowing my one-year-old daughter was sitting on the floor beside the sink, I took one step sideways, partly tripped over her, and dumped a big splash of batter on her head! Needless to say, she wasn't very pleased, and I had a mess to clean up! I don't remember for sure, but likely I was in a hurry to start with!

chatting

Strawberry Long Cake

2 cups flour
2 tsp. baking powder
6 tbsp. sugar
1 egg
½ tsp. salt
⅓ cup shortening
⅔ cup milk

Sprinkle 1 cup sugar over 4 cups strawberries. Let it set while preparing batter. Spread batter into a 9 x 13 inch cake pan and put berries over top of the batter.

Cream together:

¼ cup soft butter	3 tbsp. flour
¼ cup brown sugar	

Drop here and there over the strawberries. Bake at 350° for about 35 minutes or until done.

Strawberry *season meant a lot of work for Mom and us two oldest girls, with ten younger siblings. We three would daily pick the berries by the ten-quart bucketful. Besides being a backbreaking task, we'd occasionally meet up with garter snakes. E-ee-ck!*

Mom's spirit was undaunted. She would rise early and pick a bucketful before we girls were up and had breakfast. Her example taught us to work, too.

I remember one time when I was in charge of babysitting, Grandpa passed by and saw Mom alone in the berry patch. He quoted, "Industrious mother—lazy girls. Lazy moms—industrious girls!" Thus I got an urge to prove to Grandpa that I'm not lazy!

chatting

Judith's Shortcake

2 eggs

½ cup water

½ cup lard

1 cup milk

1½ tsp. salt

6 tsp. baking powder

4 tbsp. sugar

4 cups flour

Put everything in bowl and mix. Bake at 350° for 45 minutes or until toothpick inserted in center comes out clean.

One winter *I was along when a group of four young people went to Niagara Falls on our way to Canada for a visit. We left our baggage in lockers at the terminal. I think it was snowing when we started out on our long walk to the falls. When we got back, I was tired, but I'm so glad I got to see it.*

We could hear the roar of the falling water a while before we could see the falls. We saw both the Canadian and the American falls, but the Canadian Horseshoe Falls were by far the most majestic to me. What a beautiful and grand display of God's handiwork. The water had a green appearance, and a great mist arose from it. Many seagulls flew around above the water, and quite a bit of ice surrounded it. It was a memorable experience.

chatting

Cocoa Cupcakes

1½ cups flour
⅔ cup shortening
1 tsp. baking soda
⅔ cup milk
1 cup white sugar
1 tsp. salt
½ cup baking cocoa

Stir these ingredients vigorously by hand.
Next stir in by itself ¾ tsp. baking powder.
Then add ⅓ cup milk, 2 eggs, and 1 tsp. vanilla.
Blend by hand. Fill 24 medium cupcakes or 3 layers in cake pans. Bake at 350° for 20 minutes.

When *I was about nine, I had the privilege of stirring up these cupcakes while Mom was sewing. All went well until I came to the stir-by-hand part. "Mom, does this really mean stir by hand?" . . . "Yes." Partway through the stirring process, I asked again, and she gave another hurried yes. Suddenly the sewing machine quit its steady humming, and I heard Mom's frantic voice: "Sarah, you didn't!" Each word kept coming closer until she stood by my side. A sigh escaped her lips as she stared in disbelief at my hands sunken in the chocolate mess before her. I always thought it was nine-year-old Sarah who learned a lesson that day, but since being a mother of little girls myself now, I wonder if Mom wasn't a little wiser as well!*

chatting

Rachel's Jelly Roll

Beat

    5 egg yolks

Add:

1½ cups sugar	*3 tsp. baking powder*
10 tbsp. cold water	*½ tsp. salt*
2 large cups flour	

Add:

    5 beaten egg whites last.

Bake in a jelly roll (shallow flat) pan, greased and floured, at 350° about 5-18 minutes. While baked product is hot, turn out on damp cloth sprinkled with confectioners' sugar. Roll up, using cloth as part of roll. Cool. When ready to fill, unroll, spread on filling, roll up without towel.

Chocolate Filling

Put 2½ large cups milk in saucepan.

Mix:

1 cup sugar	*¾ cup flour*
2 heaping tbsp. cocoa	*½ cup milk*
2 eggs	*1 tsp. vanilla*

When milk boils, add ingredients to the milk and stir until it boils again. Take off and cool. Put on cooled Jelly Roll and roll up. Icing, frosting, etc., are also good.

This *jelly roll is an old recipe traced back to mother, grandmother, and great-grandmother. It's so easy to make, and it just always gets nice if you do it right. I always use this recipe; the others don't turn out right, but this one usually does. It's very good with icing, filling, or whatever you wish. One time when we had it for a family outing, my niece copied the recipe for two different people. It's that good!*

Katie's Yellow Cake

1 cup white sugar	2 tsp. baking powder
2 eggs	1½ cups flour
1 cup sweet cream	1 tsp. vanilla

Stir and bake at 350° for 30 minutes.

I was *ten years old when I baked this cake for my mother's birthday. My parents were gone for the afternoon. I had helped with baking before but had never done it alone. My fifteen-year-old brother stoked up the fire for me. When the oven was hot, I put in my cake and sat down to wait. It turned out beautifully! Because I wanted to have all evidence cleared away by the time my parents returned, I frosted it soon after taking it from the oven. Then I safely hid it away. When we celebrated Mother's birthday, the cake was rather soggy because some of the frosting had soaked in. Mother knew right away that I must have frosted it while warm! To this day, I often think of that when I frost a cake.*

Corn Pone (or Johnnycake)

1 cup cornmeal
1 cup flour
½ tsp. salt
4 tbsp. baking powder
1 egg
1 cup milk
¼ cup shortening or oil

Mix all together in a bowl and pour into a 13 x 9 inch cake pan. Bake at 350° for 30-35 minutes. (When using sour milk or buttermilk, use 1 tsp. baking soda and 3 tsp. baking powder.)

Johnnycake *is the same as what people also call Shawnee cake, journey cake, and other names, depending on regional custom.*

I remember eating this "cake" for breakfast as a little girl with milk and fruit. Our favorite was, and still is, applesauce. In fact, I really don't like it with any other fruit. We also enjoy it fresh out of the oven with honey on it. We considered it as a kind of cereal at home since we ate it for breakfast. My family now eats it as cake. One son likes his plain, with no fruit. I'm still using the same recipe my mother did and will pass it on to my daughters. A month or two ago, we had some "excitement" around here when the men hauled spoiled hay piles and lit them, pile after pile. After awhile sirens went, fire trucks passed, etc. We walked out to the end of the lane to see what all the fuss was about. We didn't know they were burning hay because they just decided to do so after being out in the field. So we were somewhat shook-up until we finally found out what was going on. Such a thankful feeling to know all is well. Yet it was rather embarrassing. A distant neighbor had reported it as a house fire.

chatting

This frosting is a favorite of mine, maybe because it's so simple to make and turns out right for me. When we make a special cake at our house, it usually gets this frosting.

We have often used it on a sponge cake and put a variety of toppings (or decorations) on top. Once we had tiny tangerines, peeled them, and put one tiny slice on each piece of cake. Another time we put heartnut pieces on each slice. One time it was chocolate cake, I believe, and we flavored the frosting with peppermint and sprinkled green sugar crystals all over. Oh, yes, we also made the frosting green to go with the peppermint flavor. So there are many ways to top it.

Fluffy White Frosting
(Two Egg Whites)

³/₄ cup sugar

¹/₄ cup light corn syrup

2 tbsp. water

2 egg whites, cooked

¹/₄ tsp. cream of tartar

¹/₄ tsp. salt

1 tsp. vanilla extract

In top of double boiler, combine sugar, corn syrup, water, egg whites, cream of tartar, and salt. Cook over rapidly boiling water, beating with mixer or rotary beater until mixture stands in peaks. Remove from heat; add vanilla extract. Continue beating until frosting holds deep swirls. Frosts two-layer 8- or 9-inch cake pans or 9 x 13 inch cake pan.

Vera's Yellow Chiffon Cake

2¼ cups sifted cake flour

1½ cups sugar

1 tsp. salt

Make a well in the mix and add:

½ cup Wesson oil (or canola oil)

yolks from eggs used (below) for whites

1 tbsp. vanilla plus water to equal ¾ cup

Beat together to make dough.

1 cup egg whites, whipped until foamy. Add:

½ tsp. cream of tartar

Whip whites until stiff. Fold in dough. Bake in tube pan at 350° for 55-60 minutes.

Many *years ago I got this recipe out of the* Lancaster Farming *magazine after it won first prize in a contest. It became our six children's special birthday cake. I often made it for my sister on special occasions. Also, it is my best cake for company.*

chatting

Hawaiian Cake (moist)

2 cups white sugar	2 tsp. baking soda
2 cups flour	1 tsp. vanilla
1 cup English walnuts, chopped	2 eggs
1 (16-ounce) can crushed pineapple, with juice	
1 tsp. salt	

Pour everything together and mix. Very simple! Bake at 350° until golden brown, approximately 45 minutes.

Topping (to put on when cool)

1 (8-ounce) package cream cheese

1 stick margarine

1⅓ cups confectioners' sugar

1 tsp. vanilla

If desired, sprinkle with nuts and coconut. Yummy!

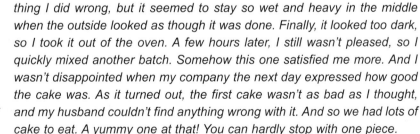

This *is a very good cake. My husband thinks I should make it more often. One time I made it for company and felt it was a flop. I didn't know of anything I did wrong, but it seemed to stay so wet and heavy in the middle when the outside looked as though it was done. Finally, it looked too dark, so I took it out of the oven. A few hours later, I still wasn't pleased, so I quickly mixed another batch. Somehow this one satisfied me more. And I wasn't disappointed when my company the next day expressed how good the cake was. As it turned out, the first cake wasn't as bad as I thought, and my husband couldn't find anything wrong with it. And so we had lots of cake to eat. A yummy one at that! You can hardly stop with one piece.*

chatting

Maplenut Chiffon Cake

2¼ cups flour

¾ cups sugar

3 tsp. baking powder

1 tsp. salt

¾ cup brown sugar

½ cup salad oil

5 egg yolks

¾ cup cold water

2 tsp. maple flavor

1 cup egg whites (from 8 eggs)

½ tsp. cream of tartar

1 cup chopped walnuts

Sift first 4 ingredients into mixing bowl. Stir in brown sugar, salad oil, egg yolks, water, and flavor. Beat until smooth. Combine egg whites and cream of tartar in mixing bowl. Beat until very stiff peaks form. Pour egg yolk batter in thin stream over egg whites. Gently fold in nuts. Bake at 325° for 55 minutes.

One year *I made this Maplenut Chiffon Cake for my mother's birthday. They live in the Grossdaadihaus (grandparents' house) adjoining our house, and we had invited the other married children who live nearby to come over that evening. This was supposed to be a surprise for my parents, the Grossdaadies (grandparents). I made the cake and covered it with plastic, being careful not to smudge the "Happy Birthday, Mommy" icing I had put on. While they were napping, I smuggled the cake into their cellar so she wouldn't see it before we sang "Happy Birthday!" We had also made custard for homemade vanilla ice cream, ready to be churned in the hand-crank ice cream freezer that evening. When Daadi got up from his nap, he went down to the cellar for something and saw the cake. He was*

chatting

keen enough not to tell Mommy, though, and we were able to surprise her. Our daughter put one candle on the cake for each decade of her life, lit them, and brought it upstairs. As soon as the cellar door opened, we all started to sing, and Mommy had to wipe away tears.

Applesauce Raisin Cake

½ cup soft butter	½ tsp. salt
1½ cups sugar	1 tsp. cinnamon
2 eggs, well beaten	1 cup raisins
1½ cups applesauce	½ cup nuts
2½ cups flour	
1 tsp. baking soda, dissolved in 2 tbsp. hot water	

Cream butter and sugar; add eggs. Mix dry ingredients and add alternately with applesauce. Add baking soda, nuts, and raisins. Bake in a 9 x 13 inch pan at 350° for about 35 minutes.

When *I was nine years old, my brother had his twelfth birthday, and I decided I wanted to make him a cake. Mom gave me permission to stir it together while he was busy in the barn doing the evening chores. I wanted to be so careful to do everything right, and thought I could do it without Mom's help. I made his favorite—applesauce cake—with raisins and chopped nuts stirred into the batter. I spread it carefully into the cake pan with a spatula and was proudly carrying it to the oven, when Mom asked, "Are you sure you added baking soda?" Oh no! How could I have forgotten? She helped me scoop it back into the bowl so I could add the soda. The cake turned out surprisingly well but perhaps not as nice as it would've been if I'd have added soda at the right time.*

chatting

Cherry Coffee Cake (or Bar)

1 cup butter	
1¼ cups sugar	
4 eggs	
1½ tsp. baking powder	
1 tsp. vanilla	
½ tsp. salt	
3 cups flour	
1 (21-ounce) can cherry pie filling	

Glaze

1 cup confectioners' sugar	
1 tbsp. butter, melted	
2 tbsp. milk	

Cream butter and sugar. Add eggs one at a time. Blend in remaining ingredients except pie filling. Place ⅔ of batter into 9 x 9 x 13 inch baking pan. Spread pie filling over batter. Drop remaining batter by teaspoonfuls over top of cherries. Bake at 350° for 30 to 40 minutes. Cool.

Glaze
Combine confectioners' sugar and melted butter. Stir in milk to reach spreading consistency.

This *is one of our favorite "cakes" to make when we want something special. We make it with or without glaze, and also in different flavors. So far we have tried apricot and plum besides sour cherries. If red (or purplish) plums are used, it colors the filling a deep ruby red; with the white drizzled frosting, it looks like something from the store.*

We like to make it because it is so special in looks and flavor and yet needs only ordinary ingredients. We use a quart jar of our own canned fruit

chatting

from the cellar, which we thickened before canning. Sometimes we use the fruit and thicken it just before baking.

We have made these as bars for family gatherings and picnics and to eat with hot school lunches. Everyone seems to like them.

One time we had an embarrassing moment when someone helped himself to a piece out of the pan, and it was very doughy. But at least that never happened again! I think it was one of the first times we made it for others. But since then we've had many successes. It's a quick, handy cake or bar to make.

Garden Huckleberry Pie

2 cups garden huckleberries, cooked and mashed
1 package grape Kool-Aid
¾ cup sugar
2 cups water
thicken with 2 rounded tbsp. ClearJel
add 1 tbsp. ReaLemon juice

Mix all ingredients together except the ClearJel. Bring to a boil. Mix the ClearJel with water to form a smooth paste, then stir into the hot mixture and return to heat. Bring to a boil again to thicken. Pour into unbaked pie shell and put top crust on (or crumbs). Bake at 375° for approximately 45-50 minutes.

This *pie is so simple and yet so delicious. It is often mistaken for blueberry or elderberry pie. Friends who dislike the strong flavor of garden huckleberries were amazed to learn what they were served. Humiliated that they did not catch on, they admitted that they had thought it was elderberry pie.*

chatting

This is a cake my husband's aunt baked. We like to go to visit them about once a year. One time a group of us went to visit them with two horses hitched to a double buggy. We started off early Saturday morning. Then we stopped at a nice pond to fish. We caught many blue gills and some big bass. We discovered we could catch big bass with little blue gills for bait. So while we women cleaned the fish, the men took some little blue gills and tried to catch a big bass yet. My husband put one little blue gill in his pliers pocket. But they didn't catch any more fish. So we loaded up and went on. We got there about 7:00 in the evening and fried some fish for our supper. The next day was Sunday, and we stayed there for dinner. My husband kept smelling something; it kept getting worse, but if he went outside, he didn't smell it much. So he thought, "Well, that's just the way my aunt's house smells." In the evening before we started home, he got a paper out of his pliers pocket, and it was wet and smelly. There was the stinky little blue gill he forgot to take out of his pocket!

White Mountain Cake

1³/₄ cup sugar	3 tsp. baking powder
1 cup cream	½ cup oil
1 cup milk	2 eggs, separated
3 cups flour	vanilla and salt

Mix everything together except egg whites. Beat the 2 egg whites until stiff peaks form and add last. Bake cake for 40 minutes at 350°. Boil topping one minute and spread over the cake. Return cake to the oven and bake 5 more minutes.

Topping

³/₄ cup brown sugar	½ cup butter, melted
1 cup coconut	1 tsp. vanilla
¼ cup cream	

Boil 1 minute.

This cake is an old-time favorite. It doesn't take any lard and you can even make it without eggs if you don't have any.

Brown Stone Front Cake

2½ cups flour

1½ cups white sugar

2 tsp. baking soda

1 tsp. salt

6 tbsp. cocoa

2 eggs

2 cups of sweet cream

1 tsp. vanilla

Combine dry ingredients first and sift. Then add eggs and cream. Bake at 350° for ½ to ¾ hour or until done.

My mother made this so often that she knew it by heart. As a child, I couldn't understand how she could bake it without a recipe. But now I also know it by heart. My parents had a family of eleven children, and I have many good memories.

My dad used to have a sawmill and did custom sawing. Every winter we filled our ice house for our use in the summer. He also tapped maple trees and boiled maple syrup, plus having a dairy. We milked twenty-eight cows, at times by hand. But with six or seven sets of hands to milk, it was quite a simple, enjoyable task! Back then, things were more simple and relaxing, although not many realized it at the time! Good luck and happy eating!

This was my mother's favorite recipe, and is still a favorite of ours to this day. I have a family of ten, and each one likes it. It is smooth and creamy if you bake it with a slow oven and do not let it boil. Use your choice of coconut, sweetened or unsweetened, fine or coarse: either is fine. My mother died about three years ago, but her recipe lives on. "Precious memories, how they linger!" (J. B. F. Wright).

Susan's Coconut Pie

½ cup sugar (scant)

1 small egg yolk

½ cup cream

½ cup milk

1 tbsp. flour

½ cup shredded coconut

2 egg whites

Mix everything together but the egg whites. Beat them until stiff peaks form; then fold into the filling. Pour into an 8-inch pie shell. Prebake the pie crust for 15 minutes before adding the filling. Bake at 325° for 45-55 minutes.

In 2001, *a neighbor with a new baby asked me to help her and do a little baking. The lady told me to make pies, whatever I wanted. Not knowing the family's likes or dislikes, I was rather undecided. Finally, after finding everything I needed, I started making pies. When suppertime came, they asked, "What kind?" so I said, "Pineapple Coconut." They had never heard of or tasted this kind before but liked it very much. The pies didn't last long. At home I also had a brother who didn't like pineapple, but we could make this kind without telling him what it was, and he'd eat it. Now I have a husband who also dislikes pineapple but loves coconut. So one of these days I'll surprise him yet.*

Pineapple Coconut Pie

| 3 eggs |
| 1 cup sugar |
| 1 level tbsp. cornstarch |
| ½ cup crushed pineapple, drained |
| ½ cup corn syrup |
| ¼ cup coconut, shredded |
| ¼ cup melted oleo or butter |

Mix all together and bake at 350° for 45 to 50 minutes. Makes one pie.

Amish Vanilla Pie

Part one

½ cup brown sugar

1 tbsp. flour

¼ cup corn syrup

1 cup water

1 egg, beaten

1 tsp. vanilla

Part two

½ cup brown sugar

¼ cup butter

1 cup flour

⅛ tsp. salt

½ tsp. baking soda

½ tsp. cream of tartar

Part one: Combine in 2-quart saucepan. Cook over medium heat, stirring until it comes to a boil. Let it cool.

Part two: Mix crumbs in a bowl until crumbly. Pour cooled mixture in an unbaked pie shell. Top with crumbs. Bake at 350° for 40 minutes or until golden brown.

Once *when we came home from church and were eating dinner, someone noticed that Dad had two vests on! He still doesn't know how it happened. But we sat there and laughed and laughed. Let's hope the men weren't as observant as the women were!*

chatting

Grape Tarts

½ cup grape juice

1 cup sugar

½ cup water

1 tsp. cornstarch, rounded

1 cup grapes

6 tart shells, baked

whipped cream

Bring the first 3 ingredients to boiling point. Blend cornstarch to a smooth paste with a little cold water and stir in. Cut grapes in halves and remove seeds. Add them to the mixture and simmer until the grapes are soft. Turn into tart shells. Top with whipped cream and 1 raw grape in each tart.

Tart Shells

1½ cups pastry flour	½ cup Crisco
1 tsp. baking powder	approximately 4 tbsp. milk
½ tsp. salt	

Combine dry ingredients. Cut in Crisco. Add milk. Roll out, put into muffin tins and flute edges. Prick with a fork, then bake at 350° until slightly browned, approximately 25 minutes.

Grape-Picking Time

A dreary day greeted us as we awoke on the fifth day of grape-picking season. A light drizzle began as we donned raincoats and hats. The truck that had come for five tons of grapes stood in the barnyard, loaded with the four and a half tons we had already picked. The driver hoped to be loaded and ready to leave by lunchtime, and it was up to us to get the last half ton picked. With wet, cold, stiff hands we tried to carefully fill the plastic boxes. Cold rain got under our sleeves and caused us to shiver! Every so often someone yelped when they happened to nip a finger! Lucky for us, with cold hands it didn't hurt so much. We became colder and wetter as box after box filled up, until finally the call came that we were finished! Hurrah! We all trooped inside, peeling off wet garments. After a hot shower and lunch we felt much better. Now what do we do to fill our lazy afternoon? Let's bake grape tarts. The misery of the forenoon is forgotten as we have fun baking.

Peanut Butter Fudge Pie

9-inch graham cracker crust	*12 ounces Cool Whip, divided*
1 cup creamy peanut butter	*1 cup fudge topping*
8 ounces softened cream cheese	*½ cup sugar*

Beat together peanut butter, cream cheese, and sugar. Gently fold in 3 cups Cool Whip. Spoon into pie shell. Place fudge topping in microwave for 1 minute. Cool slightly; then spoon over the pie filling. Refrigerate until serving time; then spread remaining Cool Whip over the fudge layer. If desired, garnish with more fudge topping. May be served partially frozen. A rich, extravagant pie that is great for special occasions or to impress special people.

Strawberry Pie

6 cups crushed berries

2½ cups sugar

12 tbsp. instant ClearJel

Mix the instant ClearJel with the sugar. Slowly sprinkle the mixture over the crushed berries and beat constantly until thick. Pour into 3 baked pie crusts and top with sweetened whipped cream. This works with peaches, too. Good luck!

We love *fresh strawberry pies topped with whipped cream fresh from our Holstein cows. I once persuaded the children to pick the last sweet but small berries from our patch. They were tired of picking for this summer, but I promised them a pie. Surprisingly, they found enough berries for two pies! It was almost time for dinner when I quickly mixed the sugar and what I thought was ClearJel. Uh! Oh! What's wrong? The moment I started beating the mixture into our last precious berries, they turned white and foamy! Here I had a bulk package of baking soda by mistake! That whole bowlful of berries had turned into "slop"! So we will need to wait until next summer to eat more fresh strawberry pie!*

chatting

Pie Plant Pie

1½ cups chopped rhubarb
1 cup milk
1¼ cup sugar
butter the size of a walnut
1 egg, beaten
2½ tbsp. flour

Mix well and pour into an unbaked pie crust. Bake at 350° for ½ hour.

I used *this recipe the first time I baked rhubarb pie, which I was so fond of. It was in the spring, and most of our family went out of state for a wedding. They left me (eleven years old) and three of my brothers at home to do chores. I, of course, felt very responsible to do the cooking. But being next to the youngest in a family of ten children, I didn't have much experience. I decided to bake a pie. I had quite a time to get the crusts rolled and fitted in the pans. But I managed and then mixed the pies. Of course, I had no idea how many crusts one recipe would make. I ended up with six pie crusts, so I made six pies.*

Well, there I was in the midst of my baking mess and here comes the egg delivery man. He brought ten dozen eggs to us every week. Since he knew most of the family was not home, he asked what I intended to do with so many pies. "Well," I replied, "I thought it would be nice to have pie on hand when the rest of the family returns home." But lo and behold, the pies were all gone by the time the others came home! The next week when he came with eggs, he complimented Mother on raising a daughter like me. By now, my face was red and I slipped into another room. Mother told him the pies were all eaten before they got home, but that I did a good job in supplying food for the table, including pies, even though it wasn't the softest crust. But I must say rolling the crust went better after that experience. And I still like rhubarb pie.

chatting

Glazed Peach Pie

7 large peaches	

7 large peaches

1 cup sugar

2½ tsp. cornstarch

1 baked pie crust

Mash three large peaches or enough to make 1 cup. Combine mashed peaches, sugar, and cornstarch; cook until thick. Cool. Put small amount of cooled glaze in bottom of pie shell. Slice 4 peaches on top and cover with remaining glaze. Top with Cool Whip.

After *my sister-in-law shared this recipe, I was amazed at how good it is for the small amount of ingredients it requires. Peeling peaches takes me back in memory to when I was a little girl. We enjoyed watching Mom peel a whole peach without breaking the "chain" it created. She told us of how her mother always made "peach peeling" pie.*

"Yuck!" was our comment until Mom reminded us of how we liked to sneak some of the peelings out of the bowl when she wasn't looking.

To our way of thinking, that was an entirely different story, but Mom didn't think it that big a difference. The only thing that changed since then, she said, was the fact that peaches weren't sprayed with harmful chemicals years ago, and she didn't know how easily it washed off.

What we liked so well with this recipe was that it tasted fresher because the peach slices weren't cooked. Each to his own preference!

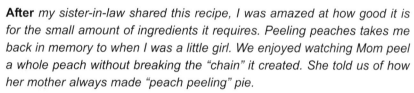

chatting

This crust can be used for your favorite pie filling, but it is especially good with apples. Bake several crusts and freeze them for a handy meal during busy seasons. Young girls can handle these crusts better than dough and rolling pin.

Oatmeal Pie Crust

³/₄ cup melted butter	¹/₂ tsp. baking soda
¹/₂ cup brown sugar	1³/₄ cups flour
¹/₂ tsp. salt	1¹/₂ cups oatmeal

Mix together and press into a 9-inch pie plate. Bake at 350° until golden brown. Delicious when filled with cooked apple pie filling.

Union Pie

2 cups sugar	2 cups molasses
2 cups sour cream	2 cups buttermilk
4 tbsp. flour	4 eggs, beaten
1 tsp. baking soda	lemon flavoring

Mix and pour in unbaked pie shells. Bake at 350° approximately 40-45 minutes or until toothpick comes clean in center. Makes 4 pies.

We got this recipe from my dad's mother. They called it buttermilk pie at home. Once when his mother wasn't at home, his sisters wanted to bake it but just couldn't find the recipe! I'm not sure if they did without pie or baked another kind. They were great pie bakers!

Mama's Mince Pies

1 cup ground beef
1 cup shredded pork
1 tbsp. melted butter

Cook together in a heavy kettle for 8-10 minutes before adding the rest of the ingredients.

6 cups apples, chopped
1 cup raisins
3 tbsp. dandelion wine or vinegar
2 cups sugar (brown)
1 tsp. cinnamon
1 tsp. allspice
salt to taste

Mix all together; then pour into 2 unbaked pie shells. Bake at 350° for 35 minutes.

When *butchering was over every winter, my mother would make a crock of mincemeat for pies. In the kitchen she would put bits of beef and pork in the old iron kettle on the big cooking range, and then add the rest of the ingredients.*

I can remember her standing in front of the stove, wearing her long gingham-checked apron, stirring and stirring with her wooden spoon, sometimes humming old-fashioned tunes. For the mincemeat she'd stir in chopped apples, raisins, brown sugar, spices, homemade dandelion wine, and probably more things I can't remember. Since we don't do our own butchering now, I hardly ever make mince pie anymore, but we do buy one every now and then, just to savor the unique taste that brings old-time memories floating back!

Another old-time memory is the half-moon pies she used to make. They were delicious!

chatting

Half-Moon Pies

1 quart applesauce	½ tsp. salt
1½ cups brown sugar	1 quart dried apple schnitz
½ tsp. cinnamon	1½ cups water

Boil dried apple schnitz (slices) in water until soft and no water remains. Put through colander; add rest of ingredients.

Make pie dough (using next recipe) and divide into balls the size of a large egg. Roll out each piece as thin as pie dough. Fold over to make crease through center. Unfold again and make 2 holes in top part of dough. On other half, place ½ cup of filling. Wet the edge and fold over. Press edges together. Cut off the remaining dough with pie crimper. Brush top with buttermilk or beaten egg. Bake at 450° until brown, approximately 25 minutes.

Never-Fail Pie Crust (Dough)

4 cups flour
1 cup Crisco
1 cup water

Mix flour and Crisco into crumbs. Add 1 cup water and mix to form dough.

Blueberry Pie

2¹/₂ cups (full) fresh blueberries

1 cup sugar

¹/₈ cup flour

¹/₈ cup Minute tapioca

¹/₈ tsp. salt

1 tbsp. lemon juice

2 tbsp. butter

9-inch unbaked pie crust

Toss blueberries with all ingredients, except lemon juice and butter. Pour into 9-inch pastry. Dribble lemon juice over blueberry mixture and dot with butter. Wet pastry edge with fingertips and cover with top pastry. Sprinkle with sugar. Bake at 350° for 45 minutes or until done.

A few *years ago we had a yard sale, and I made a dozen of these blueberry pies to sell, along with homemade bread and bars. We sold every one of the pies within a half hour of opening time, and I found myself taking orders for more. One woman happened to drop her pie on the way to her car, and she was so disappointed that she cried. She said it was her husband's birthday and his favorite kind of pie. An elderly gentleman heard her talking about it and gave her the pie he had bought! This brought more tears to her eyes. I'm thankful that there are still some kind and generous people in this world.*

chatting

Lemon Meringue Pie

1 cup sugar	¼ cup lemon juice
¼ cup cornstarch	1 baked 9-inch pie shell
1½ cups cold water	3 eggs whites, beaten
3 egg yolks, slightly beaten	⅓ cup sugar
1 tbsp. butter	

Preheat oven to 350°. In medium saucepan, combine 1 cup sugar and cornstarch. Gradually stir in water until smooth. Stir in beaten egg yolks. Stirring constantly, bring to boil over medium heat and boil 1 minute. Remove from heat. Stir in lemon juice and butter. Spoon hot filling into pie shell. In small bowl, beat egg whites until foamy. Gradually beat in ⅓ cup sugar, beating until stiff peaks form. Spread over pie, sealing the edges. Bake 15 to 20 minutes or until golden brown.

Dutch Apple Pie

3 cups sliced apples (schnitz)	1 tsp. cinnamon
1 cup brown sugar	3 tbsp. top milk
4 tbsp. butter	9-inch pastry
3 tbsp. flour	

Combine flour, sugar, and cinnamon. Cut in butter with a pastry blender. Place sliced apples in an unbaked pie shell. Sprinkle crumb mixture over top. Add milk. Bake at 375° for 35 minutes or until apples are soft and a rich syrup has formed.

Raisin Crumb Pie

³⁄₄ cup raisins

2 cups water

1 cup brown sugar

1 tsp. vinegar

2 tsp. cornstarch

Topping

1 cup flour

½ cup brown sugar

¼ cup shortening

1 tsp. baking soda

Put raisins in saucepan with water, sugar, vinegar, and salt. Bring to boil and thicken with cornstarch. Remove from heat and cool. Put in unbaked pie shell. Top with crumbs. Bake in a 350° oven 25 to 30 minutes.

I still *think back fondly to my mother's pie-making days when I wasn't old enough to go to school yet. She always gave me a little ball of dough and let me use the rolling pin to roll it out to fit a little four-inch pie tin. She usually made either cherry, apple, peach, or raisin pies, and she gave me some of the filling for my little pie. Then she showed me how to make a design on the piece I had rolled out for the top crust, using the tip of the knife. After it was on, we fluted the edge; then we poked holes in the crust to let out the steam. Sometimes we stuck dry macaroni into the holes so they wouldn't close up. Mother always made me feel like I was such a big help to her, which makes me smile now. Pie doesn't taste as good to me as it did then—maybe it was the love she put in that made the difference!*

chatting

I've always *been fond of ground cherry pies and cobblers, but my husband didn't like them, so I never bothered to plant ground cherries. I didn't real- ize that our children didn't even know what ground cherries were until one Sunday when we were at* Grossmammi's *(Grandma's) house for dinner, and she had made these pies. Our ten-year-old daughter asked, "Do ground cherries grow on trees?"* Grossmammi *thought it was a pity that her* Grossdochder *(granddaughter) didn't know about ground cherries, so she sent a sack of ground cherries and these recipes along home for us. We all like them now (even Dad), and so put plenty of ground cherry plants in our garden every year.*

Mommy's Ground Cherry Pie

3½ cups ground cherries

⅓ cup sugar

⅓ cup flour

⅔ cup brown sugar

1 tbsp. lemon juice

¼ tsp. cinnamon

2 tbsp. butter

pastry for a 2-crust pie

Mix ⅓ cup flour and ⅓ cup sugar; sprinkle on bottom crust. Fill with ground cherries. Put brown sugar on; sprinkle with lemon juice and cinna- mon. Dot with butter. Put top crust on. Bake at 400° for 15 minutes. Turn oven to 350° and bake until done (about another 40 minutes).

Ground Cherry Cobbler

Filling

1 quart canned ground cherries

1 tbsp. lemon juice

1 cup sugar

2 rounded tbsp. ClearJel

Strain the juice from the ground cherries and thicken with the ClearJel mixed with a little of the juice. Add the sugar and the ground cherries.

Crumbs

1 cup butter

2 cups brown sugar

½ tsp. salt

3½ cups flour

1 tsp. baking soda

3 cups oatmeal

Mix together until crumbly.

Press half the crumbs in a 9 x 13 inch pan; top with ground cherry filling, and then the other half of crumbs. Bake at 350° for 35 to 40 minutes.

This recipe was used at a wedding. Dad liked it so well that he asked Mother to get the recipe. It is now our family's favorite. When I ask what kind of pie they want, they all say delicious pumpkin! We never seem to have enough pumpkins in the garden.

Delicious Pumpkin Pie

Combine:

1 cup brown sugar

2 tbsp. flour

1 tsp. cinnamon

¼ tsp. salt

2 tbsp. oleo

1 tsp. vanilla

1 can pumpkin or butternut squash

2 egg yolks

2 cups milk

last: beat

2 egg whites;

add to the rest

Pour into unbaked pie shell and bake at 350° for 40 minutes.

Caramel Pecan Pie

3 eggs, well beaten	1 tbsp. melted butter
1 cup brown sugar	pinch salt
¾ cup light Karo syrup	1 cup pecans, not chopped

Bake slowly at 325° for 50-55 minutes. Serve with whipped cream.

My Best Pie Pastry (for Crusts)

5 cups flour	1½ cups lard (I use real lard)
½ tsp. salt	½ tsp. baking powder
2 egg yolks plus enough water to make 1 cup	

Combine dry ingredients; work in the lard. Place egg yolks in a 1 cup measure, stir with a fork until smooth, blend in enough cold water to make scant capful. Sprinkle gradually over the dry ingredients, toss with a fork to make a soft dough (I use my hands). Roll out as usual. Makes pastry for 3 double 9-inch crusts, but I figure on 8 single crusts. Use in recipes calling for unbaked pie shells and bake according to recipe directions.

Baking *was one of my hobbies, but I was never fond of baking pies. My crusts turned out so hard that my brothers at times suggested using a butcher knife to cut them. My pies didn't work so well for my dad, who had digestive problems and hardly any teeth.*

I worked out as a hired girl for different people, and they often gave me the job of doing the weekly baking because they knew I liked it. When I was working for a family in Bedford County, Pennsylvania, the Mrs. suggested that I could bake pies. I told her about my poor pie-baking record. She said, "Oh, I have an excellent recipe that makes such nice crusts." I didn't have much faith in it, but I tried. To my surprise, they turned out good! So I copied the recipe in my homemade cookbook to take along home. I used it to make pies for my dad. He tasted them and said, "Oh, if you bake crusts like these, I can eat pie, too." I never tried any other recipe since!

Peach Cream Pie

Filling

4 cups fresh, sliced peaches

2 tbsp. flour

¼ tsp. salt

1 cup sour cream

1 cup sugar, divided

1 egg

½ tsp. vanilla

Crust

½ cup butter

½ tsp. salt

1½ cups flour

Topping

⅓ cup sugar
_____

½ cup butter
_____

⅓ cup flour
_____

1 tsp. cinnamon
_____

Crust

Cut butter into flour and salt. Press dough into 9-inch pie pan.

Filling

Slice peaches into bowl. Sprinkle with ¼ cup sugar. Let stand while preparing rest of filling. Combine ¾ cup sugar, flour, egg, salt, and vanilla. Fold in sour cream. Stir in peaches and pour into crust. Set oven at 400°. Bake 45-55 minutes.

Our baby _thrives on goats' milk, so we keep two nannies and a billy. We've found out that goats are much harder to keep inside a pen than a cow. Whenever they have the chance, they slip out and get into mischief. Once when I had made five pumpkin pies, I set them on a little table in the washhouse to cool. One of the children was bringing in firewood and had propped the washhouse door open and forgotten to close it. The billy goat got in, was probably trying to help himself to pumpkin pie, and knocked the entire table over! He and the dog and cats had a feast!_

chatting

Aunt Elsie's Pumpkin Pie

1¼ cup cooked pumpkin (preferably butternut)

½ cup sugar

⅓ cup honey

½ tsp. salt

¼ tsp. cloves

1 tsp. cinnamon

1 tsp. flour

2 eggs, beaten

1 cup milk

2 tbsp. water

½ tsp. vanilla

Mix and pour into pie shells; makes 2 pies. Bake at 400° for 45 to 50 minutes.

We are *pumpkin pie lovers, and this recipe is a very good one. For years I'd enjoy Aunt Elsie's pumpkin pie. When we had family gatherings, it was the accepted thing: Aunt Elsie would bring pumpkin pie. I always looked forward to it.*

One time her daughters were looking through their mother's recipes, and I happened to be near and spotted this one. I was so pleased to get a copy of it. And now I, too, can make it.

My aunt once told me that the honey really puts a touch to it. Yes, it sure does! I could eat a half pie all by myself! I can almost never stop with just one piece. And then my husband likes to have whipped topping on top. It's also good to eat with vanilla ice cream. Enjoy!

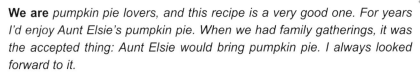

chatting

Strawberry Pudding Pie

Heat

about 1 quart milk

Mix:

⅓ cup cake flour	*2 egg yolks*
⅔ cup sugar	

Add cold milk to the mix until smooth; add to the boiling milk. Add a pinch of salt and 1 tsp. vanilla. Pour into 2 baked pie crusts.

When cold, add:

2 cups strawberry Jell-O	*2 cups boiling water*

When cold, add 2 cups fresh crushed and sweetened strawberries. When partly thick, pour on top of the pudding. Chill and put whipped cream on top.

For raspberry pie, use 2 cups black raspberry Jell-O, 2 cups hot water and 2 cups cold water. Add some sweetened fresh black raspberries.

When *we were young children, we lived on a farm. We milked cows and raised strawberries to sell. Our patch was away from our house, so in summer we packed our three meals and went to the strawberry field. We used to have shredded wheat, which was a treat. We also had other girls come in and help us. Something that happened one day was a good lesson to us all. One girl picked many more quarts than anyone else. When they checked the berry baskets in her row, she had mixed many green berries in with red ones. So my parents had to sort through all the berries so they wouldn't sell any green ones. That evening we all felt sad.*

chatting

Best-Ever Shoofly Pie

7³/₄ cups pastry flour (nice and full)	6 cups molasses (table syrup)
4¹/₂ cups brown sugar	4¹/₂ cups boiling water
7 tbsp. lard	1¹/₂ cups boiling water
6 eggs	6 tsp. baking soda

Mix dry ingredients and lard into nice, even fine crumbs. Take out 2 cups crumbs and set aside. Turn oven to 400°. In big mixing bowl, beat eggs and add molasses (use mild-flavored table syrup, not blackstrap baking molasses). Then add the 4¹/₂ cups boiling water and mix well. Dissolve baking soda in 1¹/₂ cups boiling water and add it to molasses mixture. Add crumbs and stir until smooth. Pour into 8 unbaked 9-inch pie crusts; sprinkle 2 cups of reserved crumbs evenly on top. Bake at 400° for 10 minutes, or until they start to puff up a little; then turn oven back to 350° and bake another 30 minutes until done. Always preheat the oven before putting pies in.

I was *baking bread and icing buns for a produce stand when someone informed me that a man was asking for shoofly pies, and they would send him over. Oh my! Pies are not my thing, for sure, but not shoofly pies! I tried some recipes, and the guy said they were not moist enough. I tried more recipes, and he just wasn't satisfied with them. So I started asking people in the business of baking shoofly pies for market. I got another recipe and tried it, but they cooked over so bad that I had a smoky kitchen and had to wash off the walls. I was getting discouraged. Finally I decided to try the recipe again and put the filling in eight pie crusts instead of only six. The shoofly pies turned out fine, and the guy said that's the way he likes them. I got more customers and many favorable comments. At one time I baked a hundred a day, and I have shared my recipe with others who wanted to bake shoofly pies for market.*

chatting

Sugar-Free Pumpkin Pie

2 cups cooked pumpkin

2 cups Equal Spoonful

4 eggs

4 tbsp. flour

1½ quarts milk

¼ tsp. maple flavor

1 tsp. cinnamon

Pour into blender and blend well. Pour into 2 unbaked, 9-inch pie crusts and bake at 350° for 1 hour or more, until set and done.

My *dad always loved baked goodies and desserts made out of dairy products, until at age 67 he suddenly found out that he's diabetic. What an adjustment! We discovered that Equal Spoonful can be used cup for cup like sugar, so we can make that substitution in our regular recipes for baking. Equal does not taste as bitter as some artificial sweeteners.*

chatting

Low-Sugar Pumpkin Pie

3 eggs, separated	
1 cup pumpkin	
1 tsp. salt	
1/4 tsp. pumpkin pie spice	
1 rounded tbsp. Thermflo	
1/2 cup rolled oats	
1/4 cup honey	
1/2 cup corn syrup	
3 1/2 cups milk	

Mix together egg yolks, pumpkin, salt, spice, and Thermflo. Add honey, corn syrup, and rolled oats. Mix. Stir in milk. Add beaten egg whites last. Bake at 375° for 10 minutes, decrease temperature to 350° and bake for another 35 minutes or until done.

I have *been a diabetic for two years and have learned to cut down on sugar and flour if I want to feel well. At first I thought I could not bake things that taste good, but after you get used to doing without so much sugar, they taste fine. To other diabetics: Take heart; don't become discouraged. Changing to healthy eating habits takes time. The complete changeover takes awhile, but the day will come when sweets tempt you, you take a small bite, and you find that they don't taste nearly as good as you thought they would. You will have learned to appreciate the taste of good, wholesome, food!*

chatting

Concord Grape Pie

7 cups Concord grapes
3 tbsp. cornstarch
1½ cups sugar (or ¾ cup honey and ¾ cup sugar)
¾ tsp. salt
1 grated orange rind

Wash and stem grapes. Slip skins from pulp. Heat pulp to boiling point and boil 5 minutes. Then rub through sieve to remove seeds. Combine cornstarch, sugar (or honey), salt, and orange rind with grape pulp. Cook until thickened, stirring constantly. Add grape skins and cool. Line a pie pan with plain pastry dough. Turn in mixture. Top with ⅜-inch-wide strips of pastry, laid crisscross. Bake in hot oven (425°) for 10 minutes. Reduce heat to 325° and bake 20 minutes more.

As we *headed out the lane toward the vineyard, the sun was just peeking from behind the hill beyond the lake. Beginning our second week of grape picking, we six girls split into pairs of two. Each pair grabbed a box, set it into a metal cart, and started down a row. Peering under the dense leaves, we gently snipped the first bunch. Bunch after bunch was snipped, examined for rotten and green ones, and carefully placed in the box. The warm September sun, sparkling on the distant lake, soon warmed cold hands and made us remove coats and caps. Conversation flowed as box after box filled up. Before we removed each box from the cart, we carefully checked to guarantee the correct weight. After scanning the vines to make sure we got them all, we moved on down the row. Hands and feet began lagging as the sun became hotter. Trips to the ends of the rows for boxes and a drink were welcome diversions.*

Finally came the call for lunchtime, and everybody cheered! We all trooped inside and were greeted with the delicious aroma of grape pie! The lady of the house had baked it for our lunch.

chatting

Cookies and Bars

Recipe for a Blessed Life

1 overflowing barrel of faith in the Savior

1 scoop each of repentance, confession, and forsaking of sin

1 large serving of the bread of life

generous portions of the fruits of the Spirit

1 bushel of restitution

1 peck of power to resist temptation

1 helping each of humility, self-denial, and diligence

generous sprinkling of courage to do right

Knead all together, being careful to remove any crumbs of rebellion, lukewarmness, self-seeking, and carnal-mindedness. Season with a dash of unselfish love, and constantly keep adding earnest prayer and worship until the proper consistency is reached. Be sure to share generously with others, and invite all you meet to partake of the blessings, too.

Author unknown

chatting

Clara's Sugar Cookies

6 eggs, beaten

2 cups white sugar

4 cups brown sugar

2 cups lard or butter

2 cups sour milk

2 cups sour cream

8 tsp. baking soda, dissolved in 1 cup hot water

4 tsp. vanilla

10 tsp. baking powder

2 tsp. salt

4 tbsp. lemon extract

Mix ingredients well; then add enough flour (about 12 cups) to make a stiff dough. Now drop on cookie sheets and flatten a little. Bake in 400° or 425° oven about 10 minutes.

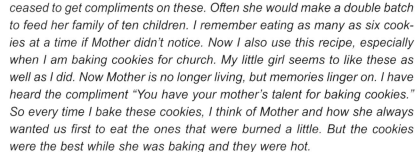

This *is the recipe my mother used when she baked cookies. She never ceased to get compliments on these. Often she would make a double batch to feed her family of ten children. I remember eating as many as six cookies at a time if Mother didn't notice. Now I also use this recipe, especially when I am baking cookies for church. My little girl seems to like these as well as I did. Now Mother is no longer living, but memories linger on. I have heard the compliment "You have your mother's talent for baking cookies." So every time I bake these cookies, I think of Mother and how she always wanted us first to eat the ones that were burned a little. But the cookies were the best while she was baking and they were hot.*

chatting

Pumpkin Cookies

1 cup pumpkin, cooked and mashed
1 cup sugar
½ cup oil
1 egg
2 tsp. baking powder
1 tsp. cinnamon
½ tsp. salt
1 tsp. baking soda dissolved in 1 tbsp. milk
1 cup chocolate chips
½ cup nuts
2 cups flour
1 tsp. vanilla

Mix first 4 ingredients; beat until smooth. Add the next 4 ingredients; then add flour. Last of all, add vanilla, chocolate chips, and nuts. Bake at 375° for 10-12 minutes.

My friend and cousins gave me this recipe. I always make about six batches. Since we have a family of nine, it always takes a lot of cookies. I like these because they are so moist and don't need frosting, and still they are everyone's favorites.

We have a dairy of forty cows. We raise our own calves and heifers. The children feed the calves, and they all love the smell of baking, especially when it's cool outside and everyone is hungry.

chatting

Chocolate Chip Cookies

2 cups butter or oil

3 cups brown sugar

2 tsp. vanilla

4 eggs

2 tsp. baking soda

2 tsp. salt

5 cups flour

Mix all ingredients, adding chocolate chips last. Bake at 350° for about 10 minutes.

These *Chocolate Chip Cookies are my favorite. Once at a yard sale, I bought some, and they were just so good and white. I decided it must be because they had all white sugar in them. So I asked for the recipe, and to my surprise, it calls only for brown sugar. My cousin and I were selling sweet corn near a mountain road when my friend brought the recipe. She said they got it out of the* Lancaster Farming *magazine. So I copied it for my cousin, and she made them the next day. We used to have cookie day in school. Once a year every family brought cookies along; we set them on the table and could eat all we wanted of any kind all day, except at recess time. These cookies are perfect for that!*

chatting

Aunt Fannie's Chocolate Chip Cookies

1½ cups vegetable oil

1½ cups brown sugar

1½ cups white sugar

4 eggs, beaten

2 tsp. baking soda

1 tsp. salt

2 tsp. vanilla

2 tsp. water

4½ cups flour

1½ cups chocolate chips

Mix oil, sugars, and eggs. Add vanilla, water, baking soda. Add chocolate chips and flour. Drop by teaspoonfuls on greased cookie sheets. Bake at 350° for 10 minutes or until light brown.

Cookies—*what a favorite for our family! We have four girls and two boys, so a batch of cookies never lasts long. In fact, most times I double this recipe. They also like plenty of milk to drink with them. Since we have a dairy farm and sixty cows, there is usually lots of good fresh milk around.*

I got this recipe from my Aunt Fannie, and since I started using it, I don't use any other chocolate chip recipe. Hope you will enjoy it, too.

chatting

Chewy Molasses Cookies

4²/₃ cups white sugar

2 cups oleo

5 beaten eggs

1 tsp. salt

1 pound raisins

10 cups flour

2 cups baking (blackstrap) molasses

Put 2½ tbsp. baking soda in ½ cup of boiling water. Combine sugar, oleo, eggs, and salt. Grind raisins and add just enough water to boil them a little, and then cool; add to oleo mixture. Add the rest of the ingredients. Drop by teaspoonfuls on ungreased cookie sheets, or make into rolls and slice. Bake at 350° for 10-12 minutes.

I was *helping out at my aunt's place when I had my fourteenth birthday. One day I was supposed to make these cookies. It was a warm time of the year to bake cookies, but it sure was worth it to make such delicious ones! One of my neighbors had a little girl who died around this time, and I had such a longing to go to her funeral, or even go before the funeral in hopes of chatting with my precious family! Homesickness was catching up with me. But in the end, I didn't go at all.*

Later my dear sisters came to accompany me one day. How enjoyable! We had some of these chewy cookies that day. Then we got the recipe from my aunt and made them for the whole family! One of our neighbors had some of these cookies and thought they were so good that she asked for the recipe. More people are just waiting for a delicious chewy cookie recipe, and this is the one!

chatting

One *Saturday afternoon about a dozen of us girls were invited to a quilting at my cousin and best friend Mary's house. We all sat around her beautiful Wedding Ring quilt in the frame, stitching away, with our tongues probably moving faster than our needles.*

I had told her I would bring something for our afternoon break, and she said she'd make some kind of a special treat, too.

At around three o'clock, Mary's mom came in with a pitcher full of iced tea and a platter full of our goodies. We were all surprised that Mary and I had made the same thing! It was Cherry Triangles: mine were on half the platter, and hers were on the other half. I was dismayed to see that hers were much bigger and lighter than mine! We couldn't figure out what had caused the difference, for we had used the same recipe. When she mentioned Occident flour, I realized that I had used all-purpose flour instead! No wonder they had not risen like they should have! I was embarrassed, but since then I haven't made the mistake of using the wrong flour.

Cherry Triangles

¾ cup milk
4½ cups Occident flour
½ cup sugar
1 cup butter
4 eggs, beaten
2 packages yeast, dissolved in ⅔ cup warm water
cherry pie filling

Scald milk, remove from heat, and cube the butter into the hot milk. When butter is melted, add the beaten eggs. Put into a large bowl; add the yeast in water, sugar, and salt. Stir in flour; this is a soft dough and can't be kneaded. Refrigerate; then roll out into small squares. Put cherry pie filling on (a diagonal) half the square, fold over to form a triangle, and seal. Cut small openings on top for steam to escape. Let rise for 1½ hours. Then bake at 350° for about 15 minutes.

Brown Sugar Oatmeal Cookies

4 cups shortening	
5 cups brown sugar	
1/2 cup honey	
8 eggs	
2 tsp. vanilla	
6 cups whole-wheat flour	
4 tsp. baking soda	
12 cups oatmeal (we use 6 cups regular and 5 cups quick)	
2 tsp. salt	
4 cups (total) raisins, chocolate chips, nuts, and/or coconut	

Bake at 350° for 12 to 15 minutes. Makes about 100 cookies.

About *two years ago, my parents took a trip, leaving my three brothers and me at home to do the chores, housework, and keep things going. We had a dairy, so milking was one of the chores. Sunday morning when my oldest brother was out in the barnyard to bring in cows, he fell and hurt his ankle. We fetched a friend to help with chores that evening and the rest of the time until our parents returned.*

Monday morning my younger brother used a neighbor's phone for the first time in his life to make an appointment at the doctor's. Then I drove my older brother to the doctor in the buggy.

After I waited for what seemed a long time in the waiting room, I was called in. What a surprise to see my brother in a wheelchair! His ankle was broken, and we needed to go to the pharmacy for crutches.

What a shock for my parents to come home and hear such news! But with time, it healed well.

chatting

Amish Hats
(or Chocolate Marshmallow Cookies)

1³/₄ cups flour	¹/₂ cup shortening
¹/₂ tsp. salt	1 egg
¹/₂ tsp. baking soda	1 tsp. vanilla
¹/₂ cup cocoa	¹/₄ cup milk
1 cup brown sugar	18 large marshmallows, cut in half

Sift together flour, salt, cocoa, and baking soda. Cream shortening and sugar; add egg, vanilla, and milk, beating well. Add dry ingredients and mix. Bake 10 minutes at 350°. Remove from oven and press ¹/₂ marshmallow, cut side down, on each cookie. Bake one minute longer. Cool and top with frosting.

Cocoa Frosting

2 cups confectioners' sugar
5 tsp. cocoa
5 tsp. cream
3 tsp. butter
pinch of salt

Mix all ingredients together and stir until creamy.

This *recipe is liked by everyone in the family. We took these cookies along on a sleep-out in our neighbor's tent. Once every summer we neighbor girls gather on a nice warm summer evening and take a good swim in the pond. Afterward everyone sits around the campfire, roasting hot dogs and marshmallows, telling stories, and eating cookies that my sister and I have taken along. What a different experience to be combing each other's hair in the dark, with only a few flashlights. It is nice to see how other girls' hair feels and how easy some stays in place. After everyone has settled down to sleep, we listen to the breezes sighing through the trees and other woodland noises. Sometimes we hear scary, eerie sounds in the bushes. At midnight we get up to stir the fire, roast more hot dogs, and go for a walk in the moonlight. Then we all crawl back in and sleep until morning. So many precious memories!*

Date Cookies

8 cups flour	1 tsp. salt
4 cups brown sugar	2 cups shortening
2 tsp. baking soda	6 large eggs
2 tsp. cream of tartar	

Blend all together and drop on cookie sheet. Bake at 375° for about 10 minutes. When cool, spread date filling between two cookies. Cookies seem a little hard at first, but several hours after the filling has been spread, they are soft and delicious.

Filling

4 tbsp. cornstarch	2 cups brown sugar
4 cups water	2 cups cut-up dates

Bring to a boil and cook until thick. Cool and spread between two cookies.

My baked *goods were getting low, and it was becoming hard to pack my husband's lunch. So I fixed some Jell-O, baked bread, and stirred up these cookies, which I had never made before. While baking them, I decided to make some in the shape of a horse. I had three M&M's, so I made three cookies and used them for the eyes. My husband works with two other guys, so that would be just right. But after a while, I had to think how happy that would make a little boy. I also made some heart-shaped ones and filled a container for a young family with two little boys whose father cannot always be at home. Now there was one horse left for the little boy next door, in his lunch the next day. So my husband didn't get a special cookie after all. Maybe he will get one next time! So when you make these cookies, don't forget to share. Bake someone happy!*

Soft Sugar Cookies

2 cups oleo

3 cups sugar

4 eggs

2 cups cream or evaporated milk

2 tsp. baking soda

6 tsp. baking powder

½ tsp. salt

1 tsp. lemon

5 cups flour or more

Cream together oleo and sugar; add eggs and stir well. Add rest of ingredients. Chill overnight. Roll out and bake at 350° for approximately 12 minutes.

Grandma's Sugar Cookies

6 cups sugar

1½ cups shortening

8 eggs

6 tbsp. vanilla

3 cups buttermilk

4 tsp. baking soda

2 tsp. cream of tartar

1½ tsp. salt

12 cups flour

Cream sugar and shortening. Add the beaten eggs and vanilla. Add the buttermilk alternately with the dry ingredients. Chill dough for several hours, roll out and cut with cookie cutters. Bake at 350° for 12 minutes.

Mm-mm-mm! *Thinking of the sugar cookies my grandma used to bake years ago, I can almost smell them again. When I was a schoolgirl, my grandma used to bake cookies for a roadside farm market. We usually went to grandma's once a week and often we were greeted by the wonderful smell of freshly baked sugar cookies.*

What a yummy treat it was to have one of those delicious mouthwatering cookies. After grandma died, my sister started working in a bakery and made these sugar cookies for the same market where grandma had supplied with them. I also worked in this bakery for a while and baked them. Due to health problems, I had to stop my job. But my sister still makes the cookies.

chatting

Soft Oatmeal Cookies

Mix together:

1 cup oil

2 eggs

1¼ cup sugar

⅓ cup molasses

Sift together and add to first ingredients:

1¾ cup flour

1 tsp. salt

1 tsp. baking soda

1 tsp. cinnamon

Mix together and add to rest of ingredients:

2 cups quick oats

1 cup raisins

½ cup nuts

Drop by teaspoonfuls on cookie sheet. Bake 10 minutes at 400°. Makes 5 dozen.

Susie's Sugar Cookies

1 cup white sugar	1 cup butter or shortening
1 cup brown sugar	2 eggs

Mix together and then add:

1 cup milk	½ tsp. salt
1 tsp. baking soda	1 tsp. vanilla
1 tsp. baking powder	

Use enough flour to make a soft dough. Drop or roll out and cut; put a raisin in the middle of each cookie. Bake in a 350° oven until golden brown, 10-12 minutes.

My brothers *are very fond of cookies, and sometimes it seems like they have bottomless stomachs. When I was still a schoolgirl, I used to be so upset when my brothers came storming in, lured by the aroma of freshly baked cookies just as I had rows and rows of them on the kitchen table to cool. They would help themselves to handfuls, and I would stamp my foot and scold. If I thought they grabbed too many, I'd be in tears. To make peace,* Mamm *(Mom) would have to come out of the other room, where she was sewing.*

One time Mamm *wasn't home, and my youngest brother came in alone. This time I was sure I'd be the winner! I shooed him off, telling him he must wait until supper. We had a fight, and finally he ran off, jumped on his bicycle, and raced down the lane. Suddenly I heard a car slam on its brakes and the terrible screech of tires. I was never so frightened, fearing he had been hit. What a relief to see him biking back in the lane, unhurt! I think we both learned a lesson that day. Now I let* Mamm *worry about how many cookies the boys eat, and I'm sure he looks both ways before crossing the road.*

chatting

M&M Jumbo Cookies

Thoroughly mix together:

2 cups soft shortening

3 cups sugar

4 eggs

Stir in:

4 tbsp. milk

2 tsp. flavor

Sift together and stir in:

7 cups flour

3 tsp. cream of tartar or baking powder

1 tsp. salt

3 tsp. baking soda

2 cups M&M's

Add:

1 cup nuts or raisins (optional)

Roll into balls the size of a walnut and place about 3 inches apart on ungreased cookie sheet. Flatten with fork dipped in flour, making a criss-cross pattern. Bake at 350° for 10 minutes or until light brown.

Gumdrop Cookies

2 cups sugar

2 cups confectioners' sugar

4 eggs

2 tsp. salt

9 cups flour

2 tsp. baking soda

2 tsp. cream of tartar

2 tsp. vanilla

1½ cups nuts

2 cups gumdrops

Mix in order given. Chill dough. Roll into 1½ inch balls and flatten. Bake at 350° for 10-12 minutes.

Cornflake Cookies

2 cups brown sugar

1 cup white sugar

2 cups oleo

4 eggs

2 tsp. vanilla

2 tsp. baking soda

2 tsp. baking powder

2 cups oatmeal

1 cup coconut

2 cups crushed cornflakes

4 cups flour

1½ cups chocolate chips or M&M's

Mix, drop onto cookie sheet, and bake at 350° for about 10 minutes. If desired, may add one cup raisins, dates, nuts, or peanuts.

Pumpkin Nut Cookies

1 pint can pumpkin

2 tsp. baking soda

4 tsp. baking powder

1 tsp. salt

2 tsp. cinnamon

4 cups flour

2 cups sugar

2 eggs, beaten

2 tbsp. milk

1 cup vegetable oil

6 ounces chocolate chips

1 cup nuts

2 tsp. vanilla

Mix sugar, oil, eggs, milk, vanilla, and pumpkin. Sift dry ingredients and add to mixture. Add chocolate chips and nuts. Drop by teaspoon onto cookie sheets and bake at 350° for 10-12 minutes.

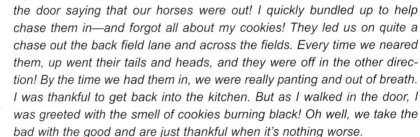

One winter *morning, I had the cookstove fired up to do some cookie baking. Just after I put the first cookie sheet full into the oven, our son burst in the door saying that our horses were out! I quickly bundled up to help chase them in—and forgot all about my cookies! They led us on quite a chase out the back field lane and across the fields. Every time we neared them, up went their tails and heads, and they were off in the other direction! By the time we had them in, we were really panting and out of breath. I was thankful to get back into the kitchen. But as I walked in the door, I was greeted with the smell of cookies burning black! Oh well, we take the bad with the good and are just thankful when it's nothing worse.*

chatting

Delicious Whoopie Pies

5 cups sugar
9 cups bread flour
2½ cups vegetable oil
5 eggs
1 tsp. salt
1½ tbsp. vanilla
2½ cups cocoa
2½ cups buttermilk or sour milk (can add 1 tsp. vinegar to 1 cup sweet milk, let set a bit, and use for sour milk)
2½ cups hot water
3 tbsp. baking soda

Mix the baking soda with the hot water and add last to mixture. Drop by teaspoonfuls onto cookie sheets. Bake at 375° for 10 to 12 minutes. Make your favorite frosting and put 2 cookies together with frosting between them.

Helpful hint: *It pays to measure your ingredients. Here's why: Once I was invited to a neighbors' baking party. We love these whoopie pies, and I was eager to share my recipe. Alas, haste makes waste! We had small bags of flour, and I thought, "A pint's a pound." So to save time, I didn't measure. Needless to say, they were quite dry and thus no prizewinners that day!*

chatting

Banana Whoopie Pies

1 cup banana, mashed

Stir in:

1 tsp. baking soda

1 egg

1 cup sugar

$\frac{1}{2}$ cup oil

$\frac{1}{2}$ tsp. salt

1 cup nuts

2 cups flour

$\frac{1}{2}$ tsp. vanilla

Bake at 350° for 15 minutes. Cool. Put your favorite icing between the cookies.

We often make these for company, and we received quite a few comments on them. Some people think they're pumpkin because they're so moist.

Chocolate Whoopie Pies

3 whole eggs

3 yolks

3 cups brown sugar

1½ cups shortening

1½ tsp. salt

3 tsp. vanilla

3 tsp. baking soda

1½ cups buttermilk

1½ cups hot water

1½ cups cocoa

5 cups flour

Dissolve baking soda in buttermilk. Mix, bake at 350° for 10-12 minutes. Fill with vanilla icing. Enjoy.

My oldest *sister used to bake chocolate and raisin oatmeal whoopie pies for a farm market. Every Wednesday was baking day. Usually there had to be at least fifty whoopie pies of each kind. Sometimes they wanted fifty of one kind and seventy-five of the other kind. We liked whoopie pie day since sometimes we could get to sample some that were too big or cracked or something. The whoopie pies had to be a certain size. Every Tuesday evening we had to make a big batch of frosting. That took quite a bit of stirring, so we sometimes took turns until it was nice and creamy. We did the baking in the forenoon. In the afternoon we took them about four miles to the market in the horse and buggy.*

We always looked forward to going along when we could. The market was beside a busy highway, and during the summer a lot of tour buses stopped there. Wednesday was one day they especially stopped, so we usually met some tourists. Sometimes they were from a different country, and they liked to take pictures of us. That farm market is still in business, but now they have a bakery of their own.

chatting

Banana Waffle Whoopie Pies

2 cups brown sugar

1 cup vegetable oil

1½ cups mashed banana

2 eggs

3 cups flour

1 tsp. baking powder

1 tsp. baking soda

1 tsp. vanilla

Beat eggs until foamy; add sugar, oil, bananas. Then add the flour and rest of ingredients. Bake in waffle pan. Oil the waffle pan before starting, and now and then between batches. Make your favorite frosting and put it between 2 waffle cookies.

Every time *I make this recipe, I remember the day I got it. We had gone to help friends work on their house. They were building an addition and had put a new roof on, several feet higher than the old part. We were making these waffle cookies when a shout was heard outside, at the north end of the house. One of the men came rushing inside, leaping up the stairs two steps at a time. We followed, reaching the top of the stairway in time to see him jump out the window and scramble up the old roof at the north end. There tarp was hung to close the gap between the new and old parts of the roof. He appeared again, holding his eighteen-month-old son. From below he had seen the child crawling on the steep roof. Any misstep would have sent the child over the edge, falling about fourteen feet. The children had been playing upstairs, and he apparently had crawled onto the roof. The little fellow had slipped under the tarp and was out in the open on the eight-foot section of the old roof. The guardian angels must have been hovering close by that day!*

chatting

Coconut Granola Bars

¾ cup packed brown sugar

½ cup corn syrup

2 tsp. vanilla

1 cup chocolate chips

½ cup sunflower seeds

2 tsp. sesame seeds

⅔ cup peanut butter

½ cup melted margarine

3 cups oatmeal

½ cup flaked coconut

⅓ cup wheat germ

In a large bowl, combine brown sugar, peanut butter, margarine, and vanilla. Combine remaining ingredients (except sesame seeds); add to peanut butter mixture and stir to coat. Press into 2 greased 13 x 9 x 2 inch pan. Sprinkle with sesame seeds. Bake at 350° for 25 to 30 minutes or until golden brown. Cool; cut into bars.

With *three sisters to help Mom, our oldest son hardly gets a chance to bake. One Saturday he asked if he might make a pan of these bars. I copy recipes I'd like to try into a "scribbler"—appropriately named since it sometimes gets pretty scribbly in there! I hadn't taken time to recopy this recipe and place it in my recipe box, where the tried and good recipes eventually land. Near the "3" in ¾ cup sugar I had written "delicious" (partly covering up the "3"). Results were very sugary bars, containing four cups of sugar and disappointing the baker!*

chatting

Favorite Granola Bars

1½ pounds marshmallows	½ cup honey
¼ cup margarine or butter	¼ cup peanut butter
¼ cup vegetable oil	

In a large bowl mix:

9½ cups Rice Krispies	1½ cups raisins
1 cup graham cracker crumbs	1 cup coconut
5 cups oatmeal	1 cup chocolate chips or M&M's
1 cup crushed peanuts	

Melt margarine and oil on quite low heat. Add marshmallows and stir until melted; turn off heat and add honey and peanut butter. Make a well in dry ingredients or have someone pour in the marshmallows while you stir; if it runs to the side of the bowl, it becomes hard and difficult to mix. Spread on greased cake pan and press quickly with the palm of the hand. Let cool. These bars do not require any baking.

Warning: The bars will disappear quickly because they're scrumptious!

These *are an all around favorite, and my mom likes to make them for family gatherings. When they're busy with produce all summer, my newlywed sister and I help out a day every week if we can. My brother's wife is always included, too. Her family lives in another county, and she blends right in with us. My little brothers and sisters are treated just like her own. Since they plan on moving out of state in a few years, we cherish the time we can spend with them now.*

One day we planned to be together that week, and in fun my sister-in-law told my little sister to make those delicious granola bars to snack on that day. We knew she was teasing, but sister decided to take her seriously anyway. Lo and behold, when we arrived, there stood a pan full of these tempting treats! Sister-in-law laughed a bit sheepishly, but by that evening we had emptied the whole thing!

chatting

S'more Bars

1 cup quick oatmeal
½ cup flour
½ cup packed brown sugar
¼ tsp. salt
¼ tsp. baking soda
½ cup oleo, melted
2 cups miniature marshmallows
½ cup chocolate chips

In a bowl, combine the first 5 ingredients; stir in oleo until crumbly. Press in a greased 11 x 7 x 2 inch baking dish. Bake at 350° for 10 minutes. Sprinkle with marshmallows and chocolate chips. Bake 5 to 7 minutes longer or until marshmallows begin to brown. Cool on a wire rack. Cut into bars and enjoy!

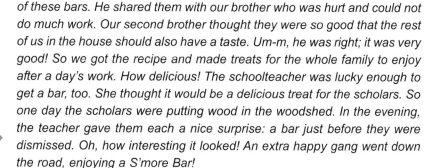

A woman *who lives in the house where my brother works gave him some of these bars. He shared them with our brother who was hurt and could not do much work. Our second brother thought they were so good that the rest of us in the house should also have a taste. Um-m, he was right; it was very good! So we got the recipe and made treats for the whole family to enjoy after a day's work. How delicious! The schoolteacher was lucky enough to get a bar, too. She thought it would be a delicious treat for the scholars. So one day the scholars were putting wood in the woodshed. In the evening, the teacher gave them each a nice surprise: a bar just before they were dismissed. Oh, how interesting it looked! An extra happy gang went down the road, enjoying a S'more Bar!*

chatting

Five-Star Brownies

3 eggs	1½ cups all-purpose flour
2 cups sugar	¾ cup baking cocoa
1½ tsp. vanilla extract	1¼ tsp. salt
½ cup butter or margarine, melted	
¼ cup shortening, melted	
1 cup chopped nuts, optional	

In a mixing bowl, beat eggs, sugar, and vanilla until well mixed. Add butter and shortening. Combine flour, cocoa, and salt; stir into egg mixture and mix well. Add nuts if desired. Line a 13 x 9 x 2 inch pan with foil and grease the foil; pour batter into pan. Bake at 350° for 30 minutes or until brownies test done when pricked, with a wooden toothpick coming out clean. Cool in pan. Turn brownies out of pan onto a cookie sheet; remove foil. Place a wire rack over brownies; turn over and remove cookie sheet. Cut with a star cutter or into bars. Yields about 3 dozen.

chatting

These *brownies have gone with us on many outings. One of the first times I made them was when the young folks were going to spend the day at a picnic. Oh, how we enjoyed those days!*

Another day that I remember well was when we went up Mahonoy Mountain on July 4. Whew, it was warm! Such sweaty, dirty girls we were by the time that was over.

Another thing I remember well from being on that mountain is how my sister and I got poison ivy or poison oak: I don't know what it was, but it was itchy! It just kept spreading, and it wasn't a nice feeling not knowing where or when it would end! We really enjoy these brownies and make them often.

Can't Leave Alone Bars

1 white cake mix	⅓ cup oil
2 eggs	

Mix with fork. Reserve ½ to 1 cup of crumbs. Pat remaining crumbs in bottom of 9 x 13 pan.

Melt:

¼ cup butter	1 can Eagle Brand condensed milk
1 cup chocolate chips	

Pour on top of crumbs. Top with remaining crumb mixture by teaspoonfuls. Bake at 300° for 20 to 30 minutes.

Lillian's Lemon Bars

1 yellow cake mix	1 stick oleo
1 egg, beaten	

Mix and press into pan. Reserve some.

1 (8-ounce) package cream cheese
3 eggs
1 box confectioners' sugar
1 package instant lemon pudding

Mix and pour over cake. Top with crumbs. Bake at 325° for 40 minutes.

Chocolate Lover's Brownies

¾ cup oleo

1½ cups sugar

1 tsp. vanilla

¾ cup flour

½ cup cocoa

3 eggs

½ tsp. baking powder

½ tsp. salt

Melt butter. Add sugar, vanilla, and eggs. Set aside. Mix remaining ingredients and add to egg mixture. Pour into 10-inch pan and bake at 325° for 30 minutes.

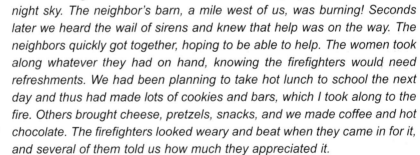

One evening we were alarmed to see an orange glow of flames in the night sky. The neighbor's barn, a mile west of us, was burning! Seconds later we heard the wail of sirens and knew that help was on the way. The neighbors quickly got together, hoping to be able to help. The women took along whatever they had on hand, knowing the firefighters would need refreshments. We had been planning to take hot lunch to school the next day and thus had made lots of cookies and bars, which I took along to the fire. Others brought cheese, pretzels, snacks, and we made coffee and hot chocolate. The firefighters looked weary and beat when they came in for it, and several of them told us how much they appreciated it.

chatting

Pecan Pie Bars

3 cups flour

¾ cup sugar

½ tsp. salt

1 cup cold butter (no substitute)

Filling

4 eggs

1½ cups sugar

1½ cups corn syrup

¼ cup butter, melted

1½ tsp. vanilla

2½ cups chopped pecans

In a large bowl, combine the flour, sugar, and salt. Cut in butter until crumbly. Press onto the bottom and up the sides of a greased 15 x 10 x 1 inch pan. Bake at 350° for 18 to 22 minutes or until crust edge is beginning to brown and bottom is set.

For filling, combine eggs, sugar, corn syrup, butter, and vanilla in a large bowl; mix well. Stir in pecans. Pour over crust. Bake 25 to 30 minutes longer or until edge is firm and center is almost set. Cool on wire rack. Cut into bars. Refrigerate until serving time. Yield: 3 to 4 dozen. Delicious!

Marshmallow Bars

¾ cup butter or margarine

1½ cups sugar

3 eggs

1⅓ cups flour

1½ tsp. baking powder

1½ tsp. salt

3 tbsp. cocoa (or 3 tbsp. flour if prefer white cake/bars)

½ cup chopped nuts

Mix all together and bake in jelly roll pan at 350° for 15 minutes. While still warm, add 4 cups marshmallows. Put in oven until melted (2 or 3 minutes). Use knife dipped in water to spread topping over cake. Cool. Cut into bars.

Topping

1⅓ cup (8 ounces) chocolate chips

3 tbsp. butter

1 cup peanut butter (can use chunky)

Melt together until smooth. Add 2 cups Rice Krispies and spoon on top of marshmallow.

I still remember the first time I had marshmallow bars. It was about twenty years ago, at the place I worked when I was a young girl. We always treated each other for our birthdays. I thought the bars were simply delicious. Since then I have made them quite often. We all enjoy them, as everyone does whenever we share them.

chatting

Coffee Bars

2²/₃ cups brown sugar
3 cups flour
1 cup cooking oil
1 cup warm coffee
2 eggs, beaten
1 tsp. salt
1 tsp. vanilla
1 tsp. baking soda
1 cup nuts

Mix everything in a bowl and beat well. Pour into a jelly roll pan and top with one cup chocolate chips. Bake at 350° for 25 to 30 minutes.

Optional: Excellent with coffee glaze on top: mix confectioners' sugar and a bit of warm coffee.

This quick and easy recipe brings back memories of our newlywed days! A close friend and her husband lived nearby, also just married. One evening she invited me to come up for a while because both of our husbands had gone hunting and weren't back yet. When I walked in the door, she was baking coffee bars, which smelled absolutely delicious! Immediately, I asked for the recipe, and she gave me a pen and paper so I could make these yummy bars for my coffee-lover husband. Now our friends have moved to a dairy farm, and we can't run up the road to them anymore. But we're still close friends and occasionally trade recipes. Precious memories remain, and our children will one day hear the stories behind the recipes we'll pass on to them!

chatting

Chocolate Nut Brownies

Fill a quart canning jar in this order:

First:

1⅛ cup flour

⅔ cup brown sugar

⅓ cup cocoa

½ cup chocolate chips

Second:

⅔ tsp. salt

⅔ cup white sugar

½ cup coconut

½ cup chopped nuts

Pour the contents of jar into a bowl.
Add:

3 eggs

1 tsp. vanilla

⅔ cup of oil

Mix well. Pour into a greased pan. Bake in a 7 x 11 inch pan at 350° for 32 to 37 minutes. Cool and cut into 2-inch squares.

We got *this recipe from an English couple. The man worked on the ambulance when my oldest brother was a baby and had to be taken to the hospital because of breathing problems. He was in serious condition. The ambulance crew got a gold medal pin because they got him to the hospital in time. Now this man always likes to give my brother something for his birthday. The last couple of years they brought vanilla ice cream, with peanuts and chocolate syrup or hot sauce for topping, enough for the*

chatting

whole family. Then one time they brought us two jars of Chocolate Nut Brownie mix and the recipe for it.

It then became a favorite brownie recipe among our family. When I heard about this cookbook, I thought it would be a good time to share this good brownie recipe with others too.

Lydiann's Granola Bars

½ cup brown sugar

3 cups quick oats

⅔ cup peanut butter

½ cup coconut

½ cup light corn syrup

½ cup melted butter

1 cup miniature marshmallows

1 cup chocolate chips

⅓ cup wheat germ

⅓ cup raisins (optional)

Mix brown sugar, peanut butter, syrup, and butter together until well blended; add remaining ingredients. Press mixture into a greased baking pan. Bake at 350° for 15 to 20 minutes.

These are my favorite bars, and I made them often. My brothers really like them for an after-school or bedtime snack.

Anna's Granola Bars

³⁄₄ cup brown sugar

¹⁄₂ cup melted butter

¹⁄₂ cup molasses

2 tsp. vanilla

²⁄₃ cup peanut butter

Mix well; then add:

3 cups oatmeal

¹⁄₂ cup raisins

¹⁄₂ cup sunflower seeds

¹⁄₂ cup chocolate chips

¹⁄₃ cup wheat germ

Press into greased 9 x 13 inch pan. Bake 15 minutes at 350°.

This *recipe comes from a mother who sent granola bars to school with her pupil for a birthday treat when I was teaching school. When I serve them to friends, they say they taste "musty" (must have more). Thus, I keep passing the recipe on.*

chatting

Candy and Snacks

The Miracle

There's a miracle called friendship
That dwells within the heart,
And you don't know how it happens,
Or where it gets its start

But the happiness it brings you
Always gives a special lift,
And you realize that friendship
Is God's most precious gift.

Author unknown

chatting

Frosted Dreams

½ cup shortening
1 (1-ounce) square unsweetened chocolate
1 cup brown sugar
1 egg
1 tsp. vanilla
½ cup sour milk
1½ cups flour
½ tsp. baking powder
½ tsp. baking soda
¼ tsp. salt
½ cup nuts
1 (6-ounce) package chocolate chips (1 cup)

Melt shortening and chocolate in pan. Stir in brown sugar. Beat in egg, vanilla, and sour milk. Sift together dry ingredients and add to chocolate mixture. Stir in nuts and chips. Drop by teaspoonfuls on greased cookie sheet. Bake at 375° for 10 minutes. Cool. Frost.

Frosting

Cream

¼ cup butter	2 tsp. instant coffee
2 tbsp. cocoa	a pinch of salt

Beat in

2½ cups confectioners' sugar
1 tsp. vanilla
enough milk for spreading consistency

Southern Buckeyes

1 pound peanut butter

1 pound butter

¼ cup ground walnuts

1½ pound confectioners' sugar

¼ cup dates, finely diced

Mix peanut butter and confectioners' sugar like pie dough; add nuts, dates, and butter. Roll into balls and let chill thoroughly. Melt 12-ounce package chocolate chips and ½ stick paraffin. Dip the balls in this.

One *wintry day we woke up to find that about two feet of snow had fallen during the night, and the wind was really whistling all around the corners of the house and barn. That meant no school, and I wanted to do something special because it was my fourteenth birthday. Mother said I could sew a new apron for myself and make any kind of candy I wished.*

It was just a week before Christmas, and I had a hard time deciding which candy I wanted to make, for they all sounded so good. So I ended up making three different kinds. I've always had a sweet tooth, but now I'm diabetic, so I let the younger set eat the Christmas candy.

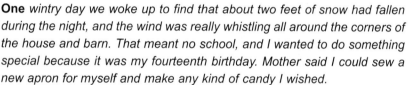

chatting

No-Bake Treats *are a very special snack at our house! We do consider it candy, much more than a cookie, and have made them for school treats, family gatherings, gifts, and picnics. They always seem to be a favorite of others, too.*

I would like to share a special experience our family had with a young pine warbler. One rainy day, I heard a bird calling over and over, but saw nothing. Later, I was upstairs and saw a bird on the windowsill. I watched in fascination and crept closer and closer, but it seemed not to mind me in the least. I put my face down to the bird's level, and it just stayed there, chirping busily. I opened the window, took the screen away, and reached for it, but he (or she) decided that was too much and flew away.

Later I heard the same bird sound when I was downstairs. So I went on a hunt for it and found it behind the house and up against the wall, hopping along. I went out in the rain after it and managed to catch it, in some weeds. It didn't like being a prisoner in the palms of my hands and struggled for freedom as I went out to the barn and produce patch, where the rest of the family was. Everyone held and admired this brown and greenish-yellow "youngster." Then I put him on a tree branch and stayed to see what he would do. He flew around a bit, but also let us put out our hand to him to step on, and he did. One time he was holding on to my finger and started stepping sideways up my arm! He also flew into the maple tree, and then flew down and landed on our son's hat. It was so amazing that a bird was so tame, but it could have been because he was so young.

Many a time since, I have heard a bird I thought sounded similar to our "friend," but I never saw it again.

No-Bake Treats

2 cups white sugar	¼ cup water
3 tbsp. cocoa	½ cup milk

Boil 1 minute. Remove from heat. Add:

3 cups oatmeal (crumbled fine)
½ cup peanut butter
1 tsp. vanilla

Drop quickly on wax paper by teaspoonfuls.

Variations: One may use coconut, nuts, or chocolate chips instead of peanut butter.

I don't bother crumbling the oatmeal; using half old-fashioned and half quick oats makes it more "nutty" if you don't have nuts. Also, nutty peanut butter does the same.

Peanut Butter Creams

1 pound confectioners' sugar	2 cups peanut butter
¼ tsp. salt	4 tbsp. butter
1 tsp. vanilla	3 tbsp. water; more if dry

Mix until candy forms a smooth dough. Shape into small balls and dip in melted chocolate.

Peanut Butter Fudge

⅔ cup canned milk

2 cups sugar

1 cup peanut butter

½ pint marshmallow crème

1 tsp. vanilla

Grease sides of a 2-quart saucepan. Combine sugar and milk in pan. Stir over medium heat. Bring to soft boil stage. Remove from heat and add peanut butter, marshmallow crème, and vanilla. Stir until well blended. Pour into 9 x 9 inch pan. Cut when firm.

I got *this recipe from a friend last Christmas. We had gone caroling on the evening before Christmas (fifteen of us cousins and friends), and all the week before we had been hoping so much for snow so we could use the big bobsled. But the weather didn't cooperate, so my brother hitched the two workhorses to the big flat wagon, and we all piled on. He had attached bells to the horses' harnesses, and they were jingling merrily as the horses clopped from house to house, to the elderly and shut-ins, which we figured could use some cheering up. At one house we sang for a good friend of ours who had been in an accident some time before and was recuperating. She served us this Peanut Butter Fudge, hot chocolate, and cookies cut in star and bell shapes, frosted with red-tinted sugar. Even though it didn't snow, I'm sure we all enjoyed the outing as we helped to spread Christmas joy and cheer.*

chatting

Taffy

1 cup sugar
1 cup honey
⅛ tsp. salt
1 tbsp. butter

Combine ingredients and cook (at 265°) until syrup forms a hard ball when dropped in cold water. Pour onto buttered plates and cool until it can be pulled. Butter hands slightly and pull until stiff. Cut in desired shapes.

Our little *Pomeranian pup, Peanut, is fond of candy, believe it or not. I know we shouldn't give him too much, but he begs so cutely that it's hard to resist him. Our married daughters come home for a candy-making day every year just before Christmas. We make about ten different kinds and then divide the candies out among ourselves. One year a granddaughter gave Peanut a piece of soft taffy. Poor Peanut chewed and chewed until his teeth were stuck together and he could only whimper. He needed help to get it out and didn't beg for any more candy the rest of the day! It's good we don't have candy year-round: we don't need any more cavities!*

chatting

Crunchy Treat

1½ pounds chocolate

1 cup peanut butter

1 pound butterscotch coating

½ box crisped rice

Melt chocolate and butterscotch. Have peanut butter and cereal at room temperature. Let coatings cool slightly. Thoroughly stir peanut butter into coatings. Add cereal. Spread on waxed paper or drop in clusters. Let candy get firm.

Perfect Peppermint Patties

1 box confectioners' sugar

3 tbsp. butter

2 to 3 tsp. peppermint

½ tsp. vanilla

¼ cup evaporated milk

2 cups chocolate chips or wafers

2 tbsp. shortening if using chocolate chips

In a bowl, combine first 4 ingredients. Add milk. Mix well. Roll into 1-inch balls and place on waxed paper. Chill for 20 minutes. Flatten with a glass to ¼ inch thick. Chill for 30 minutes. Dip in chocolate.

Vanilla Popcorn

3 quarts popped corn

1 cup sugar

½ cup butter

¼ cup light corn syrup

¼ tsp. baking soda

½ tsp. vanilla

Place popcorn in a large bowl. In a saucepan, combine sugar, butter, corn syrup, and baking soda. Bring to a boil over medium heat; boil and stir until mixture is golden—about 2 minutes. Remove from heat, stir in vanilla. Pour over popcorn and toss to coat. Cool slightly; break apart while warm.

I have *a chilling memory of popcorn. Late one dark night, the children were in bed, and I was waiting for my husband to come home. He is rarely away evenings, so I felt the quiet and the dark. After a while an unusual sound broke the silence—a sound like hail pebbling on a tin roof. And it was coming from the almost-empty popcorn bowl on the counter.*

With great apprehension, I peeked into the bowl. A poor little mouse with buttered paws was frantically trying to escape. Its frenzied attempts kicked kernels against the sides, creating quite a rattle. (It must have felt like I do some days!)

I carefully picked up the bowl and put it out the door. Two of our cats were out there, and one got the treat: they don't share. I soaked the bowl in Clorox all night!

chatting

Rocky Road Bars Candy

½ cup butter

1 cup confectioners' sugar

1 egg, beaten

6 ounces chocolate or butterscotch chips

Stir all together in top of double boiler over hot water until melted. Line a 9-inch pan with graham crackers. Sprinkle 2 cups miniature marshmallows on top. Pour chocolate mixture over all.

My sister *and I used to make these bars all by ourselves. Of course, Mom was in the kitchen, and we could ask her questions. When I wanted confectioners' sugar, she told me where to find it. I got a bag of something that looked like confectioners' sugar, never bothering to check the label on the bag. When it became hot, it got very stiff. I called Mom to come and look. Upon checking, we discovered that I had used ClearJel instead of confectioners' sugar, all because I hadn't checked the label! The bars were edible, but it was the first time (and hopefully the last) that they weren't good and sweet.*

chatting

When *I was a child, on Christmas day we always had a surprise beside our plate at the breakfast table—a small handmade gift such as new mittens, crochet-edged handkerchiefs, scarves, and always a small dish of hard candy and an orange. This was very special to us, for we never had store-bought candy at any other time. So we made it last a long time and also savored every bit of that orange. When I had a family of my own, I continued that tradition and included a big popcorn ball at each plate, too. There were also bigger gifts later in the day, when the cousins, aunts, and uncles got together for the Christmas dinner. My mother always made sure that all the children and grandchildren were aware of the real meaning of Christmas, and Dad would read aloud the Christmas story to us all after dinner.*

Party Popcorn Balls

½ cup white corn syrup

1 cup butter

1 tsp. vanilla

1⅓ cups sugar

2½ quarts popped corn

2 cups peanuts

Cook 10 to 15 minutes to hard ball stage. Pour over popcorn and peanuts, and shape into balls.

Peanut Butter Cracker Jacks

½ cup sugar

½ cup light corn syrup

½ cup peanut butter

½ tsp. vanilla

5 quarts popped corn

½ cup peanuts

Cook sugar and syrup to a rolling boil. Remove from heat and add peanut butter and vanilla. Pour over popcorn and peanuts, stirring to coat. Enjoy!

Krispie Butterscotch Candy

¼ cup butter

32 large marshmallows

Melt in pan. Keep stirring it. Pour it over:

5 cups Rice Krispies

1 cup butterscotch chips

Mix and pack into a buttered Tupperware container.

I **got** *this recipe from my girlfriends. We were all summoned to a "Come as you are" party one evening, a few months before we were old enough to start with* rumschpringe *(youthful running around). One of our gang had hired a driver with a van to come around and pick up all us girls at our homes, telling us to come along "just as we were" (without changing clothes, bathing, or combing our hair), no matter if we were in the midst of a dirty job or all* schtruwwlich *(disheveled, unkempt). I had been picking lima beans in the wet garden, and the hem of my dress was wet and muddy. But some of the others girls looked even worse: one had been helping to clean out the steer pen! Another had just finished washing her waist-length hair, and it was wet and hanging loose! We were served these tasty snacks, which we all thought were so delicious we copied off the recipes.*

Puffed Wheat Candy

1 cup brown sugar

½ cup butter

½ cup molasses

½ tsp. cocoa

8 cups puffed wheat

Mix sugar, butter, and molasses in saucepan and boil until it reaches soft ball stage. Pour over the puffed wheat. Break apart while still warm.

Pretzel and Chip Dip

2 cups mayonnaise
1½ cups sour cream
½ tsp. onion salt
½ tsp. garlic salt
1½ tsp. parsley flakes

Mix all together and store in refrigerator.

Note: This dip can also be used for celery, carrot sticks, as well as pretzels and potato chips. Delicious!

Jell-O Roll-ups

Mix 1 tbsp. gelatin in 3 ounces Jell-O (any kind). Dissolve in 1 cup boiling water. Heat a pan; add butter enough to melt 3 cups marshmallows. Add Jell-O and stir. Pour hot into a 13-inch oiled cake pan. Let set in refrigerator 20 minutes or until firm but not hard. Loosen edge with spatula and roll like pinwheel dough. Chill several hours before cutting in thin slices.

I got *this recipe from my sister-in-law, and our children really enjoy it. When she saw this recipe, my daughter asked if I remembered telling them that when they pull weeds, I will make a surprise for them; and then I made these. Making three or more colors makes them so pretty. We also took some along to school for a treat, and everyone really liked them. Children also enjoy helping. It's so simple.*

chatting

Trail Mix

1½ cups roasted peanuts

¼ cup raisins

¼ cup chopped dates

½ cup sunflower seeds

¼ cup carob chips

Mix and enjoy!

Once *I made this recipe when my family went to Greenwood Furnace. I set it out when we were having a treat with ice-cream cones, watermelon, and snacks. The next thing I knew, my niece and nephew were enjoying picking out the carob chips and only what tasted good to them. I was kind of surprised since I hadn't thought about that.*

Be sure to eat a protein snack with your fruits, preferably nuts or seeds, such as pumpkin sunflower, sesame, etc. Cheese and animal protein also works but has a tendency to overwork the kidneys and liver if too much is eaten.

chatting

Last spring *we had two cute, wooly little lambs that we bottle-fed after their mother died. At first they were weak and spindly. But soon they were as spry and lively as the healthiest of the others and became great pets. They could be a nuisance, too, and Dad was getting tired of it. One day when the children were playing over at the neighbor's place, the lambs became especially troublesome. When a milk customer drove in and the lady couldn't finish exclaiming about how adorable they were, Dad told her they were for sale. She couldn't believe her good fortune and bought them right off. Dad didn't realize how sad that would make the youngsters; their tears were almost too much for him. He hitched up the horse, drove them to the store, and got them each an ice-cream pop as a consolation.*

Homemade Fudgesicles

1 small package chocolate instant pudding	¼ cup sugar
1 cup evaporated milk	2 cups milk

Mix all together, stir well, and pour into popsicle molds. Freeze until firm.

Fruit Juice Popsicles

2 cups fruit juice	1 cup sugar
1 package unsweetened Kool-Aid	2 cups cold water
1 (3-ounce) package Jell-O (in flavor that goes well with the fruit juice)	

Heat fruit juice to boiling. Remove from heat and add the Jell-O, stirring well. Add sugar, Kool-Aid, and cold water. Fill popsicle holders and freeze.

Beverages, Jellies, and Miscellanea

Heaven's Grocery Store

I was walking down life's highway a long time ago.
One day I saw a sign that read "Heaven's Grocery Store."
As I got a little closer, the door came open wide.

I saw a host of angels, they were standing everywhere;
One handed me a basket and said, "My child, shop with care."
Everything a Christian needed was in that grocery store.
And all you couldn't carry, you could come back for more.

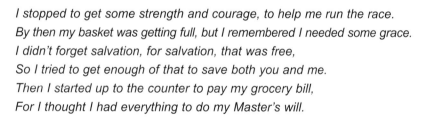

I stopped to get some strength and courage, to help me run the race.
By then my basket was getting full, but I remembered I needed some grace.
I didn't forget salvation, for salvation, that was free,
So I tried to get enough of that to save both you and me.
Then I started up to the counter to pay my grocery bill,
For I thought I had everything to do my Master's will.

As I went up the aisle, I saw prayer and I just had to put that in,
For I knew when I stepped outside, I would run right into sin.
Peace and joy were all plentiful, they were on the last shelf;
Song and praises were hanging near, so I just helped myself.

Then I said to the angel, "Now how much do I owe?"
He just smiled and said, "Just take them everywhere you go."
Again, I smiled at him and said, "How much do I owe?"
He smiled again and said, "My child, Jesus paid your bill a long time ago."

Author unknown

345

Slush Punch

1 cup strawberry Jell-O (or other flavor)

2 cups boiling water

1 cup sugar

1 small (6-ounce) can frozen orange juice concentrate

1 large (46-ounce) can pineapple juice

6 cups water

Dissolve Jell-O in boiling water; add the rest of ingredients. Freeze 1 to 2 hours before use; remove and let set until slightly slushy. Pour 2 quarts ginger ale over it (or fill tumblers half and half).

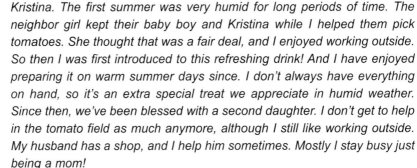

Our next-door neighbors had their sixth child a week after we had our first, Kristina. The first summer was very humid for long periods of time. The neighbor girl kept their baby boy and Kristina while I helped them pick tomatoes. She thought that was a fair deal, and I enjoyed working outside. So then I was first introduced to this refreshing drink! And I have enjoyed preparing it on warm summer days since. I don't always have everything on hand, so it's an extra special treat we appreciate in humid weather. Since then, we've been blessed with a second daughter. I don't get to help in the tomato field as much anymore, although I still like working outside. My husband has a shop, and I help him sometimes. Mostly I stay busy just being a mom!

chatting

Meadow Tea

What is more fragrant than the first meadow tea that grows along country lanes, meadows, and in our garden tea patch in the spring? Whenever I often go for a stroll to our Buschland (woodland) in the evening, when twi-light is descending and the birds sweetly singing. Or I go to fetch the cow in the morning, when everything is fresh and sparkling with dew. I can't resist picking a handful of the tea leaves, just to breathe in the sweet deli-ciousness of it. Visions of icy cold glassfuls of that good tea make my mouth water. I'm always eager to drink it when I come in hot and thirsty from hoeing in the garden or pushing the clattering reel mower. It sure is better, by far, than any store-bought variety! Years ago I heard a preacher remark that people are like tea leaves: their real flavor doesn't come out until they get into hot water. (Smiles!)

Homemade Tea Concentrate

Fill 1 quart jar with tea leaves. Pack tightly. Boil 4 quarts water. Take off heat and add tea. Allow to steep 15 minutes, tightly covered. Remove leaves and add 1 quart sugar. Stir well and freeze. Use 1 quart concen-trate to 3 quarts of water.

Four-Hour Root Beer

Mix 2 cups sugar with 4 tsp. root beer extract. Mix 1 level tsp. yeast with a little lukewarm water. Add almost a gallon of lukewarm water to the sugar mixture; then add the yeast. Makes 1 gallon. Set in the sun upright for 4 hours. Don't turn the lid on tight!

Real Lemonade

6 lemons

1½ cups sugar

2½ quarts cold water

Squeeze lemons and add sugar. Or slice the lemons thin (unpeeled), add sugar, and mash with a potato masher. Mix well before adding water.

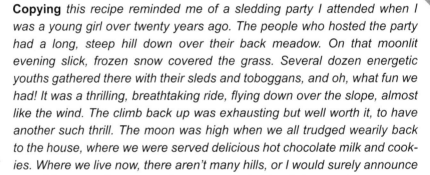

Copying *this recipe reminded me of a sledding party I attended when I was a young girl over twenty years ago. The people who hosted the party had a long, steep hill down over their back meadow. On that moonlit evening slick, frozen snow covered the grass. Several dozen energetic youths gathered there with their sleds and toboggans, and oh, what fun we had! It was a thrilling, breathtaking ride, flying down over the slope, almost like the wind. The climb back up was exhausting but well worth it, to have another such thrill. The moon was high when we all trudged wearily back to the house, where we were served delicious hot chocolate milk and cookies. Where we live now, there aren't many hills, or I would surely announce a sledding party for our sons' gang on a suitable winter evening.*

chatting

Hot Cocoa Mix

| 1 pound Nesquik | 1-pound can coffee creamer |
| 1 pound confectioners' sugar | 1 (24-ounce) box dry milk |

Mix all together and store in a dry place. Use ⅓ cup of mix in a cup and fill with hot water. This is the best!

Cherry Punch

2 packages cherry Kool-Aid	1 quart ginger ale
2 cups sugar	3 quarts water
1 (6-ounce) can frozen orange juice concentrate	
1 (6-ounce) can frozen lemon juice concentrate	

Mix all ingredients together. Pour some into ice-cube trays to use for chilling the drink.

Orange Sherbet Punch

1 package orange Kool-Aid

1 cup sugar

2 quarts water

2 quarts 7 Up

1 quart orange sherbet

1 quart orange soda

Mix and serve.

One dark *Saturday night our neighbors' shed burned to the ground. Many friends and neighbors brought food and helped to clean up and rebuild. Some gave instant chocolate mixes to make hot chocolate, which we used first. One woman gave cocoa and this recipe. It was new to me, but we all loved it. We now use it at our house; it saves money not to buy instant since we buy cocoa in bulk. Add milk to this recipe to make about 1 gallon chocolate milk.*

Chocolate Syrup

1½ or 2 cups sugar	⅓ tsp. salt
1 cup cocoa	1⅓ cups hot water

Boil 3 minutes. Cool. Add 3 tsp. vanilla. Pour into jar and store in refrigerator. Use for chocolate milk or whatever you wish.

Fresh Fruit Milkshake

½ cup fresh strawberries (or peaches, raspberries, or blueberries)

1½ cups vanilla ice cream

¾ cup cold milk

Wash and mash the fruit. Add ice cream and milk and beat until frothy. Serve.

This is great on a hot summer day when you come in from gardening, working in the fields, or playing!

Rhubarb Drink

4 pounds rhubarb
4 quarts water
2 cups sugar
1 cup pineapple juice
1 (6-ounce) can frozen orange juice concentrate

Boil rhubarb and water together until rhubarb is soft. Strain and add the remaining ingredients in order given. Pour into jars, seal, and process in boiling water bath for 10 minutes.

This *was a new recipe last spring for our family. Mom made 210 quarts, and by the middle of August, it was all gone! When we mowed the yard, we got hot and thirsty, and that's what we went for! When Dad and the boys were making hay, rhubarb drink is what they asked for, too. So be sure and try this delicious summertime drink!*

chatting

On my *twelfth birthday we were cooking apple butter most of the day. That evening I received a cute little puppy from my uncle, who was just a year older than me. On that same birthday, my mother gave me a cookbook in hopes that I would take an interest in cooking. But I was a tomboy at heart, and that puppy was much more special to me than cooking. I laid the cookbook in the drawer and barely even looked at it. I must still have been a child at heart, for I sure romped a lot with that puppy and gave it my tenderest care. When the pup was half a year old, it was hit by a car and killed instantly. What a blow this was for me! I sure moped around. Finally, my mother got me interested in trying some recipes from the new cookbook, and soon I was hooked! Ever since, I've liked to cook and try new recipes, and I am anxious to see this finished cookbook.*

Kitchen-Made Apple Butter

4 gallons apples, cored, cut, not peeled

Place in large kettle. Add:

8 pounds white sugar and let stand overnight.

Add:

1 quart good apple cider; improves flavor a lot.

The next morning, slowly cook it, covered, on range or oil stove for at least 3 hours. Drain off juice and work pulp through colander. Cook juice until it gels. Add cinnamon and cook a while longer. Can while hot. Best to cook jars in hot water bath for 15 minutes to insure seal.

Sarah's Apple Butter Recipe

4 gallons apple schnitz (slices)

1 gallon dark Karo syrup

6 pounds white sugar

Place syrup in cooker and then add schnitz and top with sugar. Let stand overnight. The next morning cook, covered, for 3 hours. Put through sieve and cook a little longer. Put in jars and seal. Cook on low heat or it will burn. Keep covered for 3 hours or it will burn. Use large cold-pack canner.

Mock Raspberry Jam

5 cups green tomatoes, ground

4 cups sugar

Bring to a full rolling boil. Boil 20 minutes. Keep stirring. Turn off heat. Add 6-ounce box raspberry Jell-O. Stir until dissolved. Place in jars, into cold-pack canner, and put in boiling water for 5 or 10 minutes. If you do not like jam thick, boil fewer minutes.

Low-Sugar Raspberry Zucchini Freezer Jam

3 cups black raspberries

3 cups zucchini

6 cups sugar

3 packages (1 cup) Sure-Jell or fruit pectin

¾ cup instant ClearJel

Peel zucchini and scoop out seeds. Cut into small pieces. Cook with raspberries and a small amount of water until zucchini is soft. Put in blender and mix until it's pulp. Then strain to remove seeds (I prefer an old, porous pillowcase as strainer). Add water or raspberries until you have 6 cups.

Mix instant ClearJel with 1 cup sugar. Add rest of sugar to fruit mix. Let set 15 minutes. Mix Sure-Jell with 2¼ cups water and boil 1 minute. Pour over fruit and stir well. Add ClearJel mixture and beat 3 minutes. Pour into freezer boxes and let stand at room temperature for 24 hours before freezing.

chatting

Our farm in the Midwest has an abundance of wild raspberries, but only a true nature lover has the patience to pick them. It takes a long time to cover the bottom of the bucket, if you can stand the bloodthirsty mosquitoes and don't mind looking like you have tangled with a wildcat!

My most frightening experience was stepping into a tangle of vines and hearing the unmistakable rattle of a snake behind me! I had two choices: run through a seemingly impenetrable jungle of vines, or go back the way I came, where the snake lay across my path. I chose to wait it out, with my heart in my throat and chills galore. I knew the snake was a bull snake, which mimics a rattler when startled. (There are no rattlers in this area.) So I waited until it slithered away; then I left without any raspberries from that patch!

That's why I mix zucchini with the raspberries: I can hardly pick enough, fast enough. But there's an abundance of zucchini—and no danger involved!

A Dark and Stormy Night

One *summer evening after supper, I was making a batch of rhubarb preserves. I added the sugar and was stirring it when the sky became dark and stormy, and thunder rumbled in the west. Big drops of rain began to fall, so I quickly ran upstairs to close the windows. The storm came fast, but I thought I could finish my jelly anyway. Suddenly there was a sharp crack of thunder, and the electricity went off. The wind was lashing the trees, and the top part of our pear tree broke off and crashed down. At bedtime the electricity still hadn't come back on. We worried that the food in the refrigerator would spoil. At eleven o'clock we were awakened by the smoke detector's beeping and hurried to the kitchen. The electricity had come back on, and my rhubarb preserves boiled until it scorched and activated the smoke detector. I had forgotten to turn off the burner under the kettle!*

Rosy Rhubarb Preserves

5 cups rhubarb, cut fine
1 cup crushed pineapple, drained
4 cups sugar
½ cup strawberry Jell-O

Combine rhubarb, pineapple, and sugar in a kettle. Place over low heat and stir gently until sugar is dissolved. Cook over medium heat until mixture becomes clear—about 10 to 12 minutes. Remove from heat and add Jell-O. Pour into jars and seal.

Wild Grape Jelly

Wash clusters and put in large kettle with only enough water to cover. Bring to boil and boil about 15 minutes. Pour into cloth bag and squeeze out all the juice. Then add as much water as juice. This is now ready for making jelly. Use 5 cups juice, 7 cups sugar, and 1 box Sure-Jell. Follow directions on Sure-Jell box for Concord-type grape jelly.

Put the remaining juice in quart cans with ½ cup sugar per quart and for later use process it 10 minutes at 10 pounds pressure or 30 minutes in boiling water bath.

Mom's Beet Jelly

6 cups beet juice (3 cups juice and 3 cups water is best)

½ cup lemon juice or ReaLemon juice

2 packages Sure-Jell

Mix and boil for 1 minute. Add:

8 cups sugar

1 large package raspberry Jell-O

Boil 5 minutes. Very good. Tastes like red raspberry jelly.

Cob Molasses

12 clean corncobs	3¼ quarts sugar
2 quarts water	¾ quart light Karo

Almost cover cobs with water. Bring to a boil. Strain through cloth. Save 2 quarts of this cob water; add sugar and Karo. Boil about 1 hour until thick enough. Makes about 3½ quarts.

Here's another cob recipe:

Corncob Syrup

12 clean corncobs	8 pints water

Boil for 30 minutes. Strain through cloth and add:

2½ pounds brown sugar	2½ pounds white sugar

Boil until syrup stage. Good on pancakes.

When *I was a small child, we lived in Iowa, and I still remember having cob syrup to put on the tables for church. I can't recall exactly how people made it, since I was only eight when we moved to another settlement. Apparently the people in the new area didn't like cob syrup. We didn't make it anytime since moving out of Iowa, to my knowledge. In my mind, I can picture it as a pinkish syrup, and it was delicious! However, I have never really figured out why people would use cobs for syrup making unless they were too poor to afford much else. Maybe we would all be better off spiritually if we wouldn't have such an easygoing time in financial matters!*

chatting

We've always *had a cow or two, with plenty of extra milk for making cheese and butter. Mom was most always too busy with her other duties, so the cheese making fell to us girls. Dad liked his homemade cheese, and so when I was fourteen years old, he got me interested in making it. My older sister (our regular cheese maker) had gotten married that year and moved far away, and I wished I had asked her more about making cheese before I tried it myself. I had beginner's luck, though, and the first time it turned out just right! But to my humiliation, the next batch was a flop, and we had to feed it to the pigs! My older brothers teased me a lot about that and still do sometimes at our family gatherings. It's really not that hard once you gain a little experience, which I should have by now: I've been making it for over twenty years. I'd encourage anyone who has a cow or extra milk to try it. With the sky-high price of cheese at the grocery stores, it sure is a savings.*

Muenster Cheese

4 gallons milk
2 cups thick buttermilk, not strong
½ cheese rennet tablet
¼ cup cold water
3 tbsp. salt

Heat milk and buttermilk to lukewarm (86°). Dissolve ½ cheese rennet tablet in water. Add to milk; let stand 1 hour. Cut into ½-inch squares. Pour off whey. Add salt; put in press overnight. Use when needed or refrigerate 2 weeks before using.

Ellen's Soda Cheese

1 gallon sour milk	1 cup cream
½ tsp. baking soda	1 tsp. salt
3 tbsp. butter	1 egg, beaten

Heat sour milk to 115°. Cut through both ways with a knife to aid heating. Pour into a cloth bag and hang overnight to drain thoroughly. When dry, crumble and stir in baking soda and butter. Let stand 5 hours. Place in double boiler and allow to melt. Add cream and stir until smooth. Add salt and egg. Boil 3 minutes or until egg is cooked. Pour into a dish.

On a low salt diet? Season foods with herbs and spices. I still use salt, but this is an excellent substitute to bring out more flavor in soups, etc.

Spiritual nugget: *Joyfulness is . . . knowing and being where God intends me to be.*

chatting

Salt Substitute (Low Salt)

1 tsp. chili powder	3 tbsp. paprika
1 tbsp. garlic powder	2 tbsp. pepper
6 tbsp. onion powder	1 tbsp. poultry seasoning
1 tsp. oregano	2 tbsp. dry mustard

Combine all ingredients, mixing well. Place in salt shaker and use instead of salt.

Homemade Cheese

Scald 3 gallons thick milk until too hot to put hand in. Stir it a few times to heat throughout. Pour it through a cheesecloth, run cold water over the curds, and wash thoroughly. Squeeze out all whey and water. Let hang in bag at least 12 hours.

Crumble curds and mix in 2 heaping tsp. baking soda and 1 tbsp. salt. Let stand 3 hours. In a large skillet, melt ½ cup butter and add the curds. Do this over very low heat, like in back of the range. After curds are melted, add 1½ cups milk. Let that cook together until smooth and pour in a buttered dish or mold.

chatting

When *I lived with my widowed Dad, we kept a cow and always had too much milk. My mother used to make cheese, and we really liked it. So I tried my hand at cheese making, too, but it just didn't turn out right. I tried different recipes, but it just didn't produce good cheese.*

We lived in a new settlement, and one day a couple stopped in, wanting to meet the Mennonites. As it turned out, they lived near a family in Pennsylvania that we both knew. Letter writing was one of my hobbies, so I wrote a letter to this family to tell them about my visitors. I also mentioned my daily work and my cheese-making failures. Some days later I received an answer to my letter. The Mrs. wrote that she makes cheese and included her recipe. I remember thinking, "Oh, groan! What would another recipe help? I've tried so many. Oh well," I decided, "I'll give it a try."

I did, and miracle of miracles! It produced excellent cheese! So I wrote back with the good news, and we exchanged letters for quite a few years.

I think the secret was in washing off the curds, since my other recipe didn't require that. I hope this recipe is successful for others, too.

Bird Treats

1 cup suet or lard, melted	
1 cup peanut butter	
1 cup cornmeal	
1 cup oatmeal	
¼ cup sugar	

Mix all together; add sunflower seeds and other birdseed in amounts desired. Serve on birdfeeder.

One day *this summer, Dad found a baby bird. We thought it had likely fallen down while trying to learn to fly.*

We kept it in a box with hopes of taking care of it until it could fly. Later we found a second bird, and now there were two hungry mouths to feed! They made enough noise that we knew they wanted something. When they opened their mouths, it was almost surprising how big they actually were. But I guess the mother bird can better drop something in for them to eat if the mouths are big!

We thought we could fill those hungry mouths at least as good as a mother bird. We took the fly swatter and went through the kitchen and on the porch in search of flies to feed them. We also dug worms for them.

Once we decided to see what our hen with three chicks would say about another "baby." She quickly put an end to that idea! She flew at that tiny bird so angrily that we were afraid she'd kill it before we could get it away. So much for that!

chatting

Homemade Baby Wipes

cut a roll of paper towels in half

2½ cups water

2 tbsp. baby bath

2 tbsp. baby oil

10-cup Rubbermaid bowl

Put toweling in bowl; mix the rest of ingredients and pour over ½ roll of toweling. To start, pull wipes out of the middle of roll. Drill or melt a hole in middle of lid and pull wipes out through hole.

We had been *a childless couple for a number of years. So our first little girl brought much joy. Then my sister shared this recipe with me. And I really like it. Wipes were so handy with a little one in the house At home, traveling, or anywhere, it was handy to have these close by. Now our little girl will soon be four years old, and we don't know if there will be any more of these precious little ones for us. But we are so thankful we are blessed with at least one. It certainly is a joy for us.*

chatting

Amazing Cleaner

1 cup ammonia

½ cup vinegar

¼ cup baking soda

1 gallon water

Mix all together. Good for washing walls and for tough jobs.

Pantry Plant Food

1 tsp. baking powder

1 tsp. Epsom salts

1 tsp. saltpeter

½ tsp. household ammonia

Mix with 1 gallon lukewarm water. Treat plants with this in place of a regular watering. It gives houseplants a boost, especially vines and ivies.

In these times *soap making is much easier than it was for our pioneer forebears. They had to set up a leach tub, which usually was a part of a large tree trunk, five or six feet long and hollowed out by burning. It was set on a big flat rock resting on stones high enough so they could set a pail under a hole drilled in the leach tub's bottom. They filled the tree trunk with wood ashes; then they poured water in again and again, and the leached lye ran out into the bucket. The lye was boiled with grease in the big copper kettle over an open, outdoor fire, and somehow or other it produced soap! They had no pleasing colors or fragrances to add to the soap, like our store-bought soap has, but it served its purpose anyway. I'm sure they didn't take baths every day, though, and maybe in wintertime not even every week.*

Kettie's Cold Soap

5 pints cold water
4 tbsp. ammonia
½ cup Borax
1 ounce oil of sassafras
1 box (laundry detergent) Tide (optional)
4 tbsp. white sugar
½ cup sal soda
2 ounces glycerin
2 cans lye

Combine all the above ingredients. Let come to the right temperature (lukewarm: heated by the lye). Then pour this mixture into 10 pounds melted lard. Be sure to pour the lye mixture into the lard (never pour the lard into the lye). Stir until it is creamy. Let harden, but cut in pieces before it gets too hard. Use a granite or iron kettle to mix it in.

Homemade Crumbly Laundry Soap

3 quarts cold water
1 can lye (1½ cups)
¾ cup Borax or Cheer
4½ to 5 pounds tallow

Mix lye and water. Add Cheer or Borax and let cool. Add melted tallow that's cooled to lukewarm or just setting up. Stir until thick. Continue to stir once in a while all day. It will be crumbly and moist. Store in plastic buckets with lids. One batch makes about 10 to 11 pounds soap. Quick and easy.

I like this *recipe because it is so quick and easy. But I like to let it age some; it seems to work better as it ages. I am using some that is three years old at present, and it works great. It will take stains out of the clothes better. I prefer this over any store-bought soaps that I have used yet. Some days I wonder how these little children's stained clothes will ever be clean again, but when I use this homemade soap, they come out nice and clean once more.*

chatting

Plain Woman's Recipe for Weight Loss and Maintenance

Written by a forty-pound loser

This plan, if followed according to directions, will cause you to lose exactly 2 pounds a week and will maintain your weight wherever you want it to stay.

•Eliminate all foods with white flour and sugar from your diet, and also all snacks like potato chips, cheese curls, party mix, corn chips, etc.

•Eat meat in moderation; eat plenty of raw and cooked vegetables and fresh fruit.

•Place ¾ quart of milk in the refrigerator every evening; next morning, skim off 1 cup of cream and top milk. Use the skimmed milk on unsweetened cereal, etc.

•Eat no more than 1 egg or 1 ounce hard cheese per day, and no more than 1 cup cottage cheese.

•Drink plenty of water and reduce salt intake. Practice eating more slowly.

•Determine your weight goal (the weight at which you look and feel best), and write it at the top of your calendar. Figure on losing 2 pounds a week, and write your desired weight-of-the-week in the Monday date of every week.

•Step on the scales every morning before you've eaten anything. If your weight is over 2 pounds above your desired weight-of-the-week, on that day you have nothing but a piece of fresh fruit and a glass of skim milk for breakfast, and nothing but Slenderizing Soup for dinner and supper and when you need a pick-me-up between meals (see next recipe).

•If your weight is below your desired weight-of-the-week, you may increase your servings of the allowed foods. Or you can adjust servings of these foods accordingly, so that you'll never need to have a Slenderizing Soup day.

•At company meals such as at Sunday invitations and weddings, you may eat one serving of everything set before you, including small servings of dessert and baked goods, regardless of what your weight was that morning. When traveling and eating at restaurants, concentrate mostly on following Step 1 of this diet whenever possible.

•Walk briskly out the back field lane or meadow for 20 minutes every morning, and again for 20 minutes each evening. Remember to enjoy the beauties of nature and commune with the Creator as you walk, casting all your perplexing problems and worries upon him. Trust him to work them out according to his will. And thank God for all your blessings and that he careth for you.

Note: Pregnant and nursing mothers should not try to lose weight; all others should consult the family doctor before starting on a diet.

Slenderizing Soup

2 quarts broth made from water, beef, or chicken bouillon, and tomato juice in the amount of your choice

Add at least 5 of these vegetables in amounts of your choice: chopped celery, carrots, turnips, broccoli, cauliflower, asparagus, spinach, cabbage, peppers, string beans, sugar peas, kale, dandelion, mushrooms, onions, summer squash, parsley, endive, Chinese cabbage, red beets, and cress. (You may also add peas and corn, but limit them to 1 cup each.)

Cook until the veggies are soft. Season to taste. Dish out in modest servings.

Food to Prepare for a Barn Raising

  50 pounds white potatoes
  30 pounds sweet potatoes
  20 plump chickens
  50 pounds roast beef
   3 hams
  15 large loaves of bread
300 yeast rolls
   2 gallons cucumber pickles
  10 dozen red beet eggs
120 shoofly pies
500 lard cakes (doughnuts)
   1 dozen sponge cakes
  15 quarts applesauce
   3 gallons soft custard
   4 gallons rice pudding
   1 large crock stewed prunes
5-gallon stone jar lemonade
5-gallon stone jar meadow tea

This is enough to feed 180 men.

I've attended *quite a few barn raisings in my time and helped to put a hearty meal on the table for the hungry, hard-working men. It sure is amazing how much can be accomplished in one day if so many willing workers get together and roll up their sleeves. We're always happy when the work is done, and thankful if no one gets hurt.*

When I was five years old, our neighbor's barn was struck by lightning and burned down. At the barn raising, we children were playing a game; I collided with another child, and my two front teeth were knocked out. I couldn't eat sweet corn off the cob that summer, but by the next summer, I had grown another set.

The next barn raising I attended was at my uncle's place; tornado-like winds had blown down their shed. Daddy used to remind us that we should always be willing to drop our own work to help others, for we never know how soon we will be the ones who need help.

chatting

Index